# Karze Ka Ishq

# OrangeBooks Publication

1st Floor, Rajhans Arcade, Mall Road, Kohka, Bhilai, Chhattisgarh 490020

Website: **www.orangebooks.in**

© **Copyright, 2024, Author**

All rights reserved. No part of this book may be reproduced, stored in a retrieval system, or transmitted, in any form by any means, electronic, mechanical, magnetic, optical, chemical, manual, photocopying, recording or otherwise, without the prior written consent of its writer.

**First Edition, 2024**
**ISBN:** 978-93-6554-976-8

KARZE KA ISHQ

# शादाब हसन

**OrangeBooks Publication**
www.orangebooks.in

# अनुक्रमणिका / Content

1. क़र्ज़ का इश्क़ (अफ़सोस).................1
   Karze Ka Ishq (Afsos)....................4

2. क़र्ज़ का इश्क़ (उम्मीद).................9
   Karze Ka Ishq (Ummeed)..............11

3. इश्क़ गवारा ..............................14
   Ishq Gawara ................................17

4. नुक़्स ......................................21
   Nukhs ........................................23

5. आँसू ........................................26
   Aansu ........................................28

6. ज़ख़्म ......................................32
   Zakhm ........................................33

7. दिल की चाभी ...........................35
   Dil Ki Chabhi .............................36

8. कायदा ....................................38
   Qaida ........................................39

9. आशिक़ ....................................41
   Aashiq........................................43

10. बेवजह ....................................46
    Bewajah ....................................47

11. मश्हूर ..................................................... 49
    Mash hoor ............................................. 50

12. पत्थर दिल ............................................. 52
    Patthar Dil ........................................... 54

13. छोटी सी कहानी ................................... 57
    Chhoti Si Kahani ................................ 58

14. झूठा ..................................................... 60
    Jhootha ................................................ 62

15. ख्वाहिश ............................................... 66
    Khwayish .............................................. 67

16. गहराई ................................................. 69
    Gahraayi .............................................. 70

17. मोहब्बत और जंग ................................. 72
    Mohabbat aur Jung ........................... 73

18. हसरत .................................................. 75
    Hasrat .................................................. 76

19. क़ैद ...................................................... 78
    Qaid ..................................................... 80

20. अख़बार ............................................... 82
    Akhbaar ............................................... 84

21. ख्यालात .............................................. 86
    Khayalaat ............................................ 87

22. ज़ालिम ................................................ 89
    Zaalim .................................................. 93

| | |
|---|---|
| **23.** तन्हाई | 98 |
| Tanhaayi | 101 |
| **24.** बाक़ी है | 105 |
| Baaqi Hai | 109 |
| **25.** सुकून | 114 |
| Sukoon | 115 |
| **26.** ज़िंदा | 117 |
| Zinda | 118 |
| **27.** उसकी बातें | 120 |
| Uski Baatein | 123 |
| **28.** बेउम्मीदी | 128 |
| Beummeedi | 131 |
| **29.** कहर | 136 |
| Qahar | 138 |
| **30.** सितम | 142 |
| Sitam | 143 |
| **31.** मुलाक़ात | 145 |
| Mulaqaat | 146 |
| **32.** हुनर | 148 |
| Hunar | 149 |
| **33.** तड़पाया | 151 |
| Tadpaaya | 153 |
| **34.** अंधेरा | 156 |
| Andhera | 158 |

**35.** हसीन चेहरा .................................................. 160
   Haseen Chehra ........................................... 163

**36.** वक्त................................................................. 167
   Waqt............................................................. 168

**37.** कुछ सवाल..................................................... 170
   Kuch sawal ................................................. 171

**38.** घायल .............................................................. 173
   Ghayal ......................................................... 174

**39.** शक ................................................................. 176
   Shaq ............................................................. 177

**40.** बदनाम नज़र ................................................. 179
   Badnaam Nazar ......................................... 180

**41.** हैवान .............................................................. 182
   Haiwaan....................................................... 185

# क़र्ज़ का इश्क़ (अफ़सोस)

कर रहा हूँ मैं क़र्ज़ का इश्क़,

किसी न किसी रोज़ तो उसे लौटाना ही पड़ेगा,

किसी और की अमानत है वो इस ज़िंदगी में,

अपने मुहाफ़िज़ के पास, तो उसे वापस जाना ही पड़ेगा।


तन्हा कर जाएगा वो शख़्स अपने जाने के बाद,

ग़मों के ढोल गुमनामी में, तो मुझे बजाना ही पड़ेगा,

उसके सहारे जीता आया हूँ मैं ये ज़िंदगी,

ख़ुद को अकेले जीना, तो मुझे सिखाना ही पड़ेगा।


ख़बर नहीं कि कौन सी मुलाकात हो जाए आखिरी,

अब हर मुलाकात में, उसे तो सीने से लगाना ही पड़ेगा,

ना कर सकूँ ऐसी मोहब्बत मैं दूसरी मरतबा,

किसी क़ातिल से अपने अहसासों का क़त्ल, तो मुझे कराना ही पड़ेगा।

जी लेना चाहता हूँ एक-एक लम्हा अपने इश्क़ का,

फिर अपने इश्क़ को क़फ़न, तो मुझे ओढ़ाना ही पड़ेगा,

उसकी डोली के साथ ही उठेगा मेरे इश्क़ का जनाज़ा,

उसके आखिरी दीदार के लिए, ये जनाज़ा तो मुझे रुकवाना ही पड़ेगा।


क्या भूल जाऊं कि कभी किया था ऐसा इश्क़ भी मैंने,

अपने इश्क़ को क़ब्र में, तो मुझे लिटाना ही पड़ेगा,

ना हो जाए बेआबरू कहीं वो मेरे नाम से,

अपने साये को भी उसके पास से, तो मुझे हटाना ही पड़ेगा!


हो चुकी है वो किसी और की, लौट के आएगी ना अब कभी,

ये सोच के सब्र का मीठा फल, तो मुझे खाना ही पड़ेगा,

अपने तसव्वुर में भी गवारा नहीं, उसके बिना ये ज़िंदगी,

और एक दिन उस शख्स को, तो मुझे भुलाना ही पड़ेगा।


के ये ज़ालिम दुनिया समझ ना जाए हाल-ए-दिल मेरा,

अपने दर्द को ज़माने से, तो मुझे छुपाना ही पड़ेगा,

चाहे अकेले में रोता रहूंगा मैं बाकी उम्र,

लेकिन इस जहाँ के सामने, तो मुझे हमेशा मुस्कुराना ही पड़ेगा!

- ❖ मुहाफ़िज़ – सुरक्षा करने वाला
- ❖ क़त्ल – हत्या
- ❖ बेआबरू – बेइज़्ज़त
- ❖ तसव्वुर – कल्पना
- ❖ गवारा – पसंदीदा

# Karze Ka Ishq - Afsos

*Kar raha hu mai karze ka Ishq,*
*Kisi na kisi roz to usey lautana hi padega,*
*Kisi aur ki amanat hai wo is zindagi me,*
*Apne muhafiz ke pas usey to wapas jaana hi padega,*

*Tanha kar jayega wo shakhs apne jaane ke baad,*
*Ghamon k dhol gumnaami me, mujhe to bajana hi padega,*
*Uske sahare jeeta aaya hu mai ye zindagi,*
*Ab khud ko mujhe akele jeena, seekhaana hi padega,*

*Khabar nahi ke kon si mulaqaat ho jaye akhiri,*
*Ab har mulaqaat me, usey to seene se lagana hi padega,*
*Naa kar saku aisi mohabbat mai dusri martaba,*
*Kisi qaatil se apne ishq ka qatal, mujhe to karwana hi padega,*

## Karze Ka Ishq

*Jee lenaa chahta hu ek ek lamha apne ishq ka,*

*Fir apne ishq ko kafan , mujhe to odhana hi padega,*

*Uski doli hi ke sath uthega mere ishq ka janaza,*

*Uske akhiri deedar ke liye, ye janaza mujhe to rukwana hi padega,*

*Ke bhul jau ke kabhi kia tha aisa ishq bhi maine,*

*Apne ishq ko qabr me, mujhe to litana hi padega,*

*Naa ho jaaye be aabru kahi wo mere naam se,*

*Apne saaye ko bhi uske paas se, mujhe to hatana hi padega!*

*Ho chuki hai wo kisi aur ki, laut ke ayegi na ab kabhi,*

*Ye soch ke sabr ka meetha fal, mujhe to khana hi padega,*

*Apne tasawwur me bhi gawara nahi, uske bina ye zindagi,*

*Aur ek din uss shakhs ko, to mujhe bhulana hi padega,*

*Ke ye duniya samajh na jaaye haal e dil meraa,*

*Apne dard ko zamane se, mujhe to chhupana hi padega,*

*Chahe akele me rota rahunga mai ye saari zindagi,*

*Lekin is jahaan ke saamne, mujhe to hamesha muskurana hi padega!*

- ❖ Muhafiz – Protector, Suraksha Karne Wala
- ❖ Qatal – Murder, Hatya
- ❖ Be Aabru – Disrespect, Baizzat
- ❖ Tasawwur – Imagination, Kalpana
- ❖ Gawara – Acceptable, Pasandeeda

# Translation

*I'm in debt of love, Someday I must repay it, it belongs to someone else in this life, to it's i guardian, it must return.*

*That person will leave me alone after they go, in the drumbeats of sorrow, I must play the tune, I've lived this life relying on their support, to live alone, I must learn how to do.*

*I don't know which meeting will be the last, in every meeting, I must embrace them tightly, I won't be able to love like this again, to kill my feelings, I must do it with a dagger.*

*I want to live every moment of my love, Then to cover my love with a shroud, I must do, Their wedding procession will take my love away, To have one last glimpse, I must stop this funeral.*

*To forget that I ever had such love, I must bury my love in a grave, I can't let my reputation be tarnished by their name, Even my shadow must be kept away from them.*

*She has become someone else's, she won't return now, Thinking this, I must taste the fruit of patience, Even in my imagination, life without her is unbearable, And one day, I must forget that person.*

*So, this cruel world doesn't understand my heart's condition, I must hide my pain from the world, Though I might cry alone for the rest of my life, In front of the world, I must always smile.*

# क़र्ज़ का इश्क़ (उम्मीद)

कर रहा हूँ मैं कर्ज़ का इश्क़,

इस इश्क़ को तो अब मुझे, अपना बनाना ही पड़ेगा,

मेरे ख़्वाब को हक़ीक़त में तब्दील करने के लिए,

अपने इश्क़ की हदों से तो, अब मुझे गुज़र जाना ही पड़ेगा।


दूरी अब बर्दाश्त नहीं, चाहे दुनिया हो जाए ख़िलाफ मेरे,

उसको पाने के लिए तो अब मुझे, ज़माने के ख़िलाफ जाना ही पड़ेगा,

बेशक कुछ फ़ासले रहे हैं हमारे दरमियान,

हमारे बीच से उन फ़ासलों को तो अब मुझे, मिटाना ही पड़ेगा।


ज़ुबान लड़ाता फिरता था, मैं उससे सारी ज़िंदगी,

मेरे आशिक़ से इश्क़ भी तो अब मुझे, लड़ाना ही पड़ेगा,

जो बस जाए मेरी रूह में, न हो पाए कभी ख़त्म,

ऐसे इश्क़ को तो अब मुझे, परवान चढ़ाना ही पड़ेगा।

रंग जाए वो मेरे इश्क़ के रंग में हमेशा के लिए,

अपने इश्क़ का रंग तो अब मुझे, उसके रुखसारों पर लगाना ही पड़ेगा,

क्या ग़ज़ब की मोहब्बत करता आया है वो मुझसे,

अपने इश्क़ की दौलत को तो अब मुझे, उस पर लुटाना ही पड़ेगा।

सारी ज़िंदगी मेरा रहे वो सिर्फ मेरा होकर,

उसके लिए अपनी तक़दीर को तो अब मुझे, हराना ही पड़ेगा,

सुना है क़िस्मत से कोई नहीं जीत पाया है इस कायनात में,

नामुमकिन को तो अब मुझे मुमकिन, करके दिखाना ही पड़ेगा।

कर रहा हूँ मैं कर्ज़ का इश्क़,

इस इश्क़ को तो अब मुझे, अपना बनाना ही पड़ेगा।

- ❖ तब्दील – बदलना
- ❖ परवान चढ़ाना – सफल करना
- ❖ तक़दीर – क़िस्मत
- ❖ रुखसार – गाल
- ❖ कायनात – दुनिया

# Karze Ka Ishq - Ummeed

*Kar raha hu mai karze ka ishq,*

*Is ishq ko to ab mujhe, apna banana hi padega,*

*Mere khwab ko haqeeqat me tabdeel karne ke liye,*

*Apne ishq ki hadon se to, ab mujhe guzar jana hi padega,*

*Doorie ab bardasht nahi chahe duniya ho jaye khilaf mere,*

*Usko paane ke liye to ab mujhe, zamane ke khilaaf jaana hi padega,*

*Beshaq kuch faasle rahe hai hamare darmiyaan,*

*Un faaslo ko to ab mujhe, mitana hi padega,*

*Zubaan ladata firta tha mai usse saari zindagi,*

*Mere aashiq se ishq to ab mujhe, ladana hi padega,*

*Jo bas jaaye meri ruh me na ho kabhi khatam,*

*Aise ishq ko to ab mujhe, parwaan chadhana hi padega,*

*Rang jaye wo mere ishq ke rang me hamesha ke liye,*

*Apne ishq ka rang to ab mujhe, uske rukhsaaro par lagana hi padega,*

*Kya gazab ki mohabbat karta aaya hai wo mujhse,*

*Apne ishq ki daulat ko to ab mujhe, uspe lutana hi padega,*


*Saari zindagi mera rahe wo sirf mera ho kar,*

*Iske liye apni taqdeer ko to ab mujhe, harana hi padega,*

*Qismat se koi nahi jeet paya hai is qaaynaat me,*

*Namumkin ko mumkin to ab mujhe, kar ke dikhana hi padega,*


*Kar raha hu mai karze ka ishq,*

*Is ishq to ab mujhe, apna banana hi padega,*

- ❖ Tabdeel – Change, Badalna
- ❖ Parwan Chadhana – To Nurture, Safal Karna
- ❖ Taqdeer – Fortune, Qismat
- ❖ Rukhsaar – Cheek, Gaal
- ❖ Kaaynaat – World, Duniya

# Translation

*I'm in debt of love, this love I must now make my own, to transform my dreams into reality, I must now cross the limits of my love.*

*I can't bear this distance anymore, even if the world is against me, to attain her, I must go against the times, though some distances have existed between us, I must now erase those distances.*

*I used to argue with her all my life, Now I must learn to fight for my love, that which settles in my soul, never to end, I must now nurture such love.*

*May she always be colored in the hues of my love, I must now apply the colors of my love on her cheeks, what a marvelous love she has shown me, I must now lavish my love's wealth upon her.*

*For my entire life, may she be only mine, for her, I must now conquer my fate, I've heard no one has ever won against destiny in this universe, I must now make the impossible possible.*

*I'm in debt of love, this love I must now make my own.*

# इश्क़ गवारा

**क़िस्मत को अगर मेरा इश्क़ ज़रा भी गवारा होता**

ना होता वो दरिया, ना महज़ मैं उसका एक किनारा होता,

ना होता मैं इतना बेबस, ना ही इतना बेसहारा होता,

ना यूँ ही घूमता रहता दर-ब-दर सुकून की तलाश में,

ना होता मैं इतना बदनाम, ना मैं कभी इतना बेचारा होता!

**क़िस्मत को अगर मेरा इश्क़ ज़रा भी गवारा होता**

होता अगर मैं मुलाज़िम, तो वो ही मेरा इदारा होता,

मेरे ज़र्रे-ज़र्रे को उसने भी अपनी रूह में उतारा होता,

रहती मेरी अहमियत उसकी ज़िंदगी में कुछ इस तरह,

होता अगर वो फ़लक जैसा, उसमें मैं ही वाहीद एक सितारा होता,

**क़िस्मत को अगर मेरा इश्क़ ज़रा भी गवारा होता**

ना होता मैं इतना मुफ़लिस, ना ही कभी इतना नाकारा होता,

ना होता मैं उसका आशिक़, ना मैं कभी इतना आवारा होता,

ना चलता कभी बर्बादी के रास्ते, ना सिलसिले होते तबाही के यूँ शुरू,

सोचता हूँ कि वो हो जाता मेरा, काश मेरे पास ऐसा कोई कफ्फारा होता,

**क़िस्मत को अगर मेरा इश्क़ ज़रा भी गवारा होता**

क्या ही होता वो मंज़र और क्या ही नज़ारा होता?

अगर होता मैं उसका, और वो शख़्स भी हमारा होता!

गुज़र जाता किसी भी हद से मैं, उसका अगर मुझे एक इशारा होता,

ना रहता मैं अकेला, ना सूना रहता मेरा वजूद,

अगर इस तरह का इश्क़ मुझे ज़िंदगी में कभी दोबारा होता!

**क़िस्मत को अगर मेरा इश्क़ ज़रा भी गवारा होता**

- ❖ गवारा – पसंदीदा
- ❖ महज़ – सिर्फ
- ❖ मुलाज़िम – नौकर
- ❖ इदारा – विभाग
- ❖ ज़र्रे-ज़र्रे – छोटी चीज़
- ❖ फ़लक – आसमान
- ❖ वाहीद – एक
- ❖ मुफ़लिस – गरीब
- ❖ कफ्फारा – तपस्या

# Ishq Gawara

***Qismat ko agar mera ishq zara bhi gawara hota***

*Na hota wo dariya, na mai mahaz uska ek kinara hota,*
*Na hota mai itna bebas, na hi itna besahara hota,*
*Na yu hi ghumta rahta dar ba dar sukoon ki talash me,*
*Na hota mai itna badnaam, na mai kabhi itna bechara hota!*

***Qismat ko agar mera ishq zara bhi gawara hota***

*Hota agar mai mulazim to wo hi meraa idaara hota,*
*Mere zarre zarre ko, usne bhi apni ruh me utaara hota,*
*Rahti meri ahmiyat uski zindagi me kuch is tarah,*
*Hota agar wo falak jaisa, usme mai hi waahid ek sitara hota,*

***Qismat ko agar mera ishq zara bhi gawara hota***

*Na hota mai itna muflis, na hi kabhi itna nakara hota,*

*Na hota mai uska ashiq, na mai kabhi itna awaara hota,*

*Na chalta kabhi barbadi ke raste, na silsile hote tabahi ke yun shuru,*

*Sochta hu ke wo ho jata mera, kaash mere paas aisa koi kaffaara hota,*

***Qismat ko agar mera ishq zara bhi gawara hota***

*Kya hi hota wo manzar aur kya hi nazaara hotaa?*

*Agar hota mai uska, aur wo shakhs bhi hamara hota!*

*Guzar jata kisi bhi hadd se mai, agar uska mujhe sirf ek ishara hota,*

*Na rahta mai akela,na soona rahta mera wajood,*

*Agar is tarah ka Ishq mujhe zindagi me kabhi dobara hota!*

***Qismat ko agar mera Ishq Zara bhi gawara hota***

- ❖ Gawara – Acceptable, Pasandeeda
- ❖ Mahaz – Only, Sirf

- ❖ Mulazim – Employee, Naukar
- ❖ Idara – Department, Vibhag
- ❖ Zarre zarre – Tiny particles, Chhoti Cheez
- ❖ Falak – Sky, Aasmaan
- ❖ Waahid – One, Ek
- ❖ Muflis – Poorer, Gareeb
- ❖ Kaffaara – Atonement, Tapasya

# Translation

*If fate had accepted my love even a little-*

*She wouldn't have been that river, nor I was a shore of it, I wouldn't have been so helpless, nor so alone, I wouldn't wander door to door in search of peace, I wouldn't be so infamous, nor would I be so miserable!*

*If fate had accepted my love even a little-*

*If I were employed, it would have been her office, she would have absorbed every particle of mine into her soul, my worth would have mattered in her life in such a way, if she were the sky, I would be the only star in it.*

*If fate had accepted my love even a little-*

*I wouldn't be so impoverished, nor would I ever be worthless, I wouldn't be her lover, nor would I ever be so aimless, I wouldn't walk the path of destruction, nor would there be a chain of ruin, I think if she were mine, how I wish I had such atonement.*

*If fate had accepted my love even a little-*

*What a scene it would have been, what a sight it would have been! If I were hers, and that person were also mine! I would cross any limits if she gave me just a sign, I wouldn't remain alone, nor would my existence be empty, If I ever experienced such love in my life again!*

*If fate had accepted my love even a little.*

# नुक़्स

मेरे नुक़्स जानने हो, तो आ जाना मेरे पास,

मेरी खूबियाँ तो तुझे खुद ही जाननी पड़ेंगी,

तेरी अच्छाइयाँ अगर सुननी हों तुझे – तो बयान कर सकता हूँ,

बेवफाइयाँ तो तेरी – तुझे खुद ही माननी पड़ेंगी,

अगर चाहूँ, तो बन सकता हूँ बेवफा तुझसे बेहतर,

बस अपनी मोहब्बत में थोड़ी सी हवस, मुझे भी सानी पड़ेंगी,

शिकायत करने का क्या है, कभी भी कर सकता हूँ तुझसे,

बस अपने ज़मीर की गर्दन – मुझे पंखे से टांगनी पड़ेगी!

अब भी तेरा साथ निभा सकता हूँ मैं ज़िंदगी भर,

फिर ना करोगी ऐसा, बात ये दिल में तुझे भी तो ठाननी पड़ेगी!

माफ़ अगर करना चाहूँ तुझे, तो कर सकता हूँ बेशक,

लेकिन अपनी गलतियों की माफ़ी – तुझे भी तो मांगनी पड़ेगी!

- ❖ नुक़्स – दोष
- ❖ बयान – प्रतिनिधित्व, चर्चा
- ❖ ज़मीर – अंतरात्मा, विवेक

# Nukhs

*Mere nukhs jaanne ho, to aa jana mere paas,*

*Meri khoobiyan to tujhe khud hi jaan ni padegi,*

*Teri achaaiya agar sunni hon tujhe – to bayan kar sakta hun,*

*Bewafayiyan to teri- tujhe khud hi maan ni padegi,*

*Agar chahun, to ban sakta hu bewafa tujhse behtar,*

*Bas apni mohabbat me thodi si hawas, mujhe bhi saan ni padegi,*

*Shikayat karne ka kya hai, kabhi bhi kar sakta hu tujhse,*

*Bas apne zameer ki gardan – mujhe pankhe se taang ni padegi!*

*Ab bhi tera sath nibha sakta hu mai zindagi bhar,*

*Fir na karogi aisa, baat ye dil me tujhe bhi to thaan ni padegi*

*Maaf agar karna chahun tujhe, to kar sakta hu beshaq*

*Lekin apni galtiyon ki maafi- tujhe bhi to maang ni padegi,*

- ❖ Nukhs – Flaws, Dosh
- ❖ Bayan – To Express, Charcha
- ❖ Zameer – Conscience, Antaraatma

## **Translation**

*If you want to know my flaws, just come to me,*

*You'll have to recognize my virtues yourself,*

*If you want to hear your goodness, I can express it,*

*But your betrayals, you'll have to acknowledge yourself.*

*If I wish, I can be unfaithful, better than you,*

*But my love must not be mistaken for mere lust.*

*What's there to complain about? I can do it anytime,*

*But I must not hang my conscience on a fan!*

*I can still stand by you for life,*

*But you must resolve not to do this again in your heart!*

*If I want to forgive you, I certainly can,*

*But you too must seek forgiveness for your mistakes!*

# आँसू

आज तू जिसके लिए अपने आँसू बहाए जा रहा है,

उसे तो कोई और अपनी ज़िंदगी की, जन्नतें दिखाए जा रहा है,

तू यहाँ रो-रो के तबाह कर रहा है अपनी ज़िंदगी,

वो किसी और की ज़िंदगी को, गुलज़ार बनाए जा रहा है,

वो जो कहती थी तुझसे, जी न सकूंगी तेरे बिना,

वो अब किसी और के साथ अपनी ज़िंदगी बिताए जा रहा है,

याद करता है तू उसकी बातें, तो हँसते में भी रो देता है,

क्या तासीर थी उसमें, जो हँसते हुए भी तुझे रुलाए जा रहा है,

वादा किया था तुझसे, उसने हमेशा साथ रहने का,

पता करो कौन सा मर्ज़ है उसको, जो वो सारे वादे भूलाए जा रहा है,

अगर तूने भी भुला दिया उसे अपनी ज़िंदगी में,

बहुत पछताएगी वो, ये सोच के दिल तेरा घबराए जा रहा है,

ज़हन में तो आता है तेरे, कि अब भूल जाऊं उसको,

लेकिन ये दिल तेरा, तेरे ज़हन से ही,टकराए जा रहा है,

ग़फलत में है तू, कि वो लौट के वापस आएगी एक दिन,

अब तो तेरा मुक़द्दर भी, तेरे ऊपर तरस खाए जा रहा है,

अगर कभी वो कहीं मिलेगी, तो बता दूंगा ऐ मेरे दोस्त,

एक आशिक़ है उसका, जो उसके लिए अपनी ज़िंदगी मिटाए जा रहा है!

- ❖ गुलज़ार – जैसे एक बगीचा, हराभरा
- ❖ तासीर – प्रभाव
- ❖ मर्ज़ – बीमारी
- ❖ ज़हन – दिमाग
- ❖ ग़फलत – उपेक्षा
- ❖ मुक़द्दर – किस्मत

# Aansu

*Aaj tu jiske liye apne aansu bahaye ja raha hai,*

*Usey to koi aur apni zindagi ki jannatein dikhaye ja raha hai,*

*Tu yahan ro ro ke tabah kar raha hai apni zindagi,*

*Wo kisi aur ki zindagi ko gulzar banaye ja raha hai,*


*Wo jo kahti thi tujhse jee na sakungi tere bina,*

*Wo ab kisi aur ke sath apni zindagi bitaye ja raha hai,*

*Yaad karta hai tu uski baate to haste hue me bhi ro deta hai,*

*Kya taseer thi usmein jo haste hue bhi tujhe rulaye ja raha hai,*


*Wada kiya tha tujhse usne hamesha sath rahne ka,*

*Pata karo kaun sa marz hai usko, jo wo saare waade bhulaye ja raha hai,*

*Agar tune bhi bhula dia usko apni zindagi me,*

*Bohot pachhategi wo, ye soch le dil tera ghabraye ja raha hai,*

*Zehan me to aata hai tere, ke ab bhul jau usko,*

*Lekin ye dil tera, tere zehan se hi takraye ja raha hai,*

*Gaflat me hai tu ke wo laut ke wapas ayegi ek din,*

*Ab to tera muqaddar bhi tere upar taras khaye ja raha hai,*

*Agar kabhi wo kahin milegi to bata dunga ae mere dost,*

*Ek aashiq hai uska jo uske liye apni zindagi mitaye ja raha hai!*

- ❖ Gulzar – Garden, Baagh
- ❖ Taseer – Effect, Prabhav
- ❖ Marz – Disease, Bimaari
- ❖ Zehan – Brain, Dimagh
- ❖ Gaflat – Delusion, Upeksha
- ❖ Muqaddar – Fortune, Qismat

# Translation

*Today, for whom you're shedding tears,*

*That person is being shown the gardens of life by someone else,*

*You are here, crying and ruining your life,*

*While they are turning someone else's life into a paradise.*

*She who once said she couldn't live without you,*

*Is now spending her life with someone else.*

*When you remember her words, even in laughter, you weep,*

*What a power she had, that even in joy, she brings you to tears.*

*She promised to always be with you,*

*Find out what illness has made her forget all her vows.*

*If you too forget her in your life,*

*She will regret it deeply; thinking this, your heart is anxious.*

*Your mind tells you to forget her now,*

*But your heart clashes with your thoughts.*
*You're in delusion that she will return one day,*
*Now even your fate is showing pity on you.*
*If she ever crosses my path, I'll let her know my friend,*
*There's a lover of hers who is sacrificing his life for her.*

# ज़ख्म

ये ज़ख्म दिल का मैं किसको दिखाऊं,

तुम एक बात पूछो, मैं दास्तान सुनाऊं,

इंसान तो क्या, मुझसे तो खुदा भी नाराज़ है,

अब खुद को मैं ले जाऊं, तो कहाँ ले जाऊं!

❖ दास्तान – कहानी

# Zakhm

*Ye zakhm dil ka mai kisko dikhaun,*
*Tum ek baat pucho, to mai dastaan sunaun,*
*Insan to kya mujhse to khuda bhi naraz hai,*
*Ab khud ko mai le jaun, to kahan le jaun!*

❖ Daastaan – Story, Kahani

# Translation

*Whom should I show these wounds of my heart to?*
*You ask me a question, and I will share my tale.*
*Not just humans, even God seems displeased with me,*
*Now, where should I take myself?*

# दिल की चाभी

अर्सा हुआ, मेरे दिल की चाभी हो चुकी थी कहीं गुम,
दिल में आने के लिए उसे इसका ताला तोड़ना ही था,

एक अर्से से जो दिल था सख़्त, एक नारियल की तरह,
लुत्फ़ उठाने के लिए उसे, इस दिल को मरोड़ना ही था,

जब ज़िंदगी में आदत सी बन गया वो शख़्स मेरे लिए,
अपनी लत लगवा के, उसे तो मुँह मोड़ना ही था,

कभी जो शख़्स करीब था मेरे, मेरी परछाई की तरह,
ज़िंदगी के अंधेरे में, मेरा साथ भी तो उसे छोड़ना ही था।

❖ लुत्फ़ – आनंद

# Dil Ki Chabhi

*Arsa hua mere dil ki chabhi ho chuki thi kahi gum,*

*Dil me aane ke liye usey iska taala todna hi tha,*

*Ek arse se jo dil tha sakht, ek nariyal ki tarah,*

*Lutf uthane ke liye usey, is dil ko marodna hi tha,*

*Jab zindagi me aadat si ban gya wo shakhs mere liye,*

*Apni lat lagwa ke, usey to muh modna hi tha,*

*Kabhi Jo shakhs qareeb tha mere, meri parchhaayi ki tarah,*

*Zindagi ke andhere me mera sath bhi to usey chhorna hi tha.*

❖ Lutf – Pleasure, Anand

# Translation

*It's been a while; the key to my heart had gotten lost somewhere,*

*To enter it, she had to break its lock.*

*For a long time, my heart was hard, like a coconut,*

*To enjoy it, she had to twist this heart.*

*When that person became a habit in my life,*

*With her addiction, she had to turn away from me.*

*Once, the person who was close to me, like my shadow,*

*In the darkness of life, she had to leave my side.*

# कायदा

काश वफ़ा निभाने का एक कायदा होता,

नुक सान इसमें कम, और कुछ ज़्यादा फ़ायदा होता!

# Qaida

*Kaash wafa krne ka ek qaydaa hota,*
*Nuksan isme kam aur kuch zada faida hota!*

# Translation

*I wish there was a rule for loyalty,*

*Where the losses were fewer and the benefits greater!*

# आशिक़

मेरे जैसे कितने आशिक़ हैं इस ज़माने में,
मसरूफ हैं वो भी किसी न किसी का दिल बहलाने में,

तक़दीर भुला कर, कर रहे हैं वो तस्वीर से मोहब्बत,
एक उनकी आशिक़ी है, जो लगी है उन्हें ही ठिकाने लगाने में!

चाहत, ज़िद और शिद्दत ही है काफी, इस दिल को जलाने में!
खुद की रूह, आबरू, शख्सियत को, यूँ ही मिट्टी में मिलाने में!

सारी कोशिशें हो चुकी हैं नाकाम उसे पाने की,
कभी सोचता हूँ, क्या ही हर्ज़ है, अब उसे भूल जाने में!

भूल नहीं सकता हूँ, या भुला देना नहीं चाहता,
नफ़ा नुक़सान देखा नहीं, मोहब्बत तो हो गई थी अनजाने में!

किसी से इश्क़ करने का हक़ तो उसे भी है बेशक,
ज़िद्दी ये दिल कोशिश में है, उसे सिर्फ अपना बनाने में!

अगर मुक़द्दर साथ देता, तो मैं भी इश्क़-ए-जंग जीत जाता,
अब लगता है भलाई है मेरी, यूँ ही खामोशी से हार जाने में!

- ❖ मसरूफ – व्यस्त
- ❖ तक़दीर – क़िस्मत
- ❖ शख़्सियत – व्यक्तित्व
- ❖ नफ़ा – फ़ायदा

# Aashiq

*Mere jaise kitne aashiq hai is zamane mein,*

*Masroof hai wo bhi kisi na kisi ka dil bahlaane mein,*

*Taqdeer bhula ke kar rahe hain, wo tasweer se mohabbat,*

*Ek unki aashiqui hai jo lagi hai, unhe hi thikane lagane mein!*


*Chahat, zid aur shiddat hi hai kaafi, iss dil ko jalane mein,*

*Khud ki ruh, aabru, izzat ko, yuhin mitti me milane mein,*

*Saari koshishe ho chuki hain nakaam usey paane ki,*

*Kabhi sochta hu, kyaa hi harz hai ab usey bhul jaane mein!*


*Bhul nahi sakta hun, ya bhula dena nahi chahta,*

*Nafa nuksaan dekha nahi, mohabbat to ho gyi thi anjaane mein,*

*Kisi se ishq karne ka haq to usey bhi hai beshaq,*

*Ziddi ye dil koshish me hai, usey sirf apna banane mein!*

*Agar muqaddar saath detaa, to mai bhi ishq e jung jeet jaata,*

*Ab lagta hai bhalayi hai meri, yun hi khamoshi se haar jaane mein!*

- ❖ Masroof – Busy, Vyast
- ❖ Taqdeer – Fortune, Qismat
- ❖ Shakhsiyat – Personality, Vyaktitva
- ❖ Nafa – Profit, Faida

# Translation

*There are many lovers like me in this world,*

*They too are busy pleasing someone's heart.*

*Forgetting fate, they are in love with the image,*

*Their love is focused on finding a place for themselves!*

*Desire, stubbornness, and intensity are enough to ignite this heart!*

*To blend one's own soul, honor, and identity into the dust!*

*All efforts to win her have been in vain,*

*Sometimes I wonder, what's the harm in forgetting her now?*

*I cannot forget her, nor do I wish to!*

*I didn't consider the gains or losses; love happened unknowingly!*

*She certainly has the right to love someone,*

*This stubborn heart is trying only to make her mine!*

*If destiny were on my side, I would have won this battle of love!*

*Now it seems that my goodness lies in silently accepting defeat!*

# बेवजह

बेवजह हुआ था इश्क़, बेवजह ही खो गया,

रूठा वो मुझसे क्यों, जो था अपना सा हो गया,

ग़मज़दा हुई ज़िंदगी उसके जाने से कुछ इस तरह,

जागा था जो मुक़द्दर, जैसे एकदम से सो गया।

❖ ग़मज़दा – दुखी

# Bewajah

*Bewajah hua tha Ishq, bewajah hi kho gaya,*
*Rutha wo mujhse kyun? Jo tha apna sa ho gaya,*
*Ghamzada hui zindagi uske jaane se kuch is tarah,*
*Jaagaa tha jo muqaddar, jaise ekdam se so gaya!*

❖ Ghamzada – Sad, Dukhi

# Translation

*The love was unwarranted, and it vanished for no reason,*

*Why did she get upset with me, when she had become so dear?*

*Life became sorrowful with her departure in this way!*

*What was once awake in my destiny suddenly fell asleep!*

# मशहूर

छोड़ा था घर मशहूर होने के लिए,

मशहूर तो हुआ, लेकिन बदनाम होकर!

# Mashhoor

*Chhora tha ghar, mash hoor hone ke liye,*
*Mashhoor to hua lekin badnaam ho kar!!*

# Translation

*I left home to become famous,*
*I got fame by becoming dishonourable!*

# पत्थर दिल

वो मेरी सोई हुई ख्वाहिशें जगा के गया,

वो मेरे अरमानों में, एक नामुमकिन सा ख्वाब सजा के गया,

खुद को हासिल नहीं करने दिया उसने मुझे,

बस वो मुझ पे, उसकी चाहत का जादू चढ़ा के गया,

वो मेरी मोहब्बत का गला, यूं हीं दबा के गया,

वो हाथ सेंकने के लिए, मेरे सुकून को जला के गया,

डूबा रहूं मैं, उसकी ही यादों में सारी ज़िंदगी,

उसकी खुमारी का ऐसा नशा, वो मुझे करा के गया,

वो मुझ पर, एक छोटा सा इल्ज़ाम लगा के गया,

वो मेरी मोहब्बत को, अपनी नफरत से हरा के गया,

कुछ तो मजबूरी उसकी भी रही होगी शायद,

तभी वो वफा को, यूं बेवफा बता के गया,

वो मेरे दिल को क्या, मेरी रूह को सता के गया,

मेरी हसरतों को, मेरी ही क़ैद में बिठा के गया,

पहले काफी नरम सुलूक करता था मैं ज़माने से,

वो पत्थर दिल, दिल मेरा भी पत्थर बना के गया,

उससे इश्क़ करने का मज़ा, वो मुझे चखा के गया,

जैसा था नहीं मैं, वो मुझे वैसा दिखा के गया,

शायद रुलाने वाला था वो मुझे सारी ज़िंदगी,

तभी आखिरी मुलाक़ात में, वो मुझे काफ़ी हंसा के गया,

वो मेरे दिल से खेल के, अपना दिल बहला के गया,

ज़ख़्म देने के बाद, इन ज़ख्मों को ज़रा सहला के गया,

मेरी शख्सियत में वफ़ा की महक से परेशान था वो शायद,

तभी वजूद को मेरे, वो मेरे आँसुओं से नहला के गया,

वो मेरे इश्क़ में, अपने ज़हर की कड़वाहट मिला के गया,

गलती से ज़हन में मेरे, वो एक चिंगारी भड़का के गया,

उससे तो उसकी शिकायत न कर सका मैं कभी,

लेकिन वो मोहब्बत के खिलाफ, मुझे लिखना सिखा के गया।

# Patthar Dil

*Wo meri soyi hui khawahishen jaga ke gaya,*

*Wo mere armaano mein, ek namumkin sa khwab saja ke gaya,*

*Khud ko haasil nahi karne diya usne mujhe,*

*Bas wo mujhpe, apni chahat ka jaadu chadha ke gaya,*

*Wo meri mohabbat ka gala, yun hi daba ke gaya,*

*Wo hath senkne ke liye, mere sukoon ko jala ke gaya,*

*Dooba rahun main, uski hi yaadon mein saari zindagi,*

*Uski khumari ka aisa nasha, wo mujhe kara ke gaya,*

*Wo mujhpe ek chhota sa ilzaam laga ke gaya,*

*Wo meri mohabbat ko, apni nafrat se hara ke gaya,*

*Kuch to majboori uski bhi rahi hogi shayad,*

*Tabhi wo wafa ko, yun bewafa bata ke gaya,*

*Wo mere dil ko kya, meri ruh tak ko jala ke gaya,*

*Meri hasraton ko, meri hi qaid me bitha ke gaya,*

*Pahle kaafi naram sulook karta tha mai zamane se,*

*Wo patthar dil, dil mera bhi pathhar bana ke gaya,*

*Usse ishq karne ka maza, wo mujhe chakha ke gaya,*

*Jaisa tha nahin main, wo mujhe waisa dikha ke gaya,*

*Shayad rulane wala tha mujhe saari zindagi,*

*Tabhi akhiri mulaqat mein, wo mujhe kaafi hasa ke gaya,*

*Wo mere dil se khel ke, apna dil bahla ke gaya,*

*Zakhm dene ke baad, in zakhmon ko zara sahla ke gaya,*

*Meri shakhsiyat me wafa ki mahak se pareshan tha wo shayad,*

*Tabhi wajood ko mere, wo mere aansuon se nahla ke gaya,*

*Wo mere ishq me, apne zahar ki kadwahat mila ke gaya,*

*Galti se zahan me mere, wo ek chingari bhadka ke gaya,*

*Usse to uski shikayat na kar saka mai kabhi,*

*Lekin wo mohabbat ke khilaaf, mujhe likhna seekha ke gaya!*

# Translation

*He awakened my dormant desires, he adorned my dreams with an impossible name, he never let me attain myself, just, cast his love's spell upon me.*

*He choked my love, leaving it gasping, burned my peace to warm his hands, I wish to drown in his memories for a lifetime, he left me under the intoxication of his charm.*

*He placed a small blame on me, defeated my love with his hatred, perhaps there was some compulsion on his part, that's why he declared fidelity as betrayal.*

*He didn't just torment my heart, but my soul too, he confined my aspirations within my own cage, I used to treat the world with kindness, he turned my heart into stone.*

*He made me taste the joy of love, made me appear as someone I wasn't, perhaps he was meant to make me cry all my life, that's why in our last meeting, he made me laugh a lot.*

*He played with my heart, soothing it afterward, after giving me wounds, he gently caressed them, he must have been troubled by the fragrance of loyalty in me, That's why he drenched my existence with my tears.*

*He mixed the bitterness of his poison into my love, by mistake, he sparked a flame in my mind, I could never complain to him, but he taught me to write against love.*

# छोटी सी कहानी

एक छोटी सी कहानी है, एक नन्हा सा फ़साना है मेरा,

ज़र्रा-ज़र्रा जोड़ के सारी ज़िंदगी, जो इज़्ज़त कमाई थी मैंने,

एक बार मोहब्बत हुई, और सब बरबाद हो गया!!

❖ ज़र्रा- ज़र्रा - छोटी छोटी चीज़

# Chhoti Si Kahani

*Ek chhoti si kahani hai, ek nanha sa fasana hai mera,*

*Zarra-zarra jod ke saari zindagi, jo izzat kamayi thi maine,*

*Ek bar mohabbat hui, aur sab barbad ho gaya!!*

❖ Zarra-zarra – Small Efforts, Chhoti cheez

## Translation

*It's a short story, a little tale of mine,*

*Every bit of respect I earned throughout my life,*

*With one love, it all got ruined!*

# झूठा

हमें अपने साथ झूठा ही रहने दो,

अपनी हकीकत बता के, अकेले हम होना नहीं चाहते,

ना कर सकेंगे रूबरू, हम अपने गुज़रे वक़्त से,

बीता वक़्त ज़ाहिर कर के, आपको हम यूँ खोना नहीं चाहते,

पास आकर बैठिए, और पूछिए हाल-ए-दिल मेरा,

खुद से बातें कर के, अब हम और रोना नहीं चाहते,

ज़िम्मेदारियों ने बना दिया बड़ा, हमें उम्र से पहले,

वरना कौन हैं वो लोग, जो बचपन में अपने खिलौना नहीं चाहते?

मुश्किल वक्त गुज़ारा है, हमने काफ़ी इस ज़िंदगी,

वो याद कर के अपनी रूह में, एक और सुई चुभोना नहीं चाहते,

बयान कर सकते हैं हम, महफ़िल में अपनी मुश्किलें,
लेकिन अपने अहसासों को हम, लफ्ज़ों में पिरोना नहीं चाहते,

मगर आप से ज़ाहिर कर सकते हैं, हम अपनी तकलीफें,
लेकिन आपके तकिए को हम, आपके आँसुओं से भिगोना नहीं चाहते,

गुनाहों में मुब्तिला रहे हैं हम, ये सारी ज़िंदगी,
इन गुनाहों को अब हम, अपने ऊपर और ढोना नहीं चाहते,

कोशिश में हैं हम, के बदल सके हकीकत मेरी,
क्योंकि जैसे थे हम, वापस से वैसे होना नहीं चाहते,

हम तो बिस्तर की सिलवटों में करवटें बदलते रहते हैं,
कौन हैं वो लोग जो कहते हैं, हम सुकून से सोना नहीं चाहते?

❖ मुब्तिला – मुग्ध

# Jhootha

*Humein apne sath jhootha hi rahne do,*
*Apni haqeeqat bata ke akele hum hona nahi chahte,*
*Naa kar sakenge rubaru, hum apne guzre waqt se,*
*Beeta waqt zaahir kr ke, apko hum yun khona nhi chahte!*

*Paas aa ke baithiye aur puchhiye haal e dil meraa,*
*Khud se baatein kar ke, ab hum aur ronaa nahi chahte,*
*Zimmedariyon ne bana diya bada hume Umar se phle,*
*Warna kaun hai wo log, jo bachpan me apne khilauna nahi chahte?*

*Mushkil waqt guzaara hai humne kaafi is zindagi,*
*Wo yaad kar ke apni ruh mein, ek aur sui chubhona nahi chahte,*
*Bayaan kar sakte hain hum, mahfil me apni mushkilein,*
*Lekin apne ahsaaso ko hum, lafzo me pironaa nahi chahte,*

*Magar aap se zaahir kar sakte hain hum apni takleefe,*

*Lekin apke takiye ko hum, apke aansuo se bhigona nahi chahte,*

*Gunaaho me mubtila rahe hai hum ye saari zindagi,*

*Ab in gunaaho ko hum, apne upar aur dhhona nahi chahte,*

*Koshish me hain hum ke badal sake haqeeqat meri,*

*Kyunki jaise the hum, wapas se waisa hona nahi chahte,*

*Hum to bistar ki silwato me karwate badalte rahte hai,*

*Kaun hai wo log, jo kahte hain hum sukoon se sona nahi chahte?*

❖ Mubtila – Trapped, Mugdh

# Translation

*Let me remain falsely together with you,*

*I don't want to reveal my reality and be alone.*

*I cannot face my past,*

*By exposing the time gone by, I don't want to lose you.*

*Come sit close and ask about the state of my heart,*

*Talking to myself, I don't want to cry anymore.*

*Responsibilities have made me grow up before my time,*

*Otherwise, who are those who don't want to play with their childhood toys?*

*I've endured difficult times in this life,*

*Remembering those times, I don't want to prick my soul again.*

*I can express my difficulties in society,*

*But I don't want to weave my feelings into words.*

*Yet I can reveal my troubles to you,*

*But I don't want to soak your pillow with my tears.*

*I've been trapped in sins all my life,*

*And I don't want to burden myself with these sins anymore.*

*I'm trying to change my reality,*

*Because I don't want to be as I was before.*

*I keep changing positions in bed,*

*Who are those who say they don't want to sleep peacefully?*

# ख्वाहिश

मैं चाहता हूं उसकी हर ख्वाहिश पूरी हो,

लेकिन वो नादान, मेरी ही बरबादी की ख्वाहिश रखता है!

❖ नादान – मासूम, नासमझ

# Khwayish

Main chahta hun uski har khwayish poori ho,

Lekin wo nadaan meri hi barbadi ki khwahish rakhta hai!

- ❖ Nadaan – Innocent, Masoom

# Translation

*I want every wish of hers to be fulfilled,*
*Yet that naïve one wishes for my destruction!*

# गहराई

ज़्यादा गहरा न सोचा कर, ए मेरे दोस्त,

सोच की गहराई की भरपाई कुछ लोग ही कर पाते हैं!

# Gahraayi

*Zyada gahraa na socha kar aye mere dost,*
*Soch ki gahrayi ki bharpayi kuch log hi kar pate hai!*

## Translation

*Don't think too deeply, my friend,*
*Only a few can bear the weight of such deep thoughts!*

# मोहब्बत और जंग

अगर मोहब्बत और जंग में सब है जायज़,

तो नाजायज़ क्या है?

पा लेने की ज़िद अगर न हो शामिल,

तो सारे ज़माने को पता है, इन्हें निभाने के फरायज़ क्या है!

❖ फरायज़ – कर्तव्य

# Mohabbat aur Jung

*Agar mohabbat aur jung me sab hai jayaz,*

*To najayaz kya hai?*

*Paa lene ki Zid agar na ho shamil,*

*To saare zamane ko pata hai inhe nibhane ke farayaz kya hai!*

- ❖ Farayaz – Duties, Kartavya

## Translation

*If everything is fair in love and war,*

*Then what is unfair?*

*If the desire to possess is not included,*

*The whole world knows what it takes to fulfill these duties!*

# हसरत

एक हसरत है तुम्हें पाने की,

बेवजह ही तुमसे दिल लगाने की,

ख्वाहिश नहीं कि तुम भी चाहो टूटकर हमें,

एक चाहत है तुम्हारे लिए फना हो जाने की।

❖ फना – नाश, बर्बाद

# Hasrat

*Ek hasrat hai tumhe paane ki,*
*Bewajah hi tumse dil lagane ki,*
*Khwayish nahin ke tum bhi chaho tut kar humein,*
*Ek chahat hai tumhare liye fanah ho jaane ki!*

❖ Fanah – Destroy, Barbad

# Translation

*There is a longing to have you,*

*For no reason, my heart is attached to you.*

*I don't wish for you to break my heart too,*

*There is a desire to be consumed by my love for you!*

# क़ैद

करते होंगे लोग यादों को क़ैद अपने ज़हन में,

उसने तो मेरे ज़हन को अपनी यादों से क़ैद कर रखा है!

होते होंगे लोग बेवफ़ा इस कायनात में,

उसने तो अपनी अदाओं से मुझे उबैद कर रखा है,

कम हो जाता होगा इश्क़ लोगों के दरमियान,

उसने तो मेरी मोहब्बत को मुस्तक़िल ज़ैद कर रखा है,

होती होगी खोट और मिलावट लोगों की नियत में,

उसने तो मेरी नियत को मुसलसल सुफैद कर रखा है!

- ❖ उबैद – वफादार
- ❖ दरमियान – बीच में

- ❖ मुस्तक़िल – अटल
- ❖ ज़ैद – बढ़ना
- ❖ मुसलसल – निरंतर
- ❖ सुफैद – शुद्ध

# Qaid

*Karte honge log yaado ko qaid apne zehan me,*

*Usne to mere zehan ko apni yaadon se qaid kr rakha hai,*

*Hote honge log bewafa is kaaynaat me,*

*Usne to apni adaon se mujhe ubaid kar rakha hai,*

*Kam ho jata hoga ishq logo ke darmiyaan,*

*Usne to meri mohabbat ko mustaqil zaid kr rakha hai,*

*Hoti hogii khot aur milawat logo ki niyat me,*

*Usne to meri niyat ko musalsal sufaid kr rakha hai!*

- ❖ Ubaid – Loyal, Wafadar
- ❖ Darmiyan – In between, Beech mein
- ❖ Mustaqil – Permanent, Atal
- ❖ Zaid – To increase, Vikas
- ❖ Musalsal – Constant, Nirantar
- ❖ Sufaid – White, Pure, Shudh

## Translation

*People may imprison memories in their minds,*

*But she has trapped my mind with her memories!*

*There may be unfaithful people in this world,*

*But she has captivated me with her charm.*

*Love may diminish between people,*

*But she has made my love everlasting.*

*There may be deceit and corruption in people's intentions,*

*But she has kept my intentions pure and constant!*

# अख़बार

तेरे चेहरे के अख़बार को देखकर मालूम होता है,

इसमें खबर है कोई, जो मैं पढ़ नहीं पाऊंगा,

इल्तिजा यही है कि, यूं तन्हा न छोड़ना मुझे,

बिन तेरे ज़िंदगी में आगे, मैं कभी बढ़ नहीं पाऊंगा,

अगर आई है तू मुख्तलिफ़ होने के लिए,

ये रस्म-ए-जुदाई के फंदे पे, मैं कभी चढ़ नहीं पाऊंगा,

तुझसे शिकवा करने का दिल तो है बहुत,

लेकिन इंसान हूं, अपनी क़िस्मत से भी तो, मैं कभी लड़ नहीं पाऊंगा!

- ❖ इल्तिजा – निवेदन
- ❖ मुख्तलिफ – जुदा
- ❖ शिकवा – शिकायत

# Akhbaar

*Tere chehre ke akhbaar ko dekh ke maloom hota hai,*

*Isme khabar hai koi Jo Mai padh nahi paunga,*

*Iltija yahi hai ke yu tanhaa naa chhorna mujhe,*

*Bin tere zindagi me aage, mai kabhi badh nahi paunga!*

*Agar aayi hai tu mukhtalif hone ke liye,*

*Ye rasm e judai ke fande pe, mai kabhi chadh nahi paunga,*

*Tujhse shikwa karne ka dil to hai bohot,*

*Magar insaan hu, apni qismat se bhi to mai kabhi lad nahi paunga.*

- ❖ Iltija – Request, Nivedan
- ❖ Mukhtalif – Separate, Juda
- ❖ Shikwa – Complaint, Shikayat

## Translation

*Looking at the newspaper of your face, I can tell,*
*There's news in it that I cannot read.*
*My plea is that you don't leave me alone like this,*
*Without you, I can never move forward in life!*
*If you've come to be different,*
*I can never rise to the occasion of this separation.*
*I have a strong desire to complain to you,*
*But I am human; I can never fight against my fate!*

# ख्यालात

ख्यालात की दुनिया में तुम्हारी रूह तक सिर्फ मेरी है,

क्या हुआ अगर हकीकत में, तुम्हारा जिस्म किसी और के पास है!

# Khayalaat

*Khayalaat ki duniya me tumhari ruh tak sirf meri hai,*

*Kya hua agar haqiqat me tumhara jism kisi aur ke paas hai!*

# Translation

*In the world of thoughts, your soul belongs only to me,*
*What if in reality, your body is with someone else!*

# ज़ालिम

**कैसा ज़ालिम है वो, एक ही ज़ुल्म बार-बार करता है,**

मेरे दिल में रहता है, और मेरे ही दिल के टुकड़े हज़ार करता है,

मेरे ज़हन को क़ैद किए हैं, अपनी यादों से वो इस तरह,

शाम ढलते ही वो मुझे, मेरे दीवानेपन से बीमार करता है।

**कैसा ज़ालिम है वो, एक ही ज़ुल्म बार-बार करता है,**

मेरा ज़हन चाल से उसकी, इस दिल को हमेशा होशियार करता है,

लेकिन मासूम दिल मेरा, उस पर हमेशा ऐतबार करता है,

कोई मौका नहीं छोड़ता, वो मेरे इस दिल को तोड़ने का,

जैसे वो शख़्स शिद्दत से, बस इसी मौके का इंतज़ार करता है।

**कैसा ज़ालिम है वो, एक ही ज़ुल्म बार-बार करता है,**


मेरा दिल उस पर अपनी जान, यूं निसार करता है,

उसको भूल जाने से हमेशा इनकार करता है,

दिल और ज़हन की होती रहती है आपस में कश-मकश,

दिल मेरा मेरे ही ज़हन से, उसकी मोहब्बत का इज़हार करता है।


**कैसा ज़ालिम है वो, एक ही ज़ुल्म बार-बार करता है,**


कुछ तो खूबी होगी उसमें, जो मेरे दिल को वो उसका तलबगार करता है,

क्या खासियत है उसमें, जो मेरा दिल उससे मोहब्बत बेशुमार करता है?

नमाज़े अदा करता हूं, सिर्फ उसे पाने के लिए,

खुदा की नज़र में अक्सर, वो मुझे इस तरह से गुनहगार करता है।


**कैसा ज़ालिम है वो, एक ही ज़ुल्म बार-बार करता है,**

कभी-कभी वो कमाल का रुख इख़्तियार करता है,

मेरी तन्हाईयों का, मुझे ही कसूरवार करता है,

उसकी मोहब्बत में पागलपन के दौर से गुज़रता हूं मैं,

और मेरी ऐसी हालत का, वो मुझे ही ज़िम्मेदार करता है।

**कैसा ज़ालिम है वो, एक ही ज़ुल्म बार-बार करता है,**

मेरी चाहत को भरी महफ़िल में, वो ज़ार-ज़ार करता है,

तौहीन मेरे इश्क़ की, वो सर-ए-बाज़ार करता है,

अब तो आलम ये है कि, लगता है कारोबारी है वो,

इश्क़ का सौदागर है, और मोहब्बत का कारोबार करता है!

**कैसा ज़ालिम है वो, एक ही ज़ुल्म बार-बार करता है !**

- ❖ ऐतबार – भरोसा
- ❖ निसार – निछावर
- ❖ कश-मकश – खींचतान
- ❖ इज़हार – बताना

- ❖ तलबगार – चाहने वाला
- ❖ रुख इख्तियार – परिवर्तन
- ❖ ज़ार-ज़ार – दुखी
- ❖ तौहीन – बेइज़्ज़ती
- ❖ सर-ए-बाज़ार – लोगों के बीच में
- ❖ सौदागर – व्यापारी

# Zaalim

**Kaisa zaalim hai wo, ek hi zulm bar bar karta hai**

Mere dil me rahta hai, aur mere hi dil k tukde hazar karta hai,

Mere zehan ko qaid kiye hai apni yaadon se wo iss tarah,

Shaam dhalte hi wo mujhe, mere deewanepan se bimaar karta hai,

**Kaisa zaalim hai wo, ek hi zulm bar bar karta hai,**

Mera zehan chaal se uski, is dil ko hamesha hoshiyar karta hai,

Lekin masoom dil mera, uspe hamesha aitbaar karta hai,

Koi mauka nahi chhorta wo mere is dil ko todne ka,

Jaise wo shakhs shiddat se bas isi mauke ka intezaar karta hai,

**Kaisa zaalim hai wo, ek hi zulm bar bar karta hai,**

*Mera dil uspe apni jaan yun nisaar karta hai,*

*Usko bhool jaane se hamesha inkaar karta hai,*

*Dil aur zehan ki hoti rahti hai kash m kash,*

*Dil mera mere hi zehan se uski mohabbat ka izhaar karta hai,*

**Kaisa zaalim hai wo, ek hi zulm bar bar karta hai,**

*Kuch to khoobi hogi usmein,jo mere dil ko wo uska talabgaar karta hai,*

*Kya khasiyat hai usme jo mera dil usse mohabbat beshumar karta hai,*

*Namaz e ada karta hu sirf usey paane ke liye,*

*Khuda ki nazar me aksar, wo mujhe is tarah se gunahgaar karta hai,*

**Kaisa zaalim hai wo, ek hi zulm baar baar karta hai,**

*Kabhi kabhi wo kamaal ka rukh ikhtiyar karta hai,*

*Meri tanhaaiyo ka mujhe hi kasoor waar krta hai,*

*Uski mohabbat mein pagalpan ke daur se guzarta hun main,*

*Aur meri aisi halat ka, wo mujhe hi zimmedaar karta hai,*

*Kaisa zaalim hai wo, ek hi zulm baar baar karta hai,*

*Meri chahat ko bhari mahfil me, wo zaar zaar karta hai,*
*Tauheen mere ishq ki, wo sar-e-bazaar karta hai,*
*Ab to alam ye hai ke lagta hai kaarobaari hai wo,*
*Ishq ka saudagar hai aur mohabbat ka kaarobaar karta hai!*

*Kaisa zaalim hai wo, ek hi zulm bar bar karta hai!*

- ❖ Aitbaar – Trust, Bharosa
- ❖ Nisaar – Sacrifice, Nyochhawar
- ❖ Kashmakash – Struggle, Khinchtaan
- ❖ Izhaar – To express, batana
- ❖ Talabgaar – Seeker, Chahne wala
- ❖ Rukh Ikhtiyar – Change in Personality, Parivartan
- ❖ Zaar zaar – Sad, Dukhi
- ❖ Tauheen – Disrespect, Baizzati
- ❖ Sar-e- bazaar – In a crowd, logon ke beech mein
- ❖ Saudagar – Merchant, Vyapaari

# Translation

*What a cruel person he is, committing the same injustice repeatedly,*

*He resides in my heart, yet breaks it into a thousand pieces.*

*He has imprisoned my mind with his memories like this,*

*As evening falls, he makes me ill with my own madness.*

*What a cruel person he is, committing the same injustice repeatedly.*

*My mind, aware of his tricks, keeps this heart always alert,*

*Yet my innocent heart always trusts him.*

*He leaves no opportunity to break my heart,*

*As if he waits with intensity for just this chance.*

*What a cruel person he is, committing the same injustice repeatedly.*

*My heart sacrifices itself for him,*

*Always refusing to forget him.*

*There's a constant struggle between my heart and mind,*

*My heart expresses his love through my own thoughts.*

*What a cruel person he is, committing the same injustice repeatedly.*

*There must be something in him that makes my heart long for him,*

*What is it about him that my heart loves him endlessly?*

*I pray only to win him over,*

*In God's eyes, he often makes me feel like a sinner.*

*What a cruel person he is, committing the same injustice repeatedly.*

*Sometimes he adopts a marvelous demeanor,*

*Blaming me for my loneliness.*

*I go through a phase of madness in his love,*

*And he holds me responsible for my condition.*

*What a cruel person he is, committing the same injustice repeatedly.*

*In crowded gatherings, he makes my love weep,*

*He humiliates my feelings in public.*

*Now it feels like he's a businessman,*

*A merchant of love, trading in affection!*

*What a cruel person he is, committing the same injustice repeatedly!*

# तन्हाई

फरमाया उससे जो इश्क़  तो मुझे फ़कत तन्हाई मिली,

मर्ज़ मिला ऐसा, न जिसकी कभी कोई दवाई मिली,

बर्बाद किया उसके इश्क़ ने आहिस्ता-आहिस्ता से ऐसे,

ना कहीं कोई सबूत मिला, ना कहीं कोई तबाही मिली,

माहिर थी जैसे वो मेरे इश्क़ को हलाल करने में,

समझ नहीं आता, माशूका मिली या कोई क़साई  मिली,

मजनून किया उसके इश्क़ ने मुझे कुछ इस तरह,

खुदा से भी दूर हुआ, और उससे भी हमें जुदाई मिली,

ताल्लुक तोड़ दिए मेरे अपनों ने, मुझे दीवाना समझ के,

फिर मैं जहाँ भी गया, वहाँ मुझे सिर्फ रुसवाई मिली,

हसरतें इतनी भी बड़ी नहीं थीं उससे मेरी,

ख्वाहिश थी वफ़ा की, लेकिन मिली तो हमें सिर्फ बेवफ़ाई मिली,

उससे मिलने से पहले, मैं भी था हंसता-खिलखिलाता,

हंसी खो गई मेरी, मुझे तो वो ऐसी हरजाई मिली,

साबित कर न पाया, अपनी मोहब्बत मैं उसे,

मेरे इश्क़ के खिलाफ मुझे, उसी से हमेशा झूठी गवाही मिली,

फ़ैसला हो सकता था मेरे हक़ में मेरे इश्क़ का,

लेकिन न मिला कोई पैरोकार, न मुझे कोई सुनवाई मिली,

ख़ामोशी तो रही नापसंद मुझे ये सारी ज़िंदगी,

फिर न जाने क्यों इस दुनिया से मुझे, इतनी ख़ामोशी से बिदायी मिली !

- ❖ मर्ज़ – बीमारी
- ❖ माहिर – विशेषज्ञ
- ❖ हलाल – मार डालना

- ❖ माशूका – प्रेमिका
- ❖ मजनून – दीवाना
- ❖ रुसवाई – अपमान
- ❖ हरजाई – बेवफा
- ❖ पैरोकार – वकील

# Tanhaayi

*Farmaya usse jo ishq to mujhe faqt tanhayi mili,*
*Marz mila aisa, na jiski kabhi koi dawayi mili,*
*Barbad kiya uske ishq ne ahista ahista se aise,*
*Na kahin koi saboot mila na kahin koi tabahi mili!*

*Mahir thi jaise wo mere ishq ko halal karne me,*
*Samajh nahi aata mashooqa mili, ya koi kasayi mili,*
*Majnoon kia uske ishq ne mujhe kuch is tarah,*
*Khuda se bhi door hua, aur usse bhi hamein judaayi mili!*

*Ta'lluq tod diye mere apno ne mujhe deewana samajh ke,*
*Fir mai jahan bhi gaya wahan mujhe sirf ruswaayi mili,*
*Hasratein itni bhi badi nahi thi usse meri,*
*Khwaish thi wafa ki, lekin mili to hamein sirf bewafayi mili,*

*Usse milne se pahle mai bhi tha hasta khilkhilata,*

*Hasee kho gayi meri, mujhe to wo aisi harjaayi mili,*

*Saabit kar na paya apni mohabbat mai usey,*

*Mere ishq ke khilaaf mujhe usi se hamesha jhuti gawahi mili,*

*Faisla ho sakta tha mere haq me mere ishq ka,*

*Lekin na mila koi pairokaar, na mujhe koi sunwayi mili,*

*Khamoshi to rahi napasand mujhko saari zindgi,*

*Fir na jaane kyu is duniya se mujhe, itni khamoshi se bidayi mili!*

- ❖ Marz – Disease, Bimari
- ❖ Mahir – Specialist, Visheshagya
- ❖ Halal – To kill, Maar dalna
- ❖ Mashooqa – Lover, Premika
- ❖ Majnoon – Crazy, Deewana
- ❖ Ruswayi – Dishonour, Apmaan
- ❖ Harjaayi – Unfaithful, Bewafa
- ❖ Pairokaar – Lawyer, Wakeel

## Translation

*What I said was love, but I received only loneliness,*

*I was afflicted with a disease for which there was no cure.*

*Her love gradually destroyed me in such a way,*

*That I found no evidence, nor any devastation.*

*She was skilled at making my love seem permissible,*

*I can't tell if I found a beloved or just a butcher.*

*Her love drove me to madness like this,*

*I became distant from God, and from her I received separation.*

*My loved ones severed ties with me, thinking I was crazy,*

*Wherever I went, I only faced humiliation.*

*My desires weren't that great for her,*

*I wished for fidelity, but only found betrayal.*

*Before meeting her, I used to laugh and smile,*

*My laughter vanished; I only found despair.*

*I couldn't prove my love to her,*

*Against my love, I always received false testimony from her.*

*A decision could have been made in favor of my love,*

*But I found no advocate, nor was I ever heard.*

*Silence has been unwelcome to me my whole life,*

*And then, I don't know why, I was bid farewell so quietly from this world!*

# बाक़ी है

क्यों हार जाऊं इस ज़माने से मैं,

के मुझमें थोड़ी हिम्मत, तो अभी बाक़ी है,

तारीफें करते जो थकते नहीं थे कभी,

करना उन्हें मेरी ग़ीबत, तो अभी बाक़ी है,

नक़ाब तो उठ चुका है चेहरे से उनके,

दिखाना उन्हें अपनी जुर्रत, तो अभी बाक़ी है,

वक्त लगेगा मुझे यूं रुसवा करने में उन्हें,

के दुनिया में मेरी थोड़ी इज़्ज़त, तो अभी बाक़ी है,

छोड़ने पड़ेंगे ख्याल उन्हें मेरी बरबादी के,

ज़माने में मेरी इतनी शोहरत, तो अभी बाक़ी है,

नासमझ समझते आए हैं काफी लोग मुझे,
दिखाना उन्हें मेरी हिकमत, तो अभी बाक़ी है,

देख रहा हूं अभी तो तमाशा मैं फिलहाल,
करना मुझे कोई हरकत, तो अभी बाक़ी है,

ज़माने ने देखा है नरम लहजा मेरा,
दिखाना अपने जलाल की शिद्दत, तो अभी बाक़ी है,

माफ करने की तो वैसे आदत रही है मेरी,
लेकिन मुझमें बदले की फितरत, तो अभी बाक़ी है,

कर रहे हैं वो लोग दुश्मनी मुझसे खामखां यूं ही,
उठाना उन्हें उनकी ज़िल्लत, तो अभी बाक़ी है,

लिख सकता हूं अपनी सारी नफरत ज़माने के लिए,
क्योंकि लिखना मुझे मेरी वसीयत, तो अभी बाक़ी है,

## Karze Ka Ishq

डरता हूं के हो न जाऊं ज़ालिम मैं भी,

मुझमें मेरे ईमान की मोहब्बत, तो अभी बाक़ी है,

वैसे अभी तो नहीं आया मुझे ख़याल-ए-बरबादी,

के दिल में मेरे थोड़ी उल्फत, तो अभी बाक़ी है,

नुकसान हुआ दौलत का, तो क्या ही नुकसान हुआ,

शुक्र है मेरे पास मेरी सेहत, तो अभी बाक़ी है,

हौसले टूट जाएं मेरे ये तो मुमकिन नहीं,

देखना मुझे अपने खुदा की रहमत, तो अभी बाक़ी है,

वैसे आज़माई है, अभी तो आधी ही तक़दीर मैंने,

आज़माना मुझे मेरी आधी क़िस्मत, तो अभी बाक़ी है।

- ❖ ग़ीबत – पीठ पीछे बुराई करना
- ❖ हिकमत – बुद्धिमानी
- ❖ जलाल – गुस्सा

- ❖ ज़िल्लत – बेइज़्ज़ती
- ❖ उल्फत – प्यार

# Baaqi Hai

*Kyu haar jau is zamane se mai,*
*Ke mujhme thodi himmat to abhi baaqi hai,*

*Taareefein karte jo thakte nhi the kabhi,*
*Karna unhe meri gheebat to abhi baaqi hai,*

*Naqaab to uth chuka hai chehre se unke,*
*Dikhana unhe apni jurrat to abhi baaqi hai,*

*Waqt lagega mujhe yu ruswa karne me unhe,*
*Ke duniya me meri thodi izzat to abhi baaqi hai,*

*Chhorne padenge khayal unhe meri barbadi ke,*
*Zamane me meri itni shohrat to abhi baaqi hai,*

*Nasmjh samjhte aye hai kaafi log mujhe,*
*Dikhana unhe meri hikmat to abhi baaqi hai,*

*Dekh raha hu abhi to tamasha mai filhal,*
*Karna mujhe koi harkat to abhi baaqi hai,*

*Zamane ne dekha hai naram lahja mera,*
*Dikhana apne jalal ki shiddat to abhi baaqi hai,*

*Maaf karne ki to waise aadat rahi hai meri,*
*Lekin mujhme badle ki fitrat to abhi baaqi hai,*

*Kar rahein hai dushmani mujhse khamakha yu hi,*
*Uthana unhe unki zillat to abhi baaqi hai,*

*Likh sakta hu apni saari nafrat zamane ke liye,*
*Kyuki likhna mujhe apni wasiyat to abhi baaqi h,*

*Darta hu ke ho na jau zaalim mai bhi,*
*Mujhme mere imaan ki mohabbat to abhi baaqi hai,*

*Wyse abhi to nahi aya mujhe khayal e barbadi,*
*Ke dil me mere thodi ulfat to abhi baaqi hai,*

*Nuksan hua daulat ka to kya hi nuksaan hua,*
*Shukr hai mere paas meri sehat to abhi baaqi hai,*

*Hausle tut jaaye mere ye to mumkin nahi,*
*Dekhna mujhe apne khuda ki rahmat to abhi baaqi hai,*

*Waise aazmaayi hai abhi to aadhi hi taqdeer maine,*
*Aazmaana mujhe meri aadhi qismat to abhi baaqi hai!*

- ❖ Gheebat – Backbiting, Peeth pichhe burayi karna
- ❖ Hikmat – Wisdom, Buddhimaani
- ❖ Jalal – Anger, Gussa
- ❖ Zillat – Dishonour, Baizzati
- ❖ Ulfat – Affection, Pyaar

# Translation

*Why should I lose to this world,*
*When I still have some courage left in me?*
*Those who never tire of praising me,*
*Let them gossip about me; that's still left to do.*
*The mask has been lifted from their faces,*
*Showing them my bravery is still to come.*
*It will take time to expose them for humiliating me,*
*Because I still have some respect in this world.*
*They will have to abandon thoughts of my ruin,*
*As I still have some fame in this life.*
*Many have misunderstood me,*
*Showing them my wisdom is still pending.*
*I'm currently observing this spectacle,*
*Taking action is still on my agenda.*
*Society has seen my soft demeanor,*
*Revealing the intensity of my majesty is yet to happen.*
*I've developed a habit of forgiveness,*
*But my nature for revenge is still alive.*
*They're acting against me for no reason,*

*Raising them from their disgrace is still pending.*

*I can write all my hatred for the world,*

*Because I still have to write my will.*

*I fear becoming cruel myself,*

*As the love for my faith is still within me.*

*I haven't yet contemplated my ruin,*

*Because there's still some affection in my heart.*

*What loss does it matter if I lose wealth?*

*I'm grateful that my health is still intact.*

*My spirit will not break; that's impossible,*

*I still have to witness the mercy of my God.*

*I've tested only half of my fate so far,*

*Testing my complete destiny is still to come!*

# सुकून

फ़ायदे में होती मेरी भी ज़िंदगी,

अगर पल-पल मैं उसे, खो नहीं रहा होता,

वायदे पर रहती अगर अपने वो क़ायम,

तो इस मोहब्बत को अकेले मैं, ढो नहीं रहा होता,

इतना दर्द न होता मुझे कभी शायद,

अगर वो इस दिल में कोई कांटा, चुभो नहीं रहा होता,

नींद मुझे भी आ जाती तसल्ली से बेशक,

अगर वो किसी और की बाहों में, सुकून से सो नहीं रहा होता!

# Sukoon

*Fayde me hoti meri bhi zindagi,*
*Agar pal pal mai usey kho nhi rha hota,*
*Wayde pe rahti agar apne wo qaayam,*
*To is mohabbat ko akele mai dhho nahi raha hota,*

*Itna dard na hota mujhe kabhi shayad,*
*Agar wo is dil me koi kaata chubho nahi raha hota,*
*Nind mujhe bhi aa jaati tasalli se beshaq,*
*Agar wo kisi aur ki baahon me sukoon se so nhi rha hota!!*

# Translation

*My life would have been better,*

*If I weren't losing her every moment.*

*If she remained steadfast in her promises,*

*I wouldn't be searching for this love alone.*

*I wouldn't feel so much pain, perhaps,*

*If she weren't piercing my heart with her presence.*

*I would also find peace in sleep, for sure,*

*If she were peacefully sleeping in someone else's arms!*

# ज़िंदा

अभी ज़िंदा हूं मैं, ये सबूत है इस बात का,

दुनिया में कोई किसी के बगैर मर नहीं जाता।

❖ बगैर- बिना

# Zinda

*Abhi Zinda hun main, ye saboot hai is baat ka,*
*Duniya mein koi kisi ke bagair marr nahi jata!*

- ❖ Bagair – Without, Bina

# Translation

*I'm still alive; this is proof of that.*

*No one in this world truly dies without someone else!*

# उसकी बातें

उसकी बातों को अपनी यादों में सजा रखा है,

मेरे अहसासों को अपने ही दिल में, दबा रखा है,

अहमियत कितनी है उसकी, मैं कैसे बताऊं उसे,

उसकी मोहब्बत में तो मैंने, अपना नाम तक भुला रखा है,

मेरे इश्क़ ने मेरे ही ज़हन में, तूफान मचा रखा है,

उसकी मोहब्बत को मेरे लिए, मेरी दवा बना रखा है,

मेरे टूटे हुए दिल की मरम्मत कर रहा वो इस तरह,

जैसे मेरे दिल को उसने, किराए पर उठा रखा है,

बीती यादों को मैंने, अपने दिल से भुला रखा है,

उसकी चाहत में मैंने, खुद की हस्ती मिटा रखा है,

वो कहती है उससे खफा-खफा सा रहता हूं मैं,

जबकि उस नादान को मैंने, अपनी पलकों पे बिठा रखा है,

उसके इश्क़ को अपनी रूह में बसा रखा है,

उसको पाने की ख्वाहिश में, खुद को सता रखा है,

उसकी हसरत में तड़पता हूं मैं इस कदर,

जैसे मैंने उसका दिया कोई, मीठा सा ज़हर खा रखा है,

एक राज़ गुज़रे वक्त का, मैंने उससे छिपा रखा है,

शर्मसार हूं, तब भी मैंने उससे नज़रें मिला रखा है,

सहम जाता हूं जब तसव्वुर करता हूं उसके बिना ये ज़िंदगी,

इसलिए काफी झूठों को मैंने, उससे सच्चा बता रखा है,

अपनी क़िस्मत को अपने ही ऊपर हंसा रखा है,

उसको पाने से पहले ही, उसको गवा रखा है,

वो सोचती है उससे जुदा-जुदा सा रहता हूं मैं,
उसे तो बस मैंने अपनी, बुरी सोहबत से बचा रखा है,

मेरी क़िस्मत ने तमन्नाओं को मेरी जला रखा है,
मेरे बीते वक्त ने, मुझे उससे दूर भगा रखा है,

टूट जाएगी वो मेरी ज़िंदगी का अफसाना सुनके,
इसलिए मैंने भी अपने होठों को बस, यूं ही सिला रखा है!

- ❖ हसरत – चाहत
- ❖ शर्मसार – शर्मिंदा
- ❖ तसव्वुर – कल्पना
- ❖ अफसाना – कहानी

# Uski Baatein

*Uski baaton ko apni yaadon me saja Rakha hai,*
*Mere ahsaaso ko apne dil me hi daba rakha hai,*
*Ahmiyat kitni hai uski mai kaise bataau usey,*
*Uski mohabbat me to maine apna naam tak bhula rakha hai,*

*Mere ishq ne mere hi zehan me toofan macha rakha hai,*
*Uski mohabbat ko mere liye meri dawa bana rakha hai,*
*Mere tute hue dil ki marammat kar rha wo is tarah,*
*Jaise mere dil ko usne kiraye pe utha rakha hai,*

*Beeti yaadon ko maine apne dil se bhula rakha hai,*
*Uski chahat me maine khud ki hasti mita rakha hai,*
*Wo kahti hai usse khafa khafa sa rahta hu mai,*
*Jabki us nadaan ko maine apni palkon pe bitha rakha hai,*

*Uske ishq ko apni ruh me basa rakha hai,*

*Usko paane ki khwayish me khud ko sata rakha hai,*

*Uski hasrat me tadapta hu mai is qadar,*

*Jaise maine uska diya koi meetha sa zehar kha rakha hai,*

*Ek raaz guzre waqt ka maine usse chhipaa rakha hai,*

*Sharmsaar hu, tab bhi maine usse nazren mila rakha hai,*

*Saham jata hu jb tasawwur karta hu uske bina ye zindagi,*

*Isliye kaafi jhuthon ko maine usse sachcha bata rakha hai,*

*Apni qismat ko apne hi upar hasa rakha hai,*

*Usko paane se pahle hi, usko gawa rakha hai,*

*Wo sochti hai usse juda juda sa rahta hu main,*

*Usey to bas maine apni buri sohbat se bacha rakha hai,*

*Meri qismat ne tamannao ko meri jala rakha hai,*

*Mere beete waqt ne, mujhe usse door bhaga rakha hai,*

*Tut jayegi wo meri zindagi ka afsaanaa sunke,*

*Isliye maine bhi apne hotho ko bas yuhi sila rakha hai!*

- ❖ Hasrat – Desire, Chahat
- ❖ Sharmsaar – Ashamed, Sharminda
- ❖ Tasawwur – Imagination, Kalpana
- ❖ Afsaana – Story, Kahani

# Translation

*I have adorned her words in my memories,*
*Concealed my feelings deep within my heart.*
*How can I express her importance to her?*
*In her love, I have even forgotten my own name.*

*My passion has stirred a storm in my mind,*
*Her love has become my remedy.*
*She mends my broken heart this way,*
*As if she has rented my heart for herself.*

*I have erased past memories from my heart,*
*In her affection, I have obliterated my own existence.*
*She says I seem angry with her,*
*While I have placed her on my lap like royalty.*

*I have enshrined her love in my soul,*
*In the desire to have her, I keep tormenting myself.*
*I yearn for her so much,*
*As if I have consumed a sweet poison meant for her.*

*I have hidden a secret from the past,*

*Though I am ashamed, I still manage to meet her gaze.*

*I tremble at the thought of life without her,*

*That's why I have called many falsehoods true regarding her.*

*I have kept my fate resting upon me,*

*I have held her even before I could possess her.*

*She thinks I remain distant,*

*When I have only protected her from my bad company.*

*My destiny has burned my desires,*

*My past has driven me far from her.*

*She would shatter upon hearing the tale of my life,*

*That's why I have kept my lips sealed for now.*

# बेउम्मीदी

इश्क़ करना है तो बेउम्मीदी के ख्याल से करो,

क्योंकि इश्क़ में अरमानों का तो तुम्हें क़त्ल-ए-आम ही मिलेगा,

करना ही है इश्क़, तो करो किसी मुसाफिर की तरह,

इस जहाँ में वफा निभाना, तो तुम्हें हराम ही मिलेगा,

एक ऐसी नीलामी की तरह होती है ये मोहब्बत,

जिसकी चाहत में तुम्हें हर आशिक़, खुद नीलाम ही मिलेगा,

बादशाहत करता आया है, ये इश्क़ इस जहाँ में ऐसे,

यहां पर हर आशिक़, तुम्हें इसका गुलाम ही मिलेगा,

ज़िंदगी का इम्तिहान लेता है ये कुछ इस तरह,

यहां हर आशिक़ इश्क़ में, तुम्हें नाकाम ही मिलेगा,

## Karze Ka Ishq

गुज़र जाओगे इश्क़ में जब तुम अपनी हदों से भी ज़्यादा,
अपनी हस्ती का तब तुम्हें, काम तमाम ही मिलेगा,

दिन की रोशनी में मिलोगे, तो मुस्कुराते हुए मिलोगे लोगों से,
रात के अंधेरों में तो, तुम्हारे हाथों में जाम ही मिलेगा,

दुनिया की भीड़ में काफी शरीफ लगोगे तुम,
तन्हाइयों में तो तुम्हारा, वजूद भी तुम्हें बदनाम ही मिलेगा,

मशवरा है कि न करना तुम, कभी किसी से मोहब्बत,
वरना इश्क़ में तुम्हारा भी, तुम्हें बुरा अंजाम ही मिलेगा।

काफी लोग पहचान तक भुला चुके हैं, इस इश्क़ में अपनी,
नाम तुम्हारा भी इस दुनिया में, तुम्हें गुमनाम ही मिलेगा,

चंद लोगों को ही नसीब होती है, उन्हें उनकी मोहब्बत,
वरना इश्क़ में तबाह लोगों का ज़िक्र, तुम्हें सर-ए-आम ही मिलेगा,

अगर लग गई हाथ तुम्हें, तुम्हारे इश्क़ में कामयाबी,

तो आशिक़ो की दुनिया में तुम्हें, सिर्फ एहतराम ही मिलेगा,

वरना ज़ख्म मिलेगा ऐसा जो सहन न होगा तुमसे,

और एक दर्द मुस्तकिल तुम्हें, सुबह व शाम ही मिलेगा,

तकसीम न कर सकोगे तुम किसी से अपनी तकलीफें,

जैसे उस दर्द पर लिखा तुम्हें, सिर्फ तुम्हारा नाम ही मिलेगा!!

- ❖ बेउम्मीदी – आशाहीन
- ❖ हस्ती – व्यक्तित्व
- ❖ जाम – शराब
- ❖ वजूद – अस्तित्व
- ❖ मुस्तकिल - कभी खत्म न होने वाला, अटल
- ❖ तकसीम – बांटना

# Beummeedi

*Ishq karna hai to beummeeedi ke khayal se karo,*
*Kyunki ishq me armano ka to tumhe katle aam hi milega,*
*Karna hi hai ishq to karo kisi musafir ki tarah,*
*Is jahaan me wafa nibhana to tmhe haraam hi milega,*

*Ek aisi neelaami ki tarah hoti hai ye mohabbat,*
*Jiski chahat me tumhe har aashiq khud neelam hi milega,*
*Badshaahat karta aya hai ye ishq is jahan me aise,*
*Yahan pe har ashiq tumhe iska ghulaam hi milega,*

*Zindagi ka imtihaan leta hai ye kuch is tarah,*
*Yahan har aashiq ishq me tmhe naqaam hi milega,*
*Guzar jaoge ishq me jab tum apni hadon se bhi zada,*
*Apni hasti ka tab tumhe, kaam tamam hi milega,*

*Din ki roshni me miloge to muskurate hue miloge logon se,*

*Raat ke andheron me to,tumhre hathon me jaaam hi milega,*

*Duniya ki bheed me kaafi shareef lagoge tum,*

*Tanhayiyon me to tumhara,wajood bhi tumhe badnaam hi milega,*


*Mashawara hai ke na karna tum kabhi kisi se mohabbat,*

*Warna ishq me tumhara bhi tumhe bura anjaam hi milega,*

*Kaafi log pehchan tak bhula chuke hai, iss ishq me apni,*

*Naam tumhara bhi is duniya me,tumhe gumnaam hi milega,*


*Chand logo ko hi naseeb hoti hai unki mohabbat,*

*Warna ishq me tabah logo ka zikr,tumhe sar e aam hi milega,*

*Agar lag gayi hath tumhe tumhare ishq me kaamyaabi,*

*To Aashiqo ki duniya me tumhe sirf ehteram hi milega,*

*Warna zakhm milega aisa jo sahan na hoga tumse,*

*Aur ek dard mustaqil tumhe subah wa sham hi milega,*

*Takseem na kar sakoge tum kisi se apni takleefen,*

*Jaise us dard pe likha tumhe sirf tumhara naam hi milega!!*

- ❖ Beummeedi – Without hopes, Ashaheen
- ❖ Hasti – Personality, Vyaktitva
- ❖ Jaam – Alcohal, Sharab
- ❖ Wajood – Existence, Astitva
- ❖ Mustaqil – Constant, Atal
- ❖ Takseem – To distribute, Baatna

# Translation

*If you want to love, do it without any hopes,*

*Because in love, you will only find the mass slaughter of desires.*

*If you must love, do it like a traveler,*

*In this world, loyalty will be forbidden for you.*

*Love is like an auction,*

*In its longing, every lover will only find despair.*

*This love reigns like a king in this world,*

*Here, every lover will be found as its slave.*

*Life tests you in this way,*

*In love, you will only find failure.*

*When you go beyond your limits in love,*

*You will find the end of your existence.*

*In the daylight, you will meet people with smiles,*

*But in the darkness of night, you will find alcohol glass in your hands.*

*In the crowd of the world, you will seem quite decent,*

*But in loneliness, your existence will only bring you shame.*


*It's advised not to love anyone ever,*
*Or else, in love, you will face a bitter end.*
*Many have forgotten their identity in this love,*
*And your name will be lost in this world.*


*Only a few are blessed with their love,*
*Otherwise, in love, you will only hear tales of devastation.*
*If you succeed in your love,*
*In the world of lovers, you will find only respect.*


*Otherwise, you will receive wounds that you cannot bear,*
*And a constant pain will greet you morning and night.*
*You won't be able to share your troubles with anyone,*
*As that pain will only bear your name!*

# कहर

मेरी तमन्नाओं ने एक सितारा चमकाया था,

मुझे ख्वाब में, एक ऐसे शख्स को दिखाया था,

धरी की धरी रह गई मेरी सारी हसरतें,

जब किसी ने मुझे, मेरी नींद से जगाया था,

रंगीन ख्वाबों ने मुझे उकसाया था,

तक़दीर के खिलाफ मुझे बाग़ी बनाया था,

काफी बेरंग सी लगने लगी मुझे ये ज़िंदगी,

जब मैंने अपनी आँखों से वो झूठा चश्मा हटाया था,

मुक़द्दर ने मुझे, मेरे सच से मिलाया था,

बिना लड़े ही मुझे, बस ऐसे ही हराया था,

## Karze Ka Ishq

तसव्वुर में तो काफ़ी खुश रखा था मुझे,
लेकिन असल जिंदगी में तो काफ़ी रुलाया था,

चलते-चलते ही मैं, एकदम से लडखड़ाया था,
कमाने से पहले ही, काफी कुछ गंवाया था,

तन्हा छूट गया था मैं बीच सफर में ऐसे,
मेरी तक़दीर ने, एक बार फिर से मुझे आज़माया था,

क्योंकि मैंने अरमानों का एक बाग़ सजाया था,
मोहब्बत का दरख्त भी उसमें लगाया था,

पनपने से पहले ही झुलस गया वो,
उस रात खुदा ने भी क्या गज़ब कहर बरसाया था!

- ❖ हसरत – ख्वाहिश
- ❖ दरख्त – पेड़

# Qahar

*Meri tamannao ne ek sitaara chamkaya tha,*
*Mujhe khwab mein, ek aise shakhs ko dikhaya tha,*
*Dhari ki dhari rah gayi meri saari hasratein,*
*Jab kisi ne mujhe meri nind se jagaya tha,*
*Rangeen khawabo ne mujhe uksaaya tha,*
*Taqdeer ke khilaaf mujhe baaghi banaya tha,*
*Kaafi berang si lagne lagi mujhe ye zindagi,*
*Jab maine apni aankho se wo jhuta chashma hataya tha,*
*Muqaddar ne mujhe mere sach se milaya tha,*
*Bina lade hi mujhe bas aise hi haraya tha,*
*Tasawwur me to kaafi khush rakha tha mujhe,*
*Lekin asal zindagi me to kaafi rulaya tha!*
*Chalte chalte hi mai,ekdam se ladkhadaya tha,*
*Kamane se pahle hi kaafi kuch gawaya tha,*

*Tanha chhut gaya tha mai beech safar me aise,*
*Meri taqdeer ne, ek bar fir se mujhe azmaaya tha,*
*Kyunki maine armaano ka ek baagh sajaya tha,*
*Mohabbat ka darakht bhi usme lagaya tha,*
*Panapne se pahle hi jhulas gaya wo,*
*Us raat khuda ne bhi kya gazab qahar barsaaya tha!*

- ❖ Hasrat – Desire, Khwaish
- ❖ Darakht – Tree, Ped

# Translation

*My desires had made a star shine,*

*They showed me a person unlike any other.*

*All my hopes remained unfulfilled,*

*When someone woke me from my sleep.*


*Vivid dreams had urged me on,*

*Making me a rebel against fate.*

*Life began to feel quite dull,*

*When I removed that deceptive veil from my eyes.*


*Destiny brought me face to face with my truth,*

*Defeating me without a fight.*

*In my imagination, I was kept quite happy,*

*But in real life, I was made to cry!*


*As I walked, I stumbled suddenly,*

*Losing so much even before earning.*

*I was left alone in the middle of the journey,*

*As my fate tested me once again.*

*I had cultivated a garden of dreams,*
*Planting a tree of love within it.*
*But before it could flourish, it was scorched,*
*That night, God unleashed a terrible wrath!*

# सितम

ऐ सितमगर, यूं न सितम कर,

मेरे दिल पर इतने गहरे न ज़ख्म कर,

मोहब्बत ही तो की है, थोड़ा तो रहम कर,

बख़्श दे मुझे, या फिर एक बार में खत्म कर!

❖ सितमगर – अत्याचारी

# Sitam

*Ay sitamgar yu na sitam kar,*
*Mere dil pe itne gahre na zakhm kar,*
*Mohabbat hi to ki hai,thoda to raham kar,*
*Bakhsh de mujhe,ya fir ek baar me khatam kar!*

❖ Sitamgar – Oppressor, Atyachari

## Translation

*O oppressor, do not be so cruel,*

*Do not inflict such deep wounds on my heart.*

*I have loved you, so have a little mercy,*

*Either spare me or finish it all at once!*

# मुलाक़ात

वो अब मेरी ज़िंदगी में मेरे साथ न होगी,
मेरी शख्सियत में अब वो बात न होगी.

जिंदगी तो चलती रहेगी बेशक,
लेकिन उससे कभी दुबारा मुलाक़ात न होगी!

❖ शख्सियत – व्यक्तित्व

# Mulaqaat

*Wo ab meri zindagi mein mere sath na hogi,*
*Meri shakhsiyat mein ab wo baat na hogi,*
*Zindagi to chalti rahegi beshaq,*
*Lekin usse kabhi dobara mulaqaat na hogi!*

❖ Shakhsiyat – Personality, Vyaktitva

# Translation

*She will no longer be in my life with me,*

*There will be no trace of her in my identity.*

*Life will surely go on,*

*But I will never meet her again!*

# हुनर

काफी लोगों की पसंद होता मैं भी,

कि अगर मुझे अपने ऐब छुपाने का हुनर आता,

अपना समझते होते काफी लोग मुझे,

कि अगर मुझे झूठा चेहरा दिखाने का हुनर आता।

- ❖ हुनर – कौशल
- ❖ ऐब – दोष

# Hunar

*Kaafi logo ki pasand hota mai bhi,*

*Ke Agr mujhe apne aib chhupaane ka hunar aata,*

*Apna samajhte hote kaafi log mujhe,*

*Ke agar mujhe jhuta chehra dikhane ka hunar aata!!*

- ❖ Hunar – Skill, Kaushal
- ❖ Aib – Flaw, Dosh

# Translation

*I would be liked by many people,*

*If I had the skill to hide my flaws.*

*Many would consider me one of their own,*

*If I knew how to show a false face!*

# तड़पाया

अगर वो मुझे देख के मुस्कुराया न होता,

उसने मुझ पर अपना हक़ जताया न होता,

ज़ायका पता न चलता मुझे ये सारी ज़िंदगी,

क्योंकि धोखा भी मैंने, कभी खाया न होता।

अगर उसके साथ इतना वक्त बिताया न होता,

उसकी यादों में खुद को उलझाया न होता,

तैरती रहती कश्ती मेरी मोहब्बत की,

अगर उसने मेरी कश्ती को, बीच सफ़र में डुबाया न होता,

चेहरे पढ़ने का हुनर, अगर मैंने पाया न होता,

उसे अपने हुनर से वाकिफ कराया न होता,

उसके मंसूबे पहचान लेता उसकी सूरत से मैं,

अगर  उसने मुझे अपना झूठा चेहरा दिखाया न होता,

अगर इश्क़ में मैंने खुद को फसाया न होता,

तो पीठ पर खंजर मैंने खाया न होता,

कोई गिला-शिकवा न रहता मुझे उससे कभी,

अगर उसने मारने से पहले, मुझे इतना तड़पाया न होता,

- ❖ ज़ायका – स्वाद
- ❖ वाकिफ – जानकार
- ❖ मंसूबा – योजना
- ❖ खंजर – छूरा

# Tadpaaya

*Agar wo mujhe dekh ke muskuraya na hota,*
*Usne mujhpe apna haq jataya na hota,*
*Zayka pata na chalta mujhe ye saari zindagi,*
*Kyunki dhokha bhi maine, kabhi khaya na hota,*

*Agar uske sath itna waqt bitaya na hota,*
*Uski yaadon me khud ko uljhaya na hota,*
*Tairti rahti kashti meri mohabbat ki,*
*Agar usne meri kashti ko dubaya na hota,*

*Chehre padhne ka hunar maine paya na hota,*
*Usey apne hunar se waaqif karaya na hota,*
*Uske mansoobe pahchaan leta uski surat se mai,*
*Agar usne mujhe apna jhuta chehra dikhaya na hota,*

*Agar ishq me maine khud ko fasaya na hota,*
*To peeth pe khanjar maine khaya na hota,*
*Koi gila wa shikwa na rahta mujhe usse kabhi,*
*Agar maarne se phle usne mujhe itna tadpaya na hota!!*

- ❖ Zayka – Taste, Swaad
- ❖ Waaqif – Aware, Jaankar
- ❖ Mansooba – Plan, Yojna
- ❖ Khanjar – Dagger, Chhura

# Translation

*If she hadn't smiled at me,*
*She wouldn't have claimed her right over me.*
*I wouldn't have known the taste of this life,*
*Because I would never have been deceived.*

*If I hadn't spent so much time with her,*
*If I hadn't gotten lost in her memories,*
*My love's boat would have kept sailing,*
*If she hadn't sunk my ship.*

*If I hadn't learned the art of reading faces,*
*I wouldn't have revealed my skill to her.*
*I would have recognized her plans by her looks,*
*If she hadn't shown me her false face.*

*If I hadn't trapped myself in love,*
*I wouldn't have been stabbed in the back.*
*There would have been no complaints or grievances,*
*If she hadn't tortured me so much before killing me!*

# अंधेरा

गहरा है अंधेरा,

और अंधेरे में तन्हाई,

और तन्हाई में यादें,

और यादों में सच्चाई,

लिखना है अफसाना,

और अफसाने में मोहब्बत,

और मोहब्बत में नज़राना,

और नज़राने में जुदाई,

ज़िंदगी है मुश्किल,

और मुश्किल है जीना,

और जीने में है दर्द,

और दर्द में गहराई।

- ❖ अफसाना - कहानी
- ❖ नज़राना – तोहफ़ा

# Andhera

*Gehra hai andhera,*
*Aur andhere me tanhaayi,*
*Aur tanhaayi me yaadein,*
*Aur yaadon me sachchayi,*

*Likhna hai afsaana,*
*Aur afsaane me mohabbat,*
*Aur mohabbat me nazraana,*
*Aur nazraane me judaayi,*

*Zindagi hai mushkil,*
*Aur mushkil hai jeena,*
*Aur jeene me hai dard,*
*Aur dard me gahraayi!*

- ❖ Afsaana – Story, Kahani
- ❖ Nazraana – Present, Tohfa

# Translation

*The darkness is deep,*
*And in the darkness, solitude,*
*And in solitude, memories,*
*And in memories, truth,*

*I want to write a tale,*
*And in the tale, love,*
*And in love, a glimpse,*
*And in the glimpse, separation,*

*Life is difficult,*
*And living is hard,*
*And in living, there is pain,*
*And in pain, depth.*

# हसीन चेहरा

एक हसीन चेहरा वहां जाल बिछाए बैठा था,

कई मासूमों को अपनी मोहब्बत में फसाए बैठा था,

लोगों के अहसासों से खेलने का शौक रखता था वो,

कितनों के दिल तोड़ के, अपना मन बहलाए बैठा था,

वो दुनिया को अपने हुस्न से रिझाए बैठा था,

अपने मंसूबों को अपने ही दिल में दबाए बैठा था,

जैसे किसी नए शिकार की तलाश में था वो,

बड़ी चालाकी से, अपना चेहरा मुरझाए बैठा था,

वो मेरी नज़रों से अपनी नज़रें मिलाए बैठा था,

मेरे इश्क़ में वो खुद को, पहले से गिराए बैठा था,

वो कोशिश में था कि जान सके शख्सियत मेरी,

लेकिन मैं तो वहां, अपनी ही पहचान भुलाए बैठा था,

वो महफिल में इश्क़ का बाज़ार सजाए बैठा था,

खुद को कितने रंगीन ख्वाब दिखाए बैठा था,

घूम रहा था मेरे इर्द-गिर्द मोहब्बत की तलाश में,

लेकिन मैं तो इश्क़ की शमा, पहले से बुझाए बैठा था,

वो वहां कितनों के दिल चुराए बैठा था,

मेरा भी दिल लूटने की आस लगाए बैठा था,

ग़मज़दा हो गया वो, जब लगी नाकामी हाथ उसके,

मैं तो पुराना आशिक था, पहले से अपना दिल गवाए बैठा था,

वो ज़माने को एक कड़वा घूंट पिलाए बैठा था,

अपनी बेवफाई से, वफ़ा को हराए बैठा था,

कई कोशिशें की उसने, मेरे दिल पर भी तीर चलाने की,

लेकिन मैं तो पहले से, किसी और की मोहब्बत का ज़हर खाए बैठा था!

- ❖ शख्सियत – व्यक्तित्व
- ❖ शमा – दीया

# Haseen Chehra

*Ek haseen chehra wahan jaal bichaye baitha tha,*
*Kayi masoomo ko apni mohabbat me fasaye baitha tha,*
*Logo ke ahsaaso se khelne ka shauk rakhta tha wo,*
*Kitno ke dil tod ke apna mann bahlaye baitha tha,*

*Wo mahfil ko apne husn se rijhaaye baitha tha,*
*Apne mansoobo ko apne hi dil me dabaye baitha tha,*
*Jaise kisi naye shikar ki talash me tha woh,*
*Badi chalaki se apna chehra murjhaaye baitha tha,*

*Wo meri nazron se apni nazren milaaye baitha tha,*
*Mere ishq me khud ko, phle se giraye baitha tha,*
*Wo koshish me tha ke jaan sake shakhsiyat meri,*
*Lekin mai to apni hi pahchan bhulaye baitha tha,*

*Wo mehfil l me ishq ka bazaar sajaye baitha tha,*

*Khud ko kitne rangeen khawab dikhaye baitha tha,*

*Ghoom raha tha mere ird gird mohabbat ki talash me,*

*Lekin main to ishq ki shama pehle se bujhaye baitha tha,*

*Wo wahan kitno ke dil churaye baitha tha,*

*Mera bhi dil lootne ki aas lagaye baitha tha,*

*Ghamzada ho gaya wo jab lagi nakami hath uske,*

*Mai to purana ashiq tha, phle se apna dil gawaye baitha tha,*

*Wo zamane ko ek kadwa ghoot pilaye baitha tha,*

*Apni bewafayi se wafa ko haraye baitha tha,*

*Kayi koshishe ki usne, mere dil pe bhi teer chalane ki,*

*Lekin main to phle se kisi aur ki mohabbat ka zahar khaye baitha tha!*

- ❖ Shakhsiyat – Personality, Vyaktitva
- ❖ Shama – Lamp, diya

# Translation

*A beautiful face sat there, spreading its web,*
*Luring many innocent souls into its love.*

*He had a penchant for playing with people's feelings,*
*Breaking countless hearts to soothe his own.*

*He enchanted society with his beauty,*
*Hiding his plans deep within his heart.*

*It seemed he was on the hunt for fresh prey,*
*With great cunning, he wilted his own charm.*

*He met my gaze, attempting to connect,*
*While I was lost, forgetting my own identity.*

*He set up a market of love in the gathering,*
*Displaying many colorful dreams to himself.*

*He was circling around, searching for love,*
*But I was already there, letting my passion fade.*

*He was stealing hearts, including mine,*
*Hoping to loot my heart too.*

*He grew dejected when failure struck,*
*While I was an old lover, already having lost my heart.*

*He was forcing the world to swallow a bitter dose,*
*Defeating loyalty with his betrayal.*

*He made several attempts to shoot arrows at my heart,*
*But I had already ingested the poison of someone else's love!*

# वक्त

लोग बोलते हैं की, वक्त तेजी से भागता है,

वक्त की रफ्तार उनसे पूछो जो किसी की क़ैद में हैं!

# Waqt

*Log bolte hain ki, waqt tezi se bhaagta hai,*
*Waqt ki raftaar unse puchho, jo kisi ki qaid mein hain!*

# Translation

*People say time flies quickly,*

*Ask those who are imprisoned about the pace of time!*

# कुछ सवाल

अगर बिछड़ना था, तो मुझे मिलाया क्यों?
अगर जाना था, तो वो आया क्यों?

अगर खोना था, तो मैंने पाया क्यों?
अगर तोड़ना था, तो ख्वाब दिखाया क्यों?

अगर गैर था, तो मैंने अपनाया क्यों?
अगर रुलाना था, तो मुझे हंसाया क्यों?

अगर इश्क़ नहीं था, तो उसने फरमाया क्यों?
अगर वो मेरा था, तो मैंने गवाया क्यों?

खाली हाथ जाते होंगे लोग दुनिया से,
मेरे साथ ये कुछ सवाल जाएंगे!

# Kuch sawal

*Agar bichhadna tha, to mujhe milaya kyun?*
*Agar jaana tha, to wo aya kyun?*
*Agar khona tha, to maine paya kyun?*
*Agar todna tha, to khwab dikhaya kyun?*
*Agar gair tha, to maine apnaya kyun?*
*Agar rulana tha, to mujhe hasaya kyun?*
*Agar ishq nhi tha, to usne farmaya kyun?*
*Agar wo mera tha, to maine gawaya kyun?*

*Khali hath jaate honge log duniya se,*
*Mere saath ye kuch sawal jaynge!*

# Translation

*If we were to part, then why did you meet me?*

*If you were to leave, then why did you come?*

*If I was to lose, then why did I gain?*

*If you were to break, then why show me dreams?*

*If you were a stranger, then why did I embrace you?*

*If you were to make me cry, then why did you make me smile?*

*If there was no love, then why did you say so?*

*If you were mine, then why did I lose you?*

*People may leave this world with empty hands,*

*But these questions will remain with me when I leave.*

# घायल

कि मर्ज़-ए-इश्क़ से घायल हूँ मैं,
कोई बता दे, जहाँ मोहब्बत की दवा मिलती है,

कि अब इस दिल का दर्द सहा नहीं जाता,
कोई बता दे, जहाँ इस दर्द से शिफा मिलती है,

काफी बेशर्म रहा है लहजा मेरे इश्क़ का,
कोई बता दे, जहाँ थोड़ी हया मिलती है,

दौलतमंद तो रहा हूँ मैं ये सारी जिंदगी,
कोई बता दे, जहाँ थोड़ी सी भी वफा मिलती है!

- ❖ शिफा – रोगमुक्ति
- ❖ हया – शर्म

# Ghayal

*Ke marz e ishq se ghayal hu mai,*
*Koi bata de jahan mohabbat ki dawa milti hai,*
*Ke ab is dil ka dard saha nahi jaata,*
*Koi bata de jahan is dard se shifa milti hai,*

*Kaafi besharm raha hai lahja mere ishq ka,*
*Koi bata de jahan thodi haya milti hai,*
*Daulatmand to raha hu mai ye saari zindagi,*
*Koi bata de jahan thodi si bhi wafa milti hai!*

- ❖ Shifa – Rogmukti
- ❖ Haya - Sharm

## Translation

*I am wounded by the disease of love,*

*Someone tell me where the remedy for love can be found.*

*I can no longer bear the pain of this heart,*

*Someone tell me where healing from this pain exists.*

*My tone has been quite shameless in love,*

*Someone tell me where I can find a little modesty!*

*I have been wealthy all my life,*

*Someone tell me where I can find a bit of loyalty!*

# शक

अपने भरोसे में थोड़ा शक बिठा के रखो,
अपनी नरमियत में, थोड़ी कड़वाहट मिला के रखो,

फूल का बाग़ तो लगाओ अपने दिल में बेशक,
लेकिन उसमें एक, नागफनी का फूल भी खिला के रखो,

अपनी ख्वाहिशों को थोड़ा रुला के रखो,
कुछ अहसासों को ज़रा दबा के रखो।

कड़वे घूटों से भरी मिलेगी तुम्हें ये ज़िंदगी,
कुछ तुम पियो, कुछ लोगो को पीला के रखो!

❖ नागफनी – कांटे वाला फूल (Cactus)

# Shaq

*Apne bharose me thoda shaq bitha ke rkho,*
*Apni narmiyat me thodi kadwahat mila ke rakho,*
*Phool ka baag to lagao apne dil me beshaq,*
*Lekin usme ek naagphani ka phool bhi khila ke rakho,*

*Apni khwaishon ko thoda rula ke rakho,*
*Kuch ahsaaso ko zara daba ke rakho,*
*Kadwe ghooton se bhari milegi tumhe ye zindagi,*
*Kuch tum piyo aur thoda logo ko pila ke rakho!!*

## Translation

*Keep a little doubt nestled in your trust,*

*Mix a bit of harshness into your softness.*

*Sure, plant a garden of flowers in your heart,*

*But also let a thorny flower bloom among them.*

*Let your wishes cry a little,*

*And suppress some feelings just a bit.*

*Life will greet you with bitter sips,*

*Drink some yourself and offer a little to others too!*

# बदनाम नज़र

शरीफ हो गई हैं मेरी बदनाम नजरें,

जबसे मुझे उस शाख़्स का दीदार हुआ है।

जो ज़माना काटने भागता था कभी,

वो तो जैसे एकदम से, खुशगवार हुआ है।

शोर-शराबा भी अब सुकून देता है मुझे,

वो इस तरह से, मेरे ज़हन पे सवार हुआ है।

आज़ादी का ऐसा अहसास हो रहा है आजकल,

जैसे किसी क़ैद से, कोई क़ैदी फरार हुआ है।

❖ खुशगवार – सुखद

# Badnaam Nazar

*Shareef ho gayi hai meri badnaam nazre,*
*Jabse mujhe us shakhs ka deedar hua hai,*
*Jo zamana kaatne bhagta tha kabhi,*
*Wo to ekdam se jaise khushgawar hua hai,*

*Maikhaana bhi ab sukoon deta hai mujhe,*
*Wo is tarah se mere zehan pe sawaar hua hai,*
*Azadi ka esa ahsaas ho raha hai aajkal,*
*Jaise kisi qaid se koi qaidi farar hua hai,*

❖ Khushgawar – Sukhad, Happy

# Translation

*My infamous gaze has become innocent,*
*Ever since I caught a glimpse of that person.*
*Who used to flee from the world,*
*Now seems suddenly serene and pleasant.*
*Even the noise and chaos bring me peace,*
*As they occupy my mind in this way.*
*I'm feeling a sense of freedom these days,*
*Like a prisoner escaping from captivity.*

# हैवान

आजकल जानवर भी यहां ये सोच के परेशान होता है,

कौन कब यहां इंसान, और कब कौन यहां हैवान होता है,

रुसवा कर रहें हैं बहन बेटियों को कुछ लोग इस क़दर,

हरकतें इनकी देखकर, खुद जानवर भी हैरान होता है,


इसमें ना कोई हिंदू और ना ही कोई मुसलमान होता है,

कभी कहीं कोई संजय तो कहीं कोई इमरान होता है,

आदमखोर बन चुके हैं ये हवस की चाहत में यूं,

इनके दिल में ना कोई धर्म ना कोई ईमान होता है,


इनके लिए ना कभी कोई नवरात न कभी रमज़ान होता है,

इनकी हरकतों से सारा मुल्क, सिर्फ गमकिन और हलकान होता है,

अपने वहशीपन की हदों से गुजर चुके हैं ये ऐसे,

इनकी दरिंदगी से शर्मसार, अब पूरा हिंदुस्तान होता है,

ऊंची शख्सियतों का तबका, क्यूं ही बे ज़ुबान होता है,

ज़ुल्म के ख़िलाफ चुप रहना, तो कायरो का निशान होता है,

क्यों सब मदहोश पड़े हैं, अपनी ही ज़िंदगी में ऐसे,

इन्हें होश में लाने का, तो अब मुझे अरमान होता है,


हुकूमत की तरफ से क्यूं नहीं, कोई बड़ा फरमान होता है,

बच निकलने का तभी, इन ज़ालिमों को हमेशा यूं ही गुमान होता है,

उनकी रूह तड़प जाएगी उनको आख़िरत मिलेगी ऐसी,

उन बेरहमो के ख़िलाफ, ये दुआ है मेरी और ये मेरा एलान होता है!


कभी सोचता हूं ये कितना घिनौना और गंदा होता है,

करने वाले होते हैं मुर्दा, या इसमें से कोई ज़िंदा होता है,

इतनी आसानी से बे आबरू कर देते हैं ये ज़माने को,

जैसे इनका ये रोज़ का ही काम धंधा होता है,

यहां क्यों नहीं खुदा का एक बंदा होता है?

जिसके हाथ में, अपने देश का तिरंगा झंडा होता है,

ऐसे वहशियो और कमज़र्फो को सबक सिखाने खातिर,

क्यों उसके पास नहीं फांसी का एक फंदा होता है?

- ❖ गमकीन – दुखी
- ❖ हल्कान – परेशान
- ❖ गुमान – घमंड
- ❖ बे आबरू – बेइज़्ज़त
- ❖ कमज़र्फ – नीच
- ❖ बे ज़ुबान – जो बोल नही पता हो
- ❖ आख़िरत – अंत

# Haiwaan

*Aajkal jaanwar bhi yahan ye soch ke pareshan hota hai,*
*Kon kab yahan insaan aur kab kon yahan haiwaan hota hai,*
*Ruswa kar rahe hai bahan betiyo ko kuch log is qadar,*
*Harkatein inki dekhkar khud jaanwar bhi hairaan hota hai,*

*Isme na koi hindu aur na hi koi musalman hota hai,*
*Kabhi kahi koi Sanjay to kahi koi Imraan hota hai,*
*Adamkhor ban chuke hai ye hawas ki chahat me yun,*
*Inke Dil me na koi dharm aur na koi imaan hota hai,*

*Inke liye na kabhi koi navraat na kabhi ramzaan hota hai,*
*Inki harkato se saara mulk sirf ghamkeen aur halkan hota hai,*
*Apne wahshipan ki hadon se guzar chuke hai ye aise,*
*Inki darindigi se sharmsaar ab poora Hindustan hota hai,*

*Unchi shakhsiyato ka tabqa kyu hi bezubaan hota hai,*

*Zulm ke khilaf chup rahna to kayaro ka Nishan hota hai,*

*Kyun sab madhosh pade hai apni hi zindagi me aise,*

*Inhe hosh me laane ka to ab mujhe armaan hota hai,*

*Hukumat ki taraf se kyun nhi koi bada farman hota hai,*

*Bach niklne ka tabhi in zaalimo ko hamesha yun hi gumaan hota hai,*

*Unki ruh tadap jaayegi unhe akhirat milegi aisi,*

*Un berahmo ke khilaf ye dua hai meri aur ye mera elaan hota hai!*

*Kabhi sochta hu ye kitna ghinauna aur ganda hota hai,*

*Karne wale hote hai murda,ya isme se koi zinda hota hai,*

*Itni asaani se beaabru kar dete hai ye zamane ko,*

*Jaise inka ye roz ka hi kaam dhanda hota hai,*

*Yahan kyu nhi khuda ka ek banda hota hai?*

*Jiske haath me apne desh ka tiranga jhanda hota hai,*

*Aise wahshiyo aur kamzarfo ko sabak sikhane khatir,*

*Kyu uske pas nhi faasi ka ek fanda hota hai?*

- ❖ Ghamkeen – Dukhi
- ❖ Halkan – Pareshan
- ❖ Gumaan – Ghamand
- ❖ Be Aabru – Baizzat
- ❖ Kamzarf – Neech

# Translation

*These days, even animals are troubled by the thought,*

*Who is human and who is a beast here,*

*Some people disgrace women and daughters to such an extent,*

*That even animals are astonished by their actions.*

*There's neither Hindu nor Muslim in this;*

*Sometimes there's a Sanjay, sometimes an Imran.*

*These people have turned into man-eaters in their lust,*

*In their hearts, there's neither faith nor belief.*

*For them, there's neither Navratri nor Ramadan,*

*Their actions only bring sorrow and grief to the entire nation.*

*They have crossed all limits of savagery,*

*With their barbarism, the whole of India feels ashamed.*

*Why is the elite class silent?*

*Silence against oppression is a mark of cowardice.*

*Why is everyone intoxicated in their own lives like this?*

*I long to awaken them from this stupor.*

*Why is there no strong proclamation from the government?*

*These oppressors always feel they will escape,*

*Their souls will writhe; they will meet their end in the afterlife,*

*This is my prayer and my declaration against these brutes!*

*Sometimes I think how vile and disgusting this is,*

*The perpetrators are dead inside, or perhaps some are still alive.*

*They dishonor others with such ease,*

*As if it's their daily business.*

*Why isn't there a single man of God here,*

*Who holds the tricolor of our nation?*

*To teach a lesson to such savages and cowards,*

*Why is there not a noose of justice ready for him?*

www.ingramcontent.com/pod-product-compliance
Lightning Source LLC
LaVergne TN
LVHW061545070526
838199LV00077B/6911

# A Known And Yet Unknown World

*Desultory Notes of a Scribbler*

Anjan Kumar Chatterjee

NewDelhi • London

**BLUEROSE PUBLISHERS**
India | U.K.

Copyright © Anjan Kumar Chatterjee 2024

All rights reserved by author. No part of this publication may be reproduced, stored in a retrieval system or transmitted in any form or by any means, electronic, mechanical, photocopying, recording or otherwise, without the prior permission of the author. Although every precaution has been taken to verify the accuracy of the information contained herein, the publisher assumes no responsibility for any errors or omissions. No liability is assumed for damages that may result from the use of information contained within.

BlueRose Publishers takes no responsibility for any damages, losses, or liabilities that may arise from the use or misuse of the information, products, or services provided in this publication.

For permissions requests or inquiries regarding this publication, please contact:

BLUEROSE PUBLISHERS
www.BlueRoseONE.com
info@bluerosepublishers.com
+91 8882 898 898
+4407342408967

ISBN: 978-93-5989-246-7

Cover design: Shivam
Typesetting: Namrata Saini

First Edition: February 2024

# DEDICATION

To my sweetest and prettiest granddaughters,
Akansha and Arya,

who are our springs of unending and unbound
joy and happiness.

# CONTENTS

Prologue ............................................................................ vi

Chapter 1: Rigmarole of Life ........................................... 1

Chapter 2: Call of the Unknown from the USSR ....................... 15

Chapter 3: St. Petersburg and the River Neva – My Russian Cradle .................................................................. 28

Chapter 4: Moscow State University - My Alma Mater ........... 44

Chapter 5: Looking Back at the Soviet Era in My Own Way ..... 53

Chapter 6: Some Recalls from the Land of Plenitude – The North America ........................................................ 81

Chapter 7: Unique Travel Instances in North America .............. 91

Chapter 8: Enjoying Kebab at the Niagara Falls ..................... 108

Chapter 9: The Hudson Riverfront at the Jersey City and Gathering of Slaves of a Different Genre ................................. 116

Chapter 10: St. Moritz – an Enchanting Winter Destination in the Swiss Alps ..................................................... 126

Chapter 11: The Baltic Sea and the Land of Vikings ............... 141

Chapter 12: China – a Land with Stunning Landscapes ........... 161

Chapter 13: The Story of Diamonds and a Revelatory Visit to an Australian Mine ..................................... 178

Chapter 14: Africa – a Variegated Continent with Surprises Galore ................................................................ 193

Chapter 15: Seychelles Archipelago – The Nature's Bounty ... 215

Chapter 16: Dubai – a Microcosmic Urban Wonder in a Desert Land ........................................................... 228

Epilogue ......................................................................... 245

About the Author ........................................................... 250

# PROLOGUE

I was born in a city called Jabalpur in central India. I had my schooling in Howrah, a suburb of Kolkata, more popularly known then as Calcutta. I did my graduate studies in the prestigious Presidency College in the same city, from where I moved to Moscow State University in the unbroken Soviet Union and then to the British Research Establishment in the United Kingdom for my research studies, before I entered into my working life. My professional pursuit made me taste the flavour of living in the campus of Indian Institute of Technology at a small town, called Kharagpur, about 200 km from Kolkata, the satisfaction of residing in the capital city of Delhi, enigma of staying and working in the city of Mumbai, and travelling to four continents, more for work than pleasure.

But I was not born with a silver spoon in my mouth, neither my early life was a bed of roses. I lost my brother, eight years senior to me, when I was only four years old. He died of typhoid, which did not have a cure those days at least in the reach of middle-class families. This loss, however, did not leave any impression on me as I was too young then. I lost my dearest grandfather, when I was about twelve years old, and performed the entire ritual of cremation myself by igniting the pyre, as desired by him. It had a lasting impression in my mind. I started realizing how transient the life was. But the most devastating tragedy was the sudden and untimely death of my father, when I was about to cross the school barrier at the age of fifteen. That was a turning point in my life as I observed how my mother struggled to bring up me and my elder sister, who was about six years senior to me. My maternal uncle, *chotomama* in my mother tongue, supported us to the hilt all along our growing up. Weathering all the perturbations of life from the teen age, I grew up academically, professionally and socially.

Having reached the fag end of my life, I often wonder how one astrologer, even now unknown to me, had predicted, when I was just a few months old, that I would be scampering round the globe virtually all my life. It was written down in my horoscope, prepared then, but kept hidden by my mother from my eyes, lest I might be guided by the favorable and unfavorable predictions made in the chart. I discovered it one day accidentally from a drawer, when my mother was not at home during my school days. I glanced through it in utter curiosity and kept it back where it was lying. I never enquired with my mother later in my life what had happened to this long scroll. However, I must confess today that quite a few predictions that I had hurriedly noticed then had happened in my life, and one was my loping and cantering in different parts of the globe.

When I was young, I derived great pleasure in seeing off my relatives and friends going abroad for studies or work at the airport. Most often than not, either the persons travelling or their parents or close relatives used to break down at the airport, perhaps, being utterly concerned about the impending separation. I used to wonder why it should happen at all, since such travels for yet unknown destinations at long distance were events to celebrate and enjoy, and not occasions to lament. I hardly understood then the pangs of temporary but prolonged separation until I myself embarked on my first trip abroad. I was in Delhi at that time with my mother and I had to see her off in the New Delhi railway station before I moved, unaccompanied by anybody, to Delhi airport for my maiden flight. I still remember the stoic face of my mother through the window of the train, as it started moving. She, being a very strong-willed person, did not break down but made me realize through her facial expression and penetrating eyes what separation meant. Nevertheless, I won over myself, rushed to the airport, and embarked on my journey with immense joy and curiosity for the unknown. Traces of 'wanderlust' of some kind stayed on in me all my life. I enjoyed visiting places, seeing what I had not seen earlier, knowing what I had not known before, being acquainted with new culture, new societies, and new ways of living, looking at the landscapes of different regions, driving along different terrains, trying and often failing to go where no man has gone before.

Now, after several decades, I find pleasure in going down the memory lane and in picking up some slices of my fairly eventful life including a few captivating journeys abroad. This booklet is an attempt to capture these frames. There is nothing spectacular in it, yet very engrossing. The reminiscences are incoherent and inherently personal in settings and scenarios that I had encountered and experienced. Some may like and some may not. Yet they were; they occurred to touch me and touch many others around me at different turns of my life. In Shakespeare's words

…. "Let not virtue seek

   Remuneration for the thing it was:

   For beauty, wit,

   High birth, vigor of bone, desert in service,

   Love, friendship, charity, are subjects all

  To envious and calumniating Time."

# CHAPTER 1

# Rigmarole of Life

Have you ever seen a tea pot or a kettle without a pouring spout? This is what I had drawn in the drawing test for admission to the Bengal Engineering (BE) college, one of the oldest engineering institutions in India, situated on the bank of the River Hooghly in the suburb of Kolkata. This was the only innovative way I could think out then to cause my disqualification, when I discovered to my utter surprise that I had done unexpectedly well in all other test papers. The urge for disqualifying myself for entry to the engineering degree course was the fondness that I, along with many of my classmates, had developed for the ambience of the Presidency College (now known as the Presidency University) and the Indian Coffee House across the street in Kolkata. This fondness was the result of our having completed already the Intermediate Science course, a two-year program after leaving the high school, at the Presidency College itself. In fact we had entered the portal of Presidency College in 1955, when it was celebrating its centenary (see Picture 01-01).

*Presidency College entrance to the main building standing witness to changing times and values (Picture 01-01) (Source: India Today Web Desk, Jan 21, 2017)*

## Streaks of Presidency College

The Hindu College that was established on January 20, 1817 as the earliest institution of higher learning in Asia was the predecessor of Presidency College, which was subsequently founded in 1855. It has, thus, a rich legacy of more than one and a half centuries. The College has been given the status of an independent university in 2010.

When we came into the fold of this college almost seventy years back, it had a magnetic attraction for us. I for one was bewildered with the hearsay of its past glory. I learnt many new things more authentically, when I became familiar with the premises and had interacted with the faculty members. I always wondered how the college had shaped the minds of the elites and radical personalities of Bengal. I read the history of Bankim Chandra Chatterji, the renowned Bengali writer, and Jadunath Basu, an able administrator, both students of Presidency College, becoming the first graduates by passing the first graduation examination conducted by the Calcutta University in 1858, though the other four candidates who appeared in the examination failed due to the obscurity of the question papers.

Standing at the foot of the magnificent staircase of the main building (see Picture 01- 02), I could imagine the controversial event that happened on the flights of this staircase concerning Professor Oaten that led to rusticating Subhas Chandra Bose from the College and the Calcutta University for some time. The one-day student life of Rabindranath Tagore in Presidency College remained an indelible memory in the annals of the college. I always carried a vicarious pride for the college to have produced polyglots like Harinath De, patriots like Ashutosh Mukhopadhyay, politicians like Rajendra Prasad, scientists like Jagadish Chandra Bose, Prafulla Chandra Ray, Meghnad Saha, Satyen Bose, P.C Mahalonobis, creative artists like Satyajit Ray, and a large number of luminaries in literature, economics, and history.

*The historical staircase of the Presidency College that had witnessed the protests of students including Netaji Subhas Chandra Bose against Prof Oaten (Picture 01-02) (Source: Wikimedia Commons)*

Over and above the attraction of the College legacy, its surroundings had a hypnotic effect on many of the students. The College is situated on the northern part of College Street, a thoroughfare named so perhaps due to the location of a large number of academic institutions and a student-centric environment there.

The Senate Hall (now demolished) of the Calcutta University with its wide staircase leading to magnificent columns used to be a rare attraction for all passers-by. It was considered the icon of Calcutta University and was even printed on the postage stamp released in India on the occasion of the University's centenary (see Picture 01-03). Other landscape features that added to the character of the locality include the Darbhanga building of the University, the College Square with its swimming pool on the eastern side of the road, the Sanskrit College, Hare School, and a plethora of colleges within walking distance.

*Postal stamp released in 1957 showing the Senate Hall (Picture 01-03) (Source: https://telegraphindia.com/my-kolkata/calcutta-universitys-senate-hall/)*

The description will remain incomplete if I do not mention about the series of bookshops on the College Street, and more particularly, the secondhand book vendors displaying books on the half-a-kilometer long college railing just outside the premises (Picture 01-04). One could spend hours there, glancing through the pages of the books one was looking for, before buying.

*Wayside bookshops on College Street (Picture 01-04)*

To top it all was the Indian Coffee House across the street from the main entrance of the college (Picture 01-05) It was the haven of the city's intellectuals and rendezvous of the student community. We used to have regular arrangements for proxy in the classes that we felt unimportant so that we could use the time more 'productively' in the coffee house with larger groups of friends. Long hours of headless and tailless gossips gave us ethereal pleasure as if we had discovered a new meaning of life. Many a time we used to notice public figures, authors, poets, and artists sitting in the adjacent tables. For no reason, however, we used to feel elevated for a while as a privileged class.

*Inside the College Street Coffee House (Picture 01-05)*

I had therefore every justification, I felt then, to adopt a dubious means to disqualify myself for admission to the faraway engineering college and stick on to Presidency College for further study, irrespective of subjects or disciplines, irrespective of any concern for my future goal. However, due to my performance in the Intermediate Science examination I had a wide choice of subjects for my graduate honors course both in humanities and science streams. The choice of the subject was a big dilemma. While debates and persuasions were going on, a piece of news floated in the college campus that the first field trip for the entrants to the Geology Department would be to Kashmir, the paradise on Earth. For some of us, this snippet was the decision-maker. A few of us made up our minds instantaneously to pick up Geology, not to become a geologist but to feel the onset of winter in a boat-house on the River Jhelum.

Another four years in Presidency College rolled on. The solidly built portico, where the rich and the beautiful used to alight from their cars, and run up the majestic staircase of the main building, was a daily sight for many of us waiting at the portico for our classmates. The cross-over path to the Baker Laboratories from the main building overlooking the large green lawns of Hare School and our college on either side of the pathway had created an indelible image in our mind. The vibrant rings of bells, the last-bench sitting habits in the classrooms, proxy presence in the 'pass' classes, free access to and endearing proximity of teachers, regular gossip sessions in the coffee house, watching and howling in the friendly cricket matches played in the winter months in the college lawns, playing table tennis and carom in the students common room are some of the many other untold flashes of those days.

I and a few other classmates had no family cars, and we used to ride crowded buses across the River Hooghly every day, at least twice, for the home-to-college journey, while some of my classmates used chauffeur-driven cars. Many of us came from suburban schools and we befriended mates from elite schools of Calcutta. Surprisingly, no divide existed amongst us. I never failed to enjoy life equally amidst the elite and extrovert city boys on one hand and coy and introvert suburbanites on the other.

A few other unforgettable memories I carry from my college days. The most indelible is the general profile of teachers I met and interacted with. Their simplicity, profundity, and way of teaching remain deeply embedded in my mind. Still I use their profiles as the yardstick to judge what the present-day teachers should be like, what values they should personify, how they should enrich the progeny. Another image of those days was the decent environment that prevailed in the co-educational institution like ours. It is not that the boys did not befriend the girls or enjoyed together the social functions of the college. But still there was an environment that was romantic but totally non-offensive. In this context it may be worth recalling a story that went round in the college then. Perhaps in the early 1950s, the head of the department of philosophy, Professor Saroj Kumar Das found the separate rows of girls and boys retrogressive and one day he made them sit next to each other around the egg-shaped seminar table during his class. The boys felt thrilled and covertly romantic to have this arrangement. After this class was over, Professor Gopinath Bhattacharya entered the same room for his class on psychology for the same group of boys and girls. He was bewildered to see the sitting pattern. He asked them to revert back to separate sitting arrangements. Hearing this story, another senior professor commented that 'The decorated garden of Saroj had withered away'. That is true. The classroom romance was never there, but outside the classroom and even in the long corridors one could see the jovial, lively but restrained intermingling of boys and girls.

Perhaps the picture of the then college ambience would remain incomplete if I do not come out with my impressions on the College Union of that vintage. We did have elections for the president and other office bearers. There were political leanings among the classmates, primarily in favor or against socialism but there was no involvement of students then in active politics, nor any kind of direct interference from the political parties. The union activities that we all enjoyed were the debating competitions, musical evenings, particularly rendered by the reputed singers of Tagore songs, dramas performed by the students themselves, special lectures by the renowned personalities, sports competitions, and so on. Perhaps this was the tradition set by the predecessors. It is difficult to believe that the college union was founded in 1877 by Professor J V S Pope, who taught English Literature, to root out the feeling of dis-union prevalent among the students even those days. Much later, the structure and objectives of the union were rejuvenated and reinforced by Dr. P K Roy, the first Indian Principal, in 1905.

It is not that the college environment was always bereft of politics. Perhaps, the most perceptible intrusion of politics was the Quit India movement in the 1940s. The Communist Party, which opposed the Quit India movement, was no more underground and the literature of Marxist philosophy was openly circulated. On the other hand, the Indian National Congress sponsored the movement. The political events at that time had enormous influence on the students of history, political science and economics in particular. Many outstanding personalities of socialistic thinking were incubated then in the intellectual environment of the college. But our times were mostly apolitical. The next wave of politics entered the college campus much later, in the 1960s.

Thus, we left Presidency College in utmost camaraderie. There was no anguish, no angst. The biggest concern was what was destined for our future.

### Tug-of-war for the Future

From my school days my mother used to argue with my father that one day I should become an IAS officer, while my father used to express his desire that I should join the Indian Navy. The sparking white dresses of the Naval Officers, the life on the blue seas, the challenges of protecting the vast coast line of India used to charm my father, while my mother's feet were firmly rooted in the awesome bureaucracy held by the Indian Administrative Services. But the victory was always with my mother and my father had to abandon the idea of me joining the Indian Navy. After my father's demise, as mentioned earlier, a new perspective for my future was introduced by my *Chotomama,* who was keen on my becoming an engineer. I had foreclosed this option for reasons elaborated in the previous pages. Finally, my predicament was that I had studied a subject, which I did not want to pursue as a profession. In a nutshell, I did not know which way to go, when I completed my Master's course. In the absence of any other immediate option, I accepted a covetable job in the geological profession, for which I had qualified, and moved out of Kolkata. Back home, my mother filled up the application form for the IAS examination and paid up the fees. Far away then I lurched in the granitic hillocks of Bhagalpur in Bihar, watching carefully the sluggish movement of pythons. I was not granted leave and missed the opportunity for appearing at the IAS examination.

To my good luck, the life of a geologist for me was a very short-lived one. One October morning in mid-1960s I flew out of Delhi to land at Sherematyevo airport in Moscow for higher studies in Materials Science. Before commencing my technical studies at the Moscow State University and Baikov Institute of Metallurgy, I was sent to Leningrad State University for learning the Russian language as the entire system of education including the teaching medium was only Russian, even for the foreign students. After completing the language course at Leningrad for about 9 months, I returned back to Moscow State University for my technical education. The days and years I lived in the Soviet Union are a cherished memory. The high standards of education, enjoyable travels within and outside the Soviet Union during vacations or on work, close interactions with scores of friends from different republics in the hostels and classes, the humility and intimacy of the academicians made our life and stay immensely pleasurable. One day I reached the destination of receiving my doctoral degree from the Supreme Academic Council of the Moscow State University. With that my change of complexion was complete. I was no more a geologist who wanders through hills and dales and unravels the mystery of the Earth. I was a Materials Scientist who learnt some tricks of making and using various man-made materials for the service of mankind.

There is a saying that time and tide wait for none. Finally, a day came for me to leave Moscow. It was perhaps the month of February. It was a gloomy winter day, white snow all around, flowery ice on the bare bushes, and snow-cutting machines clearing the road for me to bid farewell to the city I loved so much.

Then it was my stint at the Building Research Establishment in the United Kingdom (see Picture 01-06). It was a different world. I was welcome by the research stalwarts of the United Kingdom in Building Sciences there. Interestingly, I had a rare opportunity of comparing the research plans and practices of the free world and the Eastern Block of that era. The most interesting was the morning coffee break, when all of us present in the laboratories would have to assemble in a hall with coffee mugs in hand. It always turned into a session for British jokes. One day a Scottish colleague was in a very jovial mood and was narrating something very hilariously. An English guy, standing by my side, shouted: 'He has got a touch of the Sun'! Everybody laughed their hearts out. For many days I did not understand what the joke was about, though I had stretched my lips then so as not to be branded a person with no humor.

*Building Research Establishment, Garston, Watford, UK (Picture 01-06)*
*(Source: Wikipedia: Author John Webb)*

**Looming of the Silvery Turf**

It is easier to confess now that I had spurned several opportunities for staying back in the west. A definite reason was the lonely life of my mother in Kolkata and, perhaps, some undefined attraction of the motherland that often spiked up in me after several years of living abroad. As luck would have it, I got into the Indian institute of Technology, Kharagpur, as an Assistant Professor in Materials Science near my beloved city Kolkata (Picture 01-07)

*Indian Institute of Technology, Kharagpur – an impressive entrance (Picture 01-07) (Source:Wikipedia: Author: Ambuj Saxena)*

I had a brief stay there but it was memorable in many ways, one being the opportunity to get back to some of my college mates who by that time had occupied faculty positions in the Geology Department. Another memory was a transient spike in my personal value as a 'suitable boy' in the IIT campus. Several professors having marriageable daughters started taking a lot of interest in me. In fact, some of them did not even hesitate to approach my mother. It was nice to see a streak of smile on my mother's lips. It was a solace for me. Having compelled my mother to live a lonesome life for several years when I stayed abroad, I left my marriage affairs solely to her discretion. In a short time she and my *chotomama* discovered the best match for me in the city of Kolkata, leaving all the pretty girls of the IIT campus in despair! Apart from being chased by the daughter-ridden fathers, and the eventual wedding, the brief stay at the IIT also gave me an opportunity to experience living in huge bungalows with acres of front and back yards, bicycle rides from the residence to the institution, facing the most brilliant cross section of students in the classes, evening sessions with the Russian faculty members in the campus then, visits and counter-visits of neighbours and new friends, snakes crossing the ill-lit campus roads, and a flavour of rural India in the surroundings.

But soon I realized that if I were to live all through my professional life in that environment, the cons would overtake the pros. I was doubtful if my enthusiasm and spirit would keep on driving me and push me up in the ladder of life. Should I not look for opportunities outside the campus, more urban, more competitive, more challenging, and mentally more rewarding for myself?

**Leap from Academia to Industry**

Within a few months of making up my mind I landed, bag and baggage, in Delhi to join the second tier of management at a cooperative research institution set up jointly by the cement industry and the Council of Scientific and Industrial Research of the Government of India, now called the National Council of Cement and Building Materials with its main complex in Haryana near Delhi border (Picture 01-08). For a change, in my own country, I got the flavour of industrial research. I worked for technology transfer to the industry. I took an active role in the dialogues between the industry and government ministries. I travelled to many African and South Asian countries as a subject expert in the government delegations. I started acting as an active member in several national and international bodies and committees. Even now, I consider my stay in Delhi, that lasted for almost eight years, with this organization as "the best of times and the worst of times" for me. It was the best as my son was born then and it was the worst because I damaged one of my legs severely in a car accident outside Delhi, when I was returning in a December night after completing an official assignment.

*National Council of Cement and Building Materials (NCB), Ballabgarh, Haryana (Picture 01-08) (Courtesy: NCB)*

When I was recovering from my leg injury and was learning to walk second time in my life, I received an invitation from a very reputed cement company, then having a sprawling R&D center in the outskirts of Bombay (now Mumbai), to head their establishment after due induction. That was the beginning of a corporate life. Suddenly my vista enlarged, my path widened, my objectives changed, my destination became clear but distant. I crossed all the hurdles speedily and steadily. One day I entered the Board Room of the company as a Whole-Time Director. In subsequent years I was nominated as a Director or the Chairman of several joint ventures and subsidiaries of the company. In the years that followed I was instrumental in bringing a few important multinational companies as joint venture partners of my company in India. I cherished the success of starting a manufacturing company in Advanced Ceramics. I still remember multiple visits I made to Iran those days to start up the first joint-venture company there in industrial consultancy service. It is a matter of joy to recall that my company was generous enough to release me for a considerable length of time to act as Cement

Production Expert under UNIDO (United Nations Industrial Development Organization) for some countries.

I have, therefore, every reason to feel gratified for achieving a large number of notable successes in the corporate endeavors. Then, a day came for me to lay down my office of employment. Who can defy age? But you can certainly defy retiring from being active. That is what I chose to do. I indulged in freelance operation, not limited to a single organization as we normally do in our employment tenure. I led the setting up of a not-for-profit knowledge center, devoted to repair and rehabilitation of buildings, under the auspices of an industrial house in Mumbai and ran it as the Director-in-charge. In parallel, I established a new consultancy outfit in Kolkata. Furthermore, I continued to serve the corporate sector in various capacities and to serve the international research programs in my fields of interest and expertise.

The intention is not to be self-congratulatory or to get lost in self-aggrandizement. The purpose is to unfold the labyrinthine life of an ordinary person. I do not know how to communicate to my mother today that her son has not been a loser by not being an IAS officer. I cannot convey to my father that his son, perhaps, has not been a less achiever than what would have happened to him as a Naval Officer. I cannot convince my *chotomama* at this juncture of life that my ploy not to get admitted to an engineering college has not been a disaster. But I must say at this stage, as Michel de Montaigne, the French philosopher, had said: "I cannot keep a record of my life through my actions; fortune has buried them too deep". Let me keep my records hereafter through my fantasies.

# CHAPTER 2

# Call of the Unknown from the USSR

Having revealed the cards of my life's rigmarole in a broad canvass in the previous Chapter, let me be more specific on why and how I had embraced a sojourn in the erstwhile Soviet Union.

During my college days in early nineteen sixties, I had the dream, like many others, to go to a foreign university to do higher studies after obtaining my master's degree. Most of the serious students those days carried the same ambition and were busy in applying for admission to and financial support from primarily the universities and institutions in the United Kingdom, the United States and Canada. Even in the society we lived in then, the academic success for one meant a degree from an American or British university. In this environment, hidden in my mind was a desire to go to some other country but I did not know where and how. As my luck would have it, an announcement appeared in the newspapers inviting applications from the Indian students completing master's degree courses for award of scholarships for post-graduate studies in the universities and academic institutions in the Soviet Union under a new collaboration agreement between the two governments. I ventured an application, passed through the entire rigmarole of assessment and selection, and turned out to be one of the first few to proceed to Moscow without knowing a word in the Russian language.

### My First Journey Abroad

I was in my twenties and that was my first flight to a country outside India. The flight was operated by Air India. It originated from New Delhi with full load of passengers, the majority of whom seemed to be the Russian with only a handful of Indians dispersed here and there in the aircraft, but none familiar to me. On the whole, it was an uneventful journey, except enjoying the on-board services of the airlines of that vintage and flying over the Himalayas with a picturesque view of snow-clad mountains peeping through occasional breaks in thick and white clouds trying to conceal the blue sky. However, interesting moments waited for me, when I landed at the Sheremetyevo International Airport in Moscow.

It was an afternoon in the month of October. I felt cold even in the jacket I wore, but it was bearable. In Delhi, I had been briefed that an official from the concerned department in Moscow would receive me at the airport. I started looking for a placard but could not find any. When I was looking around perhaps with a concerned face, a pretty girl in her late twenties, as I guessed, walked towards me and came out with some smattering of English. Although it took time for me to make out what she was trying to convey, I could understand that she was my savior in that unknown world. I had a sigh of relief that I was not in high seas. She made me stand at a corner and went away to come back with two more Indian students like me. Apparently, they had reached Moscow by different flights earlier. They were as illiterate in the Russian language as I was. They, like me, did not know what was in store for them next. Unfamiliarity in all senses turned out to be a strong bond to unite the three of us, speaking only in English, as our mother tongues were different and their command over Hindi was as poor as that of mine. In a few minutes, the girl who received us led us to a vehicle that resembled a 'matador' van of those days in India, pushed us in along with our suitcases, sat next to the driver, and asked the driver to start. The van slogged along a clean wide road, without much of vehicular and pedestrian traffic. She turned back and said, '*dobro pozhalovat*, welcome, welcome to Moscow' Then, she continued narrating that we were moving along a highway, called '*shosse'* in Russian, in the southeast direction towards the city and the city center was about 30 km from the airport. On either side of the *shosse* we could see only a few scattered hutments, a few monuments and sculptures, and vast stretches of vacant land.

We learnt from our companion that this highway was an important thoroughfare as it connected some of the suburbs of Moscow and ultimately with Leningrad, now called St. Petersburg. The highway was very well made but the adjacent landscapes were too bleak and empty at that time. Compared to this desolate scenario of the 1960s, in my subsequent trips to Moscow in 1980s and in more recent years I noticed a sea change. There were signs of significant modernization and urbanization everywhere with new construction, massive renovation, and aesthetic renewal of the road and airport infrastructure, as evident in the following images (Pictures 01-03). In 2019, the airport was named after the immortal Russian Poet Alexander Pushkin and a statue of the poet was unveiled inside the airport.

*The present-day scenario of the highway to Sheremetyevo airport in Moscow with its high traffic density (Picture 02-01) (Source: Wikimedia Commons)*

*Monument to the conquerors of Space on way to Moscow airport (Picture 02-02) (Source: Atlas Obscura: Lynn Greyling/ public domain)*

*Sheremetyevo airport in Moscow – an impressive inside dome of Terminal 3D (Picture 02-03) (Source: www.flickr.com/photos/vasilykuznetsov/4902308018/)*

Let me now come back to my original story. After a drive of about 20 km or so, we started having a glimpse of the city with massive buildings, wide and clean streets with familiar public buses plying on it. We saw for the first time electric trolley buses running in the designated tracks. We observed certain spots, where people were streaming out from the underground, which she called the metro stations. Yes, we were on the outskirts of Moscow along the outer ring road with glimpses of monolithic housing estates (Picture 03-04).

*A massive monolithic suburban housing estate of the Soviet era in Moscow (Picture 03-04)*

A few more minutes of drive and our grandiose vehicle stopped in front of a building with an impressive columnar façade with quite a few steps leading to a wide landing, where an aged woman was sitting close to the door with a small table. Each person, entering the building, was displaying a card to the woman, perhaps their photo identity we guessed, but she never made any effort to check what was being displayed. It appeared to be a routine exercise. Our guide, however, had to go close to her, exchanged some words with her, and showed her some papers. Finally, we were allowed to go inside the building. We, then, learnt that it was a student hostel of an academic institution, where some arrangements had been made for us to rest for a few hours till we would be met by another official for the next phase of movement to our destination, which were still unknown to us.

It was about five in the afternoon by the time we were taken to our room with three single cots on the first floor. Later, our guide disappeared after showing us the 'stolovaya' (dining hall) in the basement. Since we were to expect further instructions in an hour's time, we decided to lie down for a while to get over our travel fatigue. In reality, we dozed off only to be woken up some time later by the official who was expected. He informed me that I was to leave for Leningrad (now called St. Petersburg) the same midnight and handed over some roubles (the local currency) to defray my incidental expenses. My new Indian acquaintances were to proceed to Kiev in Ukraine (now a separate country) next day. I was told to be ready by 11:00 pm to be taken to the railway station to board a prestigious train named 'krasnaya strelka' (red arrow) for Leningrad. Still a few hours to pass and we did not know how to spend the time. A possible way, we felt, was to go down to the stolovaya as we were feeling hungry then. We went down, discovered a counter with a middle-aged woman apparently to take orders and receive payments, but we did not know what to order. There was not a trace of English anywhere. The woman in the counter did not understand us and we did not understand her. We checked out with a few students sitting in the dining hall to see if they could help us to overcome the language barrier. 'Nyet' was the only word we heard and guessed it meant 'no'. Without being nonplussed, we were looking around to find a way out, when I saw one of the students picking up a dish with meat and smashed potato from the service window. I caught hold of him, took him to the person in the counter, pointed to the dish, and took out the roubles in my palm. It worked. She picked up the money required for the dish, returned some coins, which, I later learnt, were 'kopek', and handed over a small printed coupon to me. I gave the coupon to the person at the service counter and my problem was solved. I got an identical dish in a few minutes, followed the student to pick up some bread pieces and salad, which were laid on a table obviously as free supply. I told my friends to do a similar exercise, but they were less adventurous than I was and did not venture. They found it safer to pick up the bread and salad to satisfy their stomach that evening.

Right at 11:00 pm, the official, who had met me in the evening, came back to take me to the railway station. His English was comprehensible. On our way to the railway station he explained that Moscow had several stations and the train to Leningrad would leave from 'Leningradskii vokzal'. It would leave exactly at midnight and reach Leningrad punctually at 7: 00 am the following morning. I wondered how I would know that the train has reached Leningrad as the platform would not be displaying the name in English. 'You need not worry', he said, 'Leningrad is the final destination for the train and wherever the train stops at 7:00 am will be Leningrad and you should get down there. Somebody from the Leningrad University will come and meet you on the platform'.

When I reached the departing platform of the station, the 'Red Arrow' was standing proudly on the track. The platform was spick and span, the train was impressive, no pushing, no bumping, no jostling along the way – an experience so different for a young Indian like me. My usher took me to the door of the train car where my coupe was located, handed over two sheets of paper – one was the ticket and the other was a letter addressed to the university, and disappeared. A smiling elderly lady met me at the entrance, took away the ticket, showed me where the big suitcase was to be kept, and ushered me to my berth in a coupe for four passengers. It was a lower birth and other passengers were yet to turn up. I sat down and started thinking about what was in store for me the next morning. It was nearing midnight. There was a spurt of checking in of passengers. Soon I found that our coupe was full. There was a youngish female and two middle-aged male passengers in our coupe. While I was still debating in my mind whether to take out my nightie for sleeping, I found other passengers including the girl undressing to their undies without any embarrassment and moving to their respective berths. After overcoming the initial hesitation, I followed them suit, covered myself up with the blanket, and slept off.

The larking fear of missing the destination woke me up much before the arrival time. I got up, dressed up and looked through the window. It was still dark and nothing much was visible but the train had slowed down. When it was nearing seven, the co-passengers got ready to disembark. It was exactly at 7:00 am the train stopped at the platform but I had no means to understand that it was Leningrad. However, as instructed, I took out my luggage, got down at the platform and waited for someone to meet me. Meanwhile, all the passengers got off the train and walked away. The train was empty. There was hardly any person on the platform. I stood there with my luggage. No body met me and I did not know what to do. I started moving in the same direction in which all other passengers moved. Suddenly I remembered that there was a letter addressed to the University. I took it out to find that it was all in Russian. Nevertheless, I started using the letter as my pathfinder. I tried to show it to a few passers-by but nobody responded. Finally, I met a messiah, who stopped, looked at the piece of paper and understood my needs but could not express in English. On the reverse side of the letter he sketched a trolley bus, wrote down a number, showed me the direction of movement with an arrow, and indicated that the sixth stop was the University on the bank of the River Neva.

I came out from the station and looked back to realize that the station had an impressive architecture (see Picture 02-05). In some features it resembled the Howrah railway station in my native city of Kolkata. Interestingly, both the stations were built in the middle of the nineteenth Century, I did not have any other clues for their apparent similarity.

*Leningrad railway station known as 'Moskovskii Vokzal' (Picture 02-05)*

As directed by my newly found unknown friend inside the station, I crossed the road, reached the trolley bus stop, got into the bus without any hassles, counted the number of stops, and reached the University stop, bag and baggage, on the bank of the River Neva..

As I alighted from the bus, despite my travel fatigue, I could not stop beholding the University building across the street (see Picture 02-06). It was a feast for the eye. The river strand stretched over a kilometer as I looked on, nicely paved and walled, and the University building stood like a royal palace. Finally, I entered the portals of the University that morning, a new and uncertain destination for me.

*Leningrad University on the bank of the River Neva (Picture 02-06)*

When I entered the edifice, as my luck would have, I saw an unmistakably Indian face at a distance. I rejoiced in my mind to see the dark-complexioned lanky guy of my age group. He appeared as an angel to me. I rushed to him. Before I could introduce myself, he extended his hand and said, 'I am Narayan Rao. What can I do for you?' 'At this moment you can save my life', I said, briefly introduced myself, and showed him the letter, my prized possession. He looked at me, looked at my disheveled hair, my unshaven face and a big suitcase on my side. No further narration was necessary. He took me to the right place and the right person, Boris Ivanov, in the department of affairs for foreign students at the University, who conversed well in English. At the outset, he was apologetic that his representative, who had turned up at the station on time but failed to identify me, and then completed all formalities quite fast. My hostel allocation was done. I was told that my Russian language course would start the following day.

Rao then introduced me to the department of Russian language for foreign students in the University premises. He entertained me with lunch and took me thereafter to the department of Geology, where he was carrying out his research studies after completing his language course. I had to wait there until he was free to take me to the hostel. Fortunately, the hostel was the same, where he was staying. It was some distance away from the university premises and involved a short bus ride, which was a surprising experience for me. Those days there were no bus conductors in the bus, neither any automat for buying the ticket. A passenger was required to drop the requisite coin in a box and tear his ticket from a role placed on the side of the box. My friend Rao did not have enough small coins to drop for buying our tickets. He pushed in a rouble currency into the box and waited for the subsequent passengers to board the bus. He collected the balance from them after announcing that he had inserted a rouble. Surprisingly they all trusted him and paid him off. Rao collected only the amount due to him after adjusting the cost of our two tickets and moved inside the bus. I wondered how such a practice was working in that country then!

Anyway, I reached the hostel with all my belongings in the evening after almost two days of ordeal.

## The first days in the hostel

My hostel room was something like a dormitory. There were four cots and three residents then, including me. Each bed had a small wooden side-shelf. A moderately large table stood at the center with four chairs. All furniture, except the side-shelves, was made of steel and quite heavy to move. Both my companions in the room were Russian and did not know a word in English. Alex was thin and tall, with sharp features and a somber mien. He hailed from Minsk in Belarus. The other roommate, Shasha, was stubby with a round and smiling face. He was from the Ural region. As I entered the room, both of them uttered some words in Russian, which I obviously did not understand then but took it as their welcome gesture. I said 'hello' and extended my hand. They had a very strong grip and I for the first time, understood what a Russian handshake meant. I kept my suitcase below the bed and went out to the room where Narayan Rao was staying. The intention was to be acquainted with the hostel building and facilities with his help.

The building had three floors and a basement, laid out in three segments at right angles to each other. The ground floor had some offices, a huge dining hall with kitchen and associated paraphernalia, and a small kiosk for selling bread, sausage, cheese and butter, when the dining hall was not in operation. The rooms were in the upper two floors on one side of the corridor – one after another. All the rooms were like dormitories with multiple occupants. There were two large common toilets in each floor - one for the male and the other for the female residents, as there were no separate wings for the girls. The rooms occupied by the girls and boys were often next to each other. The basement had all the utilities including a huge common facility with hot water for taking bath. This facility was common – three alternate evenings for the boys and the other three evenings for the girls. There were two staircases at the two ends of the edifice.

Living in this hostel was not very comfortable, not very hard either. The main difficulties, however, were the absence of privacy and the non-availability of common toiletries, which we were used to, in India. For example, one practice we had to adopt was using newspaper instead of toilet rolls, which were perennially in short supply those days, and another was not to take bath daily. To some extent, living without major compromises was not possible there those days. After a few days of suppressed feelings, we not only got used to the new mode of living but started enjoying it as well. Our daily routine started with waking up at 06:30 am, queuing up at the common toilet, rushing to the dining hall for breakfast, getting dressed up for going out to the street, running to the bus stop, reaching the university premises, occupying the class room chairs and being ready to receive the language teacher. Our classes including self-learning sessions and practices at the phonetic labs used to continue till about four in the afternoon. Then it was the time to return to the hostel, change to informal dresses, visit the hostel mates for chit-chatting, go for the supper and enjoy the free time till we went to bed.

Interestingly, we were a small group in the language class, just ten, three from India, two from East Pakistan (now Bangladesh), two from West Pakistan, two from Egypt and one from Indonesia and our teacher was Lyudmila Yakovlevna, a slim, tall and pretty Russian in her forties, who did not know a word in English. We seven from the subcontinent became good friends, tied by easy communication amongst ourselves. We were of similar age group as we had come after completing our master's degree in respective countries for our doctoral studies, whereas the other three students from Egypt and Indonesia were younger in age and came for graduate courses. They kept a distance from us, although they were quite friendly towards us. Lyudmila was a very sincere teacher. She resisted all our attempts to communicate with her and amongst ourselves in English. The teaching methodology from day one was direct and not through any other medium. It was hard, to start with, but it started yielding results in no time. We started to read, write and speak in Russian in less than a month, to the extent that we could carry on with our daily needs without any help of seniors. Of course, there were situations that sometimes seemed like comedy of errors. One day, my Bangladeshi friend, Mohabubul Karim, and I returned to the hostel after our classes. He confused his room number and entered the next room, where a girl was undressing. We were taught that in all embarrassing situations we must say 'izvenite', which meant 'excuse me'. Looking at the girl in that posture he wanted to beg her pardon but in that tense moment he uttered 'spasibo' or 'thank you'.

It took about seven months for most of us, barring some laggards, to be sufficiently fluent in reading, writing, and communicating in Russian. In the meantime, we experienced the advent of the golden autumn with unforgettable color of tree leaves, often strewn along the roadsides, followed by the freezing winter months, when the outside temperature was minus twenty five degree Celsius. The entire city was dazzlingly white in snow cover. The River Neva and its tributaries were frozen to a hard solid surface on which we could walk and cross over as an alternative to using the bridge. Heavy fur coats and fur shoes were our attire for several months. The day light was virtually missing then. The euphoria of enjoying snow with the onset of winter did not last long. Long exposure to the outdoor environment became less and less enjoyable, and we waited impatiently for the spring to appear. The real surprise, however, came when the summer set in with its White Nights. These memories and many other recollections are in the chapters that follow. The sweet and sour memories of the first welcoming days in the beautiful Arctic city will never be forgotten.

# CHAPTER 3

# St. Petersburg and the River Neva - My Russian Cradle

Though stated earlier, let me recapitulate that my initial upbringing was in a small town on the outskirts of Calcutta, which my grandfather used to call a "Coolie Town" because of the social environment. This, however, was followed by the next phase of my upbringing amongst the most elite student circles at the Calcutta Presidency College during its glorious days of 1950s. The final stage of my upbringing started circumstantially in 1960s in a city that was the fountain of the Russian culture – Leningrad or St. Petersburg as it is called now, where I had my first lessons of the Russian language, was acquainted with the Russian history and literature, met with several outstanding teachers and academicians, developed enduring friendships with fellow students, and personally visited magnificent imperial edifices standing as witnesses to the Soviet Revolution. I have no hesitation to confess that this city created a deep interest in me in the Russian history, culture and literature. I therefore call this city as my Russian cradle. Some snapshots of what I had learnt and seen are presented here.

### The River Neva – a Feast of the Eyes

Love at first sight was all that I felt, when I stood for the first time on the bank of the River Neva. A wide river with clear blue water flowing along mile-long straight edges with granite embankment on either side was a rare sight. A river flowing through the heart of a city was not new to me, as I hailed from Kolkata, where the river Ganga flows as its lifeline. But the parallel edges of the Neva, its attractive embankments, architectural beauty of the buildings on both the sides, and the colour and clarity of the flowing water made it so different that one could spend hours along the banks. Later, I learnt that the river was different in many other features. It is one of the shortest rivers with a length of hardly 75 km but one of the highest in terms of the volume of discharge. The river originates from Lake Ladoga in northwest Russia, takes a U-course, and merges into the Baltic Sea. It is one of the most fascinating rivers of Europe apparently carrying the largest volume of water in the shortest span of flow.

A walk along the river bank was our best pastime, whenever we had breaks in our classes. It was cold, often windy, as the autumn was on. Yet a brisk walk out from the university campus along the river was quite refreshing. With days and weeks passing, we could witness how the golden autumn was gradually turning into bare trees. The winter was setting in. We started seeing white flakes of ice floating on the River (Picture 03-01). Soon thereafter, the transparency of water and floating ice disappeared from the river surface. The days became dark and gloomy and our beloved Neva turned itself into white wilderness. It was a shining white frozen river with thick layer of snow. Our pleasure of walking along the river banks was lost.

*Floating ice sheets on the Neva (Picture 03-01)*

We often used to wonder how, under such adverse conditions the river was so artistically embanked and the beautiful city of St. Petersburg developed. The story goes that the river served as an important trade route in the past for the Russians, Finns and Swedes and perhaps Peter the Great, the emperor and the founder of the city, realized its strategic importance after he re-conquered the land from Sweden in the Great Northern War and founded the city along the bank of the river and its delta. The city was obviously built under very adverse climatic and geographical conditions. One of the daring attempts made at that time was to build embankments along the river. The legend goes that the entire embankment was constructed with the help of thousands of conscripted serfs, one from every ten or twelve households. The Emperor had also hired a large number of engineers and architects from different European countries to help construct the city. St. Petersburg flourished with magnificent granite embankments along with luxurious stone edifices on either side of the river.

In addition, a network of waterways, resembling Venice city, was planned. A large number of bridges were constructed, mostly of bascule type, which could be opened at night to facilitate the movement of large vessels at night time during the navigational season. Since the Emperor was highly impressed with the French architecture, the cityscape also developed a strong resemblance with Paris. There were a large number of emigrant scientists, engineers, architects, shipbuilders and artists from other parts of Europe, who had then settled in the city. Thus, it became a vibrant and cosmopolitan place to live and work. In 1712, the capital of the Russian Empire was shifted from Moscow to St Petersburg. It remained as the country's capital for more than two centuries untill the end of the Russian Revolution in 1918, barring a gap of four years (1728-1732), when Peter II had made an unsuccessful attempt to shift the capital to Moscow.

## Our Adventure on the Frozen Neva

As stated earlier, that with the onset of winter, notwithstanding all our protective gears from head to toe, we could hardly enjoy the walk along the bank of the Neva. The splendid cityscape that we enjoyed during the autumn days became objects of diminishing attraction and we concentrated more and more on studies and indoor pastimes in the centrally heated rooms, both in the university campus and in the hostel. However, on an unusually bright January day our teacher declared that we all would be going out to walk across the Neva and enjoy the real Russian winter. Although it was a surprising proposition, we didn't want to miss the opportunity, amassed enough courage, dressed up again, keeping only the cheeks and nose uncovered, and queued up behind the teacher, leading us the way. We got down to the edge of the Neva. We wondered how the blue water had hidden itself and saw, instead, carpets of dazzling white snow across the river and scores of people, young and old, walking on the foot tracks to cross the river (Picture 03-02). The bridge over the river remained a forlorn witness to the human adventure! Led by our teacher, we accomplished the task, and to our good luck, we even witnessed how a middle aged person, in his undergarment with a bare body, took advantage of a big hole in the snow to enjoy ice swim. It was also a spectacle to watch.

*The Frozen Neva (Picture 03-02)*

## St. Petersburg – an Archive of the Imperial History

The history of the city is so interwoven with the Russian imperial history that all the 'babushkas' (senior female citizens) on duty in different building complexes to check the identity cards of the visitors or perform similar light duties, had some interesting stories to share. Furthermore, the faculty members of the Leningrad University were so proud of the heritage of the city that with the slightest provocation, they used to narrate various historical anecdotes regarding how the city was built, how the different generations of the Romanovs, the imperial dynasty, ruled the Russian empire for three centuries, and how the common people lived and revolted with reformist or autocratic scions of the royal dynasty. Even without being a student of history, I was deeply absorbed in unraveling the past of the city in my own way.

Peter the Great (1672-1725), as we all know, was the first emperor of Russia and founded the city in May 1703, known then more in the German style as 'Sankt Petersburg'. The city was named not after the founder but in honor of the apostle St. Peter. The name of the city was changed to 'Petrograd' in 1914 and the name continued till 1924, when it was renamed as 'Leningrad'. In 1991 the name 'St. Petersburg' was reinstated. These changes were obviously in sync with the Russian history. During the World War I in 1914 the name of the city appeared too German and it was renamed as Petrograd. The next rechristening of the city as Leningrad was done in commemoration of Vladimir Lenin, who led the Russian Revolution, three days after his demise on 24 January 1924. Later, on July 12, 1991, during the first presidential election of Russia there was a public referendum on selecting the name of the city and the majority view was in favour of reinstating the old name.

St. Petersburg prospered under the rule of two of the most powerful women in Russian history: Empress Elizabeth, who reigned from 1740 to 1762 and Empress Ekaterina (Catherine in

English), who ruled from 1762 to 1796. The city expanded and became architecturally more attractive during their reigns. The Winter Palace and the Summer Palace of the royal family were done up, which became residences of Empress Catherine the Great. Alongside such unstinted demonstration of pomp and grandeur, the city's history was replete with several revolutions, uprisings, assassinations of Tsars, and power takeovers, which shaped the entire course of history in Russia and influenced the world. In 1801, after the assassination of the Emperor Paul I, his son Alexander I ruled Russia during the Napoleonic Wars and expanded his Empire by acquisitions of Finland and part of Poland. His mysterious death in 1825 was followed by the Decembrist revolt, which was suppressed by the Emperor Nicholas I, who ordered execution of leaders and exiled hundreds of their followers to Siberia. Nicholas I then pushed for Russian nationalism by suppressing non-Russian nationalities and religion. Emperor Alexander II, his son, however, is remembered for a great social reform undertaken by him to emancipate the serfs. It caused an influx of the poor and the hapless into the capital and led to erection of labour tenements in the city's outskirts, springing up of small industries, and converting the city of riches to a city of rags and riches. The net result was the onset of social unrest, initiation of radical movements and nucleation of Socialist organizations. St. Petersburg is strewn with memories of such social unrests, along with relics of imperial grandeur. There is hardly any city in the world, which reflects the history of the entire nation as vividly as this one.

### Siege of Leningrad: a Memorable Tale

The grandmotherly widows, who were specifically employed, as mentioned above, to carry out light jobs in residential complexes or as small pavement vendors formed a very interesting stratum of the society in Leningrad of the nineteen sixties, when I visited the city for the first time as a language student. After my communication skills in the Russian language became reasonably good and I could speak comprehensibly to others, I used to interact with the babushkas without missing a single opportunity. They were not educated but literate enough to narrate the heroic tales of the World War II. Interestingly they had huge stocks of historical snippets to share. Many of them had the pathetic experience of losing their husbands and other near and dear ones during the war. One of the episodes that they seldom forgot to narrate was the 'Siege of Leningrad' by the Germans. It was a great pride for the people of Leningrad. I was told that about three million German soldiers had streamed into the Soviet frontier for a surprise invasion planned by Adolf Hitler with a three-pronged attack on Moscow, Ukraine and Leningrad. The target of Leningrad apparently was to vanquish the Russian Baltic naval fleet and to destroy several hundreds of productive factories, which were in operation in the region. The German army moved through Lithuania, Latvia and Estonia, the Baltic states and reached Leningrad, destroyed the railway link, and blocked the waterways from Lake Ladoga. The Finnish army, which was an ally of the Germans then, covered the northern routes. Thus, the entire Leningrad was encircled and besieged. The historians say that the siege of the city continued for 900 days from the 8th September 1941 to the 27th January 1944 and over a million people had died due to aerial and artillery bombing by the German forces and due to starvation, infection, severe exposure to unprotected cold and stress. The memories of such loss of life were extremely tragic. A touching story that I heard many times was about a twelve-year old girl called Tanya Savicheva. The story goes that she used to record in a journal the dates when each of her family members died. After she lost her mother, she scribbled 'everyone is dead and only Tanya is left'. Tanya's diary became a symbol of the blockade and was one of the many documents submitted at the Nuremburg trial. As the Soviet Army held out against the Nazi siege, in early 1942 about half a million population of the city was promptly evacuated via Lake Ladoga. The rest of the population continued to survive on what the Russians called 'Cheorni Khleb' (black bread, similar to the present-day brown bread), which was strictly rationed.

## Historical Landmarks on the River Banks

Edifices built and sculptures erected on both the banks of the Neva River carry grand evidences of the entire imperial history. It is impossible to enlist them comprehensively, though I still remember a few landmarks that I had visited together with my friends or used to pass by while strolling. One of the most remarkable buildings is the 'Peter and Paul Cathedral' (Picture 03-03).

*Peter and Paul cathedral on the northern bank of the Neva (Picture 03-03)*

The cathedral was built by Peter the Great in early eighteenth century on the last upstream island of the riverine delta. The original purpose was to construct a fortress to save the city from the Finns, but this objective was never met. Instead, it became the citadel of St. Peter. The premises were also used as prison cell. In fact, even in the early 1920s it was used as prison and execution ground by the Bolshevik government. Presently, it has been converted into a very important state museum of the city's history.

Another interesting piece of history is the cruiser Aurora (Avrora in Russian), floating on the Neva (Picture 03-04). It was a naval ship belonging to the Baltic fleet. It is a memorable museum now, as on 25 October 1917 at 9:40 pm, the story goes, a blank shot was fired from its gun, signalling the start of the October revolution.

*The cruiser ship Aurora on the Neva (Picture 03-04)*

Other landmarks that I fondly remember, inter alia, are the Winter Palace of the Tsars, called 'Zimnii Dvorets' in Russian, the statue of the Bronze Horseman ('mednii Vcadnik' in Russian), and two Egyptian sphinxes, all on the river banks. The Winter Palace was the official residence of the Russian emperors from 1732 to 1917. In the course of about two centuries, the palace was enlarged to a mammoth size at different points of time and accumulated innumerable pages of the imperial history, which cannot be recounted here. Today, it is one of the most splendid museums of the world. One really interested in Russian history may take days to walk around the museum, now known as 'The Hermitage' (Pictures 03-05 and 03-06).

*The Winter Palace (now known as the Hermitage) viewed from the other bank (Picture 03-05)*

*The inside painting of the Palace Dome with famous paintings of European artists (Picture 03-06)*

The equestrian statue, the Bronze Horseman, depicting Peter the Great astride his horse, was an attempt of Catherine the Second to immortalize herself and Peter the Great in the eyes of the progeny (Picture 03-07). It is interesting that later the world-famous Russian poet Alexander Pushkin used this sculpture as the centrepiece of his epical poem bearing the same name. In fact, the poet's creation was around the flooding tendency of the river Neva caused by either the melting of ice in the Lake Ladoga or by the west wind blowing back the river flow. There were devastating floods on record, once in 1777 and again in 1824 during Pushkin's time, and the poem was a poetic imagery coupling the river flooding with the statue. Although, in reality, the flood threat of the river receded later with the construction of an upstream dam, the poem survived as a classic creation of a famous poet.

*The Bronze Horseman (Picture 03-07)*

Two of the sphinxes lying on the bank of the Neva in front of the Academy of Fine Arts are the finest examples of ancient Egyptian colossal sculptures, erected outside their homeland (see Picture 03-08). For almost two centuries, the gaze of these two sphinxes is fixed during summer on the blue water of the Neva and in winter on its white frozen layer of snow, but not on the Nile flowing through the sandy Giza.

*One of the two sphinxes on the bank of the Neva (Picture 03-08)*

## The White Nights in St. Petersburg

During the severe winter, despite our best endeavour to overcome the gloom in the surroundings, we could hardly suppress our feelings of dismay and fatigue. Our teacher understood the drooping spirit of her pupils from the tropical lands. One day, perhaps to cheer us up, she showed us a book authored by the famous Russian novelist Fyodor Dostoyevsky. In English language, the title of the book read 'White Nights and Other Stories'. Our language proficiency at that time was not good enough to read Dostoyevsky's writings in original, which she knew. She, therefore, narrated the story in a non-literary way, reading out some selected portions directly from the original novel. It was an unforgettable day in our class, when we heard 'The story from the diary of a dreamer'. The story narrated by our teacher left us awfully inquisitive about how the 'Belye Nochi' or 'White Nights' would be in Leningrad for us then. We eagerly waited for the spring and summer to arrive.

Gradually, we discovered that from May to July, the sun did not, in effect, set in St. Petersburg as geographically, the city lies in the Arctic Circle. We found that the city apparently did not sleep.

It remained as lively after midnight as it was during the day. The streets remained crowded. The restaurants were full. Scores of concerts and cultural events took place at various locations. Comparable to our dusk, the sun dimmed a little between 1:00 to 4:00 am, when the bridges over the river opened to pass the large boats to move.

Sleeping at night was a difficult task. We did not have any curtains on the glass windows, nor did we possess any masks. Often, we used to lie down on the bed and cover our eyes with some cloth pieces for sleeping off. During the weekends, we could not overcome the temptation of loitering on the streets after midnight. There were many occasions, when we crossed the river, did not have any sense of time, bridges opened for the night traffic of boats, and we could not return to our hostel even for a nap. Yet the life was full of joy and merry making. One such night, walking along the street, we reached the famous Palace Square (Dvortsovaya Ploshchad as called in Russian). This is a huge square connecting the Nevsky Prospekt with a bridge in front of the Winter Palace leading to Vasilievsky Island. It was early morning hours then but there was not a trace of darkness (see Picture 03-09). Instead, the entire area was lit with sun rays of orange tinge.

*The Palace Square during the White Nights (Picture 03-09)*

We loitered across the Square and appalled to recall that this was the place where the massacre of Bloody Sunday took place in January 1905, in which unnamed demonstrators were fired upon by the soldiers of the Imperial Guard as they marched towards the Palace to present a petition to Tsar Nicholas II. This was the place that stood witness to the significant events of the October Revolution in 1917.

**The Nevsky Prospekt – an Avenue with a History**

One of our top favourite strolling areas was the avenue named 'Nevsky Prospekt' (Picture 03-10). It is the most popular shopping and dining streets in St. Petersburg even today, I presume. It runs straight without curves and turns over a long stretch with impressive heritage buildings standing on either side.

*The Nevsky Prospekt (Picture 03-10)*

I liked roaming on this street for some other reasons. It had a lot of history concealed in it. The first and foremost is the name itself. It took its name from Alexander Nevsky Lavra, the monastery, which stands at the eastern end of the street, and it connects the Palace Square on the other end as mentioned earlier.

The history goes that Alexander Nevsky, a Prince from the Imperial family, provided the leadership in defeating the Swedes in the Northern War of the 12$^{th}$ century. A monastery was built by

Peter the Great in 1710, just a few years after the founding of Petersburg City, near the spot where there was a Swedish Fort earlier. The first church was built there in 1713 and the monastery began working shortly thereafter. A new church, designed by an Italian architect, came up there in 1724, and since the Russian Prince Alexander Nevsky (1221-1263) led the battle of victory and was also considered a Saint by the Russian Orthodox Church, his holy remains were brought from an old city called Vladimir to the new church. What is more interesting is the later part of the history. In 1750, Empress Elizabeth issued an order to fabricate a shrine made of one-and-a-half tons of pure silver to shelter the holy remains and the shrine was decorated with the victory pictures of Alexander Nevsky and others. The shrine was moved to a new cathedral in 1790 and in 1797 Emperor Paul gave the monastery the highest rank in the Orthodox hierarchy and named it the Alexander Nevsky Monastery of the Holy Spirit (Picture 03-11).

*The courtyard of Alexander Nevsky Monastery (Picture 03-11)*

The Monastery complex is home to some of the oldest buildings in the city and also to some cemeteries having the graves of several stalwarts of the Russian culture and literature such as Tchaikovsky, Dostoyevsky and Glinka. There were many attempts made to rename the street before and immediately after the Russian revolution but all attempts were unsuccessful. The overwhelming popular demand was to retain the original name of the historical avenue. Another historical trait of this street that remained ingrained in me was its popularity with the famous Russian authors of the nineteenth century. Nikolai Gogol narrated the feverish life of the avenue in his story "Nevsky Prospekt', published in 1835. Fyodor Dostoyevsky used this avenue as a setting in many of his works and particularly in 'Crime and Punishment'. There is a café, called 'Literary Café', on this street, which served as rendezvous for many of the writers.

## Concluding Remarks

Saint Petersburg is a unique city in Russia that has been called by different names such as Petrograd, Leningrad, Petersburg, etc., in its long history but it never failed to maintain its pleasing ambience, its cosmopolitan flavor, and its intoxicating attractiveness. Those who had opportunities of being there once have always remained its admirer with intents of revisiting and walking along the strand of the river Neva or along the Nevsky Prospekt or looking at the Hermitage. It is the city, where I had learnt the first letters of the Russian language in the middle of nineteen sixties and learnt to love the language as a very dear medium of communication for the rest of my life. The historical aroma of the city, the river Neva flowing through its heart, the waterways, bridges and the monumental edifices have remained embedded in my mind, coupled with the intimate and affectionate touch of numerous friends and families. True to what I have said, I have revisited the city several times in the last four decades on work and leisure. If there is another opportunity, I would rush again to my beloved city – my Russian cradle.

# CHAPTER 4

# Moscow State University - My Alma Mater

We were standing in front of the magnificent edifice of *Moskovskii Gosudarstvenni Universitet* (Em-Gay-Eu in the Russian acronym), one of the top universities of the world. My wife and I gazed and gazed from a distance (Picture 04-01). It was a kind of revisiting my alma mater after about four decades, a visit, though not planned in advance, was immensely invigorating to us. Isn't it a moment of pride to come back to a seat of education which is 265 years old and where I had spent quite a few of my younger years? I felt deeply nostalgic, and that is why I had agreed to my wife's insistence to return via Moscow from a conference in St. Petersburg. I wanted to unlock some of the past golden moments of my life and my wife perhaps looked for an opportunity to verify a few of the gossips and narrations about the University she had heard from me and from my friends.

*Moscow State University (Courtesy: Dmitry A. Mottl (Picture 04-01))*

My story goes back to the middle of nineteen sixties, when I had for the first time entered the portals of the most magnificent and imposing monolithic building of the Moscow State University for my doctoral studies. As a young lad then I stood for a while on the wide and long steps leading to the portal and was bewildered simply with the grandeur of the building. Looking at the main entrance, I could see a high central tower with a star on top almost piercing the sky (Picture 04-02), and looking behind, I saw aesthetically paved walkways leading towards a promenade overlooking the Moscow River (Picture 04-03) . It was a splendid landscape in front of the University.

*Central tower and the spire at the top (04-02)*

*Paved walkways towards the promenade overlooking the Moscow River (Picture 04-03)*

While revisiting my beloved university this time, both of us stopped at the doorstep of the main portal to reinvent our views and feelings on the grandiose structure. I wondered if I would still find the university premises as impressive as I used to find it as a student. I must admit that there was no change in my feelings and the level of my appreciation of the building architecture remained the same. I found the entire structure as imposing and magnificent as it was during my student days. Since my wife was looking at the structure for the first time, I tried to excite her to come out with her impressions. The reaction was unspoken but visible on her face. I could see in her eyes a tinge of disbelief that such a university building was constructed in the early 1950s in the Stalinist era and survived the vicissitudes of time. She was sipping the grandeur and splendour of the building.

It is true that there were no apparent changes in the external view of the premises. The 240m-high central tower with 36 floors still makes you feel small. The star at the top of the tower is still shining as it used to. Kudos to the university staff that despite its mind-boggling dimension, the star at the top of the tower is so well maintained! From the ground level it is so difficult to imagine that it weighs 12 tons and has enough space to accommodate a small room with a viewing platform. The giant clocks, barometers, thermometers, statues, carved wheat sheaves, all on the building facades, remain unchanged. The terrace, where the steps end before the entry portal, still carries the statues of male and female students gazing with utter optimism and confidence into the future. The most impressive were the massive columns at the main entrance (Picture 04-04).

*Massive columns at the main entrance to the central tower (Courtesy: Fred Shaerli) (Picture 04-04)*

We had not come prepared to enter the building. There were no invitations, no passes. Chances were that we would fail. Nevertheless, we ventured up to the security guard and tried to explain that I had studied in the sixties and my wife was keen to see where her husband had studied. The guard demanded a proof, which obviously I did not carry with me. But still I cajoled him in Russian. Finally, looking at the tearful eyes of my sari-clad wife, the guard relented, allowed us to go inside, but cautioned not to hang around for long.

Inside the building I took my wife through some stretches of marbled internal corridors and roofed walkways (see Picture 04-05). With mounting fatigue, she realized that walking even inside the building will be a herculean task as the entire building had almost 33 km of corridors, 5000 rooms, a concert hall, a theatre, a museum, a library, a swimming pool, a police station, a post office, a laundry, a hairdresser's salon, banks, shops, cafeterias and even a bomb shelter.

*Inside view of the University (Picture 04-05)*

During my days there were four interconnected wings of this building, where students and scholars were housed. I wanted to take my wife to one such wing where I had spent quite a few years of my young life. The inevitability of a pretty long walk, though all inside the building, discouraged her. We stopped and sat on the stairs leading to the dancing floor, which was of the size of a tennis court.

While resting, I whispered into her ears that when I started living in this building, for days and months I did not have occasions to go out. I lived in one floor, my laboratories and classrooms were in other floors of the same building, the shops for my daily needs were in the basement, the cafeterias for breakfast, lunch and dinner were accessible from inside the building, the cinema hall was on the ground floor; book shops, bank and post office were around. Certainly, there were no needs to go out but still we used to come out of the building almost every afternoon or evening, be it summer or winter. It was so refreshing in the summer evenings to walk along the square in front of the building with straight spic-and-span streets covered on either side with trees beatified with blossoming green foliage. The streets lead us to the river bank overseeing the Moscow stadium and provided a bird's eye view of the entire city (Picture 04-06).

*Bird's eye view of the city and the stadium from the Lenin Hill (Picture 04-06)*

But in the December and January months, the landscape dramatically changed. The verdant place turned into white wilderness in stark contrast! The entire stretch that was green converted to sparklingly white with snow (Picture 04-07). The temperature used to fluctuate around (-) 20-25$^0$C. Most trees turned bare and their branches were decorated by nature with icicles forming flower-like shapes. Some trees that refused to be oppressed by the forces of winter were covered with snow contrasting with the green leaves left on them. We covered ourselves from head to toe and used to walk over the place to have a glimpse of the frozen river, shining brilliantly white even in the midnight.

*The white wilderness during the winter months (Picture 04-07)*

Coming back to where we were, we got up from our remembrances, started walking again, and came near the elevators of the central tower. I remembered the days, when we used to literally run through the corridors to get into the elevator for timely attendance in our classes. But as the luck would have it, many of us would find all the elevators simultaneously moving up to either $26^{th}$ or $32^{nd}$ floors. An American friend of mine, who was studying Russian history at the university, would quietly come to my side to bet which elevator would come down first so that we could stand at a vantage point. Both of us used to lose the bet almost equally and celebrated the wins in the cafeteria in the evening.

Suddenly from a distance, I noticed at the end of the corridor the same book kiosks where I used to buy scores of books including translations of English publications. I never afforded to buy most of those books in original versions in India as a student but I could procure the same books in Russian language at throw-away prices. In fact, knowledge and information were in the reach of the masses. Was the situation same now? Just to check my curiosity, I went up to one of the book kiosks. I was glad to find after so many decades that the prices of books have remained affordable. As a memento I bought and carried a couple of books in the Russian language.

Many more memories crowded my mind. I could see, of course from outside, the hostel room where I lived and studied for several years. I remembered my neighbours from Ukraine and Siberia, who used to treat me, whenever they received their packets of special food items from home. I remembered our get-togethers with friends in the common room on our floor of the hostel block to celebrate different occasions, some real and some fabricated. Those and many other sweet memories and anecdotes flashed in my mind. It was time for us to leave so that we could keep our word with the security guard. We came out and came to the grand steps leading to the huge square. It was the month of April. Snow had disappeared but the roads were still wet. Greens were trying to stage their come-back. We walked down to the promenade overlooking the Moscow River. I had a pleasant feeling to see that the ski stations, where we had our first lessons of skiing on the hill slope, were still there, and the track that we used to take to reach the river bank was still in use.

On the river strand I saw a big change. There used to be no vendors on this strand in my olden days but now there were several of them. The delight of quiet enjoyment had disappeared. It was perhaps a gift of free economy! I also learnt about another big change. We knew the place, where the University was situated, as 'Leninskie Gory' (meaning Lenin Hill). In 1999, after the fall of the Soviet Union, the name was changed and its old historical name 'Vorobievskie Gory' (meaning Sparrow Hill) was restored. Yes, the world has changed and names do matter.

Notwithstanding such political changes, Em-Gay-Eu remains Em-Gay-Eu, an excellent centre of education and research that was created by a great scientist of all times, Mikhail Lomonosov, by a decree of the Russian Empress Elizabeth on January 25, 1755. This date is celebrated as the Students' Day all over Russia even now. In 1940 the University was renamed in honour of Mikhail Lomonosov. Over the decades the campus has grown and some of the faculties are housed in separate buildings detached from the central interconnected structure. The whole campus has now a floor area of more than a million square meters. The population of graduate and postgraduate students, I was told, had crossed forty thousand. More than 6000 teachers and about 5000 research scholars work in different faculties and the university enrols about 4000 international students from all over the world. I shall be failing in my duties if I do not mention about the University library. It has a collection of 9 million books and an average readership of 55.000 using 5.5 million books per year. As of 2019, I was told that the university boasts of having the affiliation of 13 Nobel laureates, six Field Medal winners, and one Turing Award winner.

Coming back to the beauty and the uniqueness of the building, the history goes that in the post-war period Joseph Stalin had ordered seven huge multi-storied "neoclassic" structures to be built all over the city of Moscow. These structures did come up over a period of time and remain as landmarks of the city. The Em-Gay-Eu building was by far the largest. I am told it still remains the tallest educational building in the world. Hats off to the Architect Lev Rudnev!

It was our 'Yarrow Revisited'. We looked at the Moscow River from the strand of the Sparrow Hill. It reminded us of the following few immortal lines of the poet:

> "For busy thoughts the Stream flowed on
> In foamy agitation;
> And slept in many a crystal pool
> For quiet contemplation:
> No public and no private care
> The freeborn mind enthralling
> We made a day of happy hours,
> Our happy days recalling."

# CHAPTER 5

# Looking Back at the Soviet Era in My Own Way

I became curious about the Soviet life and society during my school days in 1950s, when I used to overhear my father heatedly discussing with his friends in our living room on the 'Sinews of Peace' address delivered by Winston Churchill. I overheard the expression 'Iron Curtain' for the first time then without, of course, understanding what it really meant. Later, of course, I did not take much time to unravel the significance, particularly when I reached the portals of the Presidency College. More gossips and little facts floated around us those days about the Soviet Union and its satellite countries in East Europe, which probably justified the nomenclature of Iron Curtain.

Considering the number of years that I had spent in the Soviet Union, I feel obliged to narrate how I had spent so many eventful years of my life behind the Iron Curtain, when I was young and prone to impressionism. It may also be relevant to mention that by the sheer turn of events in my professional life I could revisit the country several times later. Thus, I gathered a plethora of sweet and sour memories of the country when it was behind the Iron Curtain and when the curtain was dismantled. I had a large network of friends and well-wishers in that country then, many of whom remained in touch with me for decades. The Russian teachers occupied a special place in my heart. Their affectionate behaviour left an indelible impression in me. I enjoyed the great experience of observing how Marxism-Leninism had been unfolding in the country. I could also notice the expanding cracks and ultimate collapse of the Soviet regime during my later visits. With all these experiences I felt an urge to scribble my reminiscences of the Soviet life, academia and society even without being a historian. It is not a political critique. There are no references, no authentication. It is wholly based on memory and some diarised noting of mine. Let me start with my sketchy notes on Red Square - the centrepiece of Russian history.

## Red Square – an Indelible Witness to Changing Times in Russia

I was always curious to find out why the place is called 'Red' as I didn't find anything red there, barring a few crimson coloured buildings (Picture 05-01). In my young days, I carried the same misconception that many others might be carrying even today that the name was connected with the "communist movement", because of the latter's association with colour red. Later I realized that it could not be the case anyway, as the Red Square was called so since centuries before the advent of communism there. From the gossips in my university days I was given to understand that in the ancient Russian language the word "krasnyi" meant "beautiful", from which the name of the place was derived as "Krasnaya Ploshchad", meaning a beautiful square, though the meaning of the word got mutated to signify "red" in the modern Russian.

*The Red Square with Kremlin entrance on the right and St. Basil's Cathedral on the left (Picture 05-01)*

The history of Red Square dates back to the later part of the 15th century and has been a focal point of most social and political happenings in the Imperial Russia, during the Soviet era, and even in Russia of post 1990s. Standing in the middle of Red Square, covering an area of more than 70,000 m², one can see the Russian heritage all around: Kremlin, GUM (State Departmental Store), the State History Museum, Lenin's Mausoleum and St. Basil's Cathedral, each having its own history. The Red Square was declared a World Heritage Site by UNESCO in 1990.

In its earliest incarnation, Red Square was known as Trinity Square as Trinity Cathedral stood at the southern fringe during the rule of Ivan III, who is credited to have reconstructed Kremlin in the early years of the 15th century. The Trinity Cathedral was later replaced by the nine-towered Cathedral of Saint Basil the Blessed during 1554-1560 by Ivan IV, better remembered as Ivan the Terrible and the first Grand Prince to be proclaimed as Tsar of Russia in 1547, to commemorate the defeat of Tatars (Mongols) of Kazan and Astrakhan. This Cathedral continues to be a landmark of Moscow city.

The adjacent Kremlin is a fortified complex, having five palaces and four cathedrals inside it with an enclosing wall and towers. Though Kremlin carried the rich legacy of imperial Russia, it turned out to be the prime centre of politics during the Soviet era. The Soviet Government moved from Petrograd (today's St Petersburg) to Moscow on the 12th March 1918. Vladimir Lenin chose to use the Kremlin Senate as his residence and Joseph Stalin had his private rooms in the Kremlin as well. The story goes that Stalin was eager to remove all the relics of the Tsarist regime. But it seems that, in reality, instead of massive destruction of properties, the premises underwent extensive renovation and restoration. A visible change was the replacement of the golden eagles on the towers by shining stars. The Grand Palace in Kremlin, overlooking the Moscow River to the south, St. Basil's Cathedral and Red Square to the east, and Alexander

Garden to the west, became the Presidential Palace of the ruling government.

The major changes in Red Square came apparently in 1930, when the construction of Lenin's Mausoleum was completed along with granite paving of the square. After the collapse of the Soviet Union, the Red Square missed the grand military parades of May Day and October Revolution Anniversary on the 7$^{th}$ November for several years till the parades were revived in 2008.

The Red Square remains a unique symbol of the historical past and the modern history of Russia, as unique as the Tsar Bell, probably the largest and the heaviest bronze casting in the world, standing as an imperial heritage on the grounds of Kremlin in a cracked state due to some fire occurrence in the olden days (Picture 05-02).

*The Tsar Bell standing on the Kremlin grounds (Picture 05-02)*

**Tell Tales about Gorky Street**

When we were studying in Moscow State University in the late 1960s, a street named in honour of Maxim Gorky, the famous socialist writer, in the central part of the city, not far from the Red Square, was a very popular road for us to have occasional leisurely strolls for window shopping or for a drink (Picture 05-03). My special attraction for this street was its interesting history in keeping with the changing times.

The road, it is said, existed even in the 12$^{th}$ century and it was called Tverskaya Street. In the 17$^{th}$ and 18$^{th}$ centuries the street was the centre of Moscow's social life with fashionable shops, luxurious hotels, and grand houses. The wealthiest aristocrats were passionate to live there. The street was the main thoroughfare for the movement of the royalty from the Northern Capital to Moscow Kremlin for residence. On the street stood the residence of the Governor of Moscow and in its front a large square was created for parades and celebrations.

*A stretch of the Gorky Street in the 1980s (Picture 05-03)*

The post-revolution period gave a new look to the historically famous street and it was renamed in 1932 as Gorky Street after Maxim Gorky, the renowned author, who was admired by both Vladimir Lenin and Joseph Stalin. Later, the relatively narrow street was widened by tearing down several churches and old buildings, and subsequently the low-rise buildings were replaced with massive apartment-block buildings, typical of the Soviet era. The entire rebuilding effort was to proclaim "socialist realism". However, in 1990, perestroika of the Soviet regime by Gorbachev became an active force. There was a deliberate attempt to reinvent the future by returning to the country's past. The Gorky Street was again renamed as Tverskaya Street. Interestingly, in 1947, the Tverskaya Square was decorated with an equestrian statue of Prince Dolgoruky, the founder of the Moscow City.

**Foreign Students and Scholars in the USSR**

In the universities and academic institutions, both at St. Petersburg and Moscow, there were three groups of foreign students and researchers. The first group belonged to the East European countries, particularly from Poland, the then East Germany, and Bulgaria. Sprinklings of students from Czechoslovakia, Hungary, and Romania were met with, but not very frequently. Most of the students I came across from the East European countries were pursuing research in their fields of interest. The second group came from the Asian, African and Latin American countries such as Algeria, Afghanistan, Congo, Cuba, Egypt, Indonesia, Iran, Kenya, Peru, Sudan, Syria, Vietnam and some other developing nations. Most of these students came after their schooling and pursued courses in polytechnics or institutions. A limited number were in the university degree courses. In total numbers, they constituted a large bulk. The third group was from the developed countries such as the USA, UK, Australia, France, Italy, and others. These students were mostly on short-term visits and came to study the Russian language, ballet, music, etc. or to familiarize themselves with specialized institutions as permitted by the Soviet authorities.

I did not mention about India in the above categories. The Indo-Soviet student exchange programmes started in the early 1960s and were limited to studying the Russian language or to undertaking researches in specified fields of science and technologies as agreed between the two governments. Outside of the above scheme, there were industrial trainees from India, particularly from the steel and oil sectors. Interestingly, during this period the relation between the Chinese and the Soviet governments were highly strained and all the Chinese students were asked to return home. As a result, all the Soviet cities that were permitted to have foreign nationals were totally devoid of the Chinese students. However, several Mongolian students were studying in Moscow, some of whom have kept contacts with me even today.

Inviting foreign students into the Soviet Union was an extremely carefully crafted strategy for spreading the message of goodwill in the cold war times. The cities where the foreign students were permitted to live, the institutions they were admitted to, the academic courses they were offered, hospitality that they enjoyed were well planned by the authorities, leaving nothing to the choice of the foreign students or the countries they were coming from. Yet the influx of foreign students was large. There were hardly any deserters as they were taken care of in a planned manner. Those polytechnics, institutes or universities that were approved for foreign nationals had a separate department or cell for them. Such cells had officials who could converse and communicate in English and some other foreign languages. They tracked smartly the enrolled students, who by regulations prevailing then could not travel beyond 40 km from the city limits on their own. This was perhaps intended to ensure that the foreigners were not exposed to the rural living conditions or the lack of infrastructure there.

It is important to mention here that the living expenses and the academic fees of the foreign students and scholars were covered through monthly scholarships. The public transport was cheap. The cities had good and affordable entertainment facilities. Barring a few fashionable hotels and restaurants, the normal lunch and dinner places, 'stolovaya' in the Russian, within the institute campuses or outside on the streets were not at all expensive. Broadly, the Soviet regime had created an environment and a supporting infrastructure in some of the major cities that attracted the foreign students. Another important feature was the absence of apartheid in the minds of the Russians. Creed and colour never came in the way of befriending the foreigners. Thus, with many positives, the strategy of the Soviet regime to send out messages to the world, from behind the iron curtain, but with the help of sponsored education, that the USSR was a country to reckon with, worked well in those days. Perhaps, this success prompted the regime to set up Patrice Lumumba University of Friendship, essentially for the African and Latin American youngsters, who could join after completing their schooling in their own countries. The University has now been renamed as the Russian University of Peoples' Friendship and the infrastructure has been significantly upgraded (see Picture 05-04).

*Russian University of Peoples' Friendship (Picture 05-04)*

## Inheritance and Nurturing of Science and Technology Infrastructure

It is remarkable how the Soviet regime inherited and nurtured the academic and scientific infrastructure that was created during the imperial era. The Moscow State University, The St. Petersburg State University and The Novosibirsk State University are the glaring examples along with a host of specialized institutes scattered throughout the country. But one may find a more mind-boggling scenario if one tries to track the history of the Russian Academy of Sciences (Picture 05-05).

*The President's office of the Russian Academy of Sciences in Moscow in 2013 (Picture 05-05)*

Historically speaking, the Academy of Sciences was set up in 1725 by an imperial decree by Peter the Great in St Petersburg. In its journey up to the October Revolution, it was a highly recognized international organization, although it passed through ups-and-downs during the world war times or even with the change of emperors. Nevertheless, it survived and in 1925, the Soviet government recognized the academy as the highest all-union scientific institution. It was renamed as the Academy of Sciences of the USSR. In 1934, the headquarters of the academy was shifted from St. Petersburg to Moscow. It is strongly believed that the academy was behind the success of the Soviet Union becoming the superpower in the cold war era. All the military and space successes of the 1950s and 1960s can be traced back to this academy.

The academy faced the biggest crisis in 1990s after the collapse of the Soviet Union. There were hardly any state supports to nurture the scientific temper of the country. It is believed by many that during this crisis the Soviet Union lost scores of scientific talents that were born between the mid-1960s and mid-1970s to other countries.

Keeping aside the above historical tracing, it is important to state that the full membership or even the next lower level of corresponding membership of the academy was the most covetable and prestigious target for the scientific and academic community in the Soviet era. My close interactions with a large cross section of faculty members of the universities and institutions revealed that the membership of the political party was an unwritten qualification, in addition to the professional excellence. Since many talented teachers and researchers kept themselves away from active politics, they suffered in not moving up the ladder. The Soviet hypothesis of 'technical change' begetting 'social change' did not work in practice and many warriors of science languished. Still, one should not ignore the continuing efforts of the Soviet regime to nurture science and technology. Even after the collapse of the USSR, the academy was revived in 2017. The agricultural and medical sciences were added to the academy. As far as I know, more than 1000 institutes are in its fold now, apart from a large number of individual members. It is claimed that as of April 2023 there are close to 2000 individual members, of which 450 are the foreign members.

## V I Lenin State Library

To my mind, another remarkable academic infrastructure, inherited and developed by the Soviet regime, is the V.I. Lenin State Library of the USSR, situated in Moscow. It is the largest in the country and probably the fifth largest in the world. It was founded in 1862 as Moscow's free public library along with the Rumiantsev Museum, the history of which is different from my present discourse, and hence, not discussed here.

I was encouraged to be a member of the library by my research guide in 1967. In fact, as a foreign research scholar I enjoyed the privilege of bypassing the normal entry queue, which used to be quite long every day. I could also requisition the books and journals for consultation and reading on priority. The special treatment given to the foreigners by the library was not at all liked by the Soviet readers. We often had to ignore their unfriendly glance and silent grudges while carrying on with our work in the library. The library officials, however, were highly accommodative and extremely helpful.

On the first day, I was impressed with the imposing columnar architecture of the library building. The artistic sculpture of Dostoyevsky in the front was a landmark feature (Picture 05-06). When I was given a tour of the library and saw the 250-seater reading hall and hundreds of kilometres of shelves storing millions of items, I was flabbergasted. I was especially impressed with the huge collection of items in foreign languages. I was given to understand that there were books, journals, sound recordings, music, etc. in about 250 world languages and it constituted about 30% of the total collection. In fact, I could get a feel of it, when I had to refer to several publications in Italian, French, German, Japanese, Chinese and Korean languages for my dissertation, and to obtain the copies of the publications for subsequent translation to the Russian language. The imperial inheritance of the library and its expansion was, to my mind, a very positive endeavour of the Soviet regime.

*Dostoyevsky's statue at the entrance to Lenin's Library (Picture 05-06)*

## The Socialist System of Education and the Academic Environment

Having gone from India with a high level of illiteracy and poor academic infrastructure, I was keen to explore the socialist education system. In principle and strategy, I found it quite different from the systems prevailing in many developed and developing countries. In the late sixties, from the media reports I could make out that the literacy in the Soviet Union was over 99%, while the same country had reported less than 60% literacy in 1926. How was it achieved? Because of the policy, or the system, or the way it was implemented? Frankly speaking, I could not do a proper analysis of the factors responsible. I believe it had happened because of the conviction, priority, continuous course correction over the decades, and unfaltering implementation. I read about the policy of 'Likbez' (Liquidation of illiteracy), pronounced by Lenin in 1919, which led to massive implementation of the system of universal compulsory education. There were many components of implementation. I found the following steps of implementation as important and relevant:

- adult literacy drive;
- mobilisation of Komsomol (the youth wing of the Party), and the Young Pioneers detachments to carry the mission forward;
- massive drive for vocational certification for the majority of those who could not complete the secondary education;
- emphasis on diploma-level technical education in 'Tekhnikums' for others;
- filtered and limited admission of only deserving students to degree or university level education.

What was often not highlighted but which I thought was especially important was the early identification of deficient children and bringing them up through correction schools.

Interestingly, during our informal chats with the Russian friends, it was evident that this young generation that had successfully completed the secondary education and succeeded to secure admission to Moscow State University lacked in general global information and world history. At the same time, their understanding of the Soviet history and unfolding of Marxism-Leninism in the country was not of an order that offered some opportunity for us to learn what we did not know from outside. Strikingly different, however, were our teachers and academicians. Their profundity in the concerned fields, their inquisitiveness about the bigger world and their inherent love for the teaching profession were exemplary. Most of the teachers I came across in science and technology had deep insight in the fundamentals of mathematics, physics, chemistry and materials science. More than five decades back they passed on the concepts of simulation and modelling in structure-property relationship of materials to us, which is a big talk in today's world. Surprisingly, most of them were detached from politics and did not hold membership of the Party. The academic environment in the institutes of higher education in the then Soviet Union was highly conducive for research and education, notwithstanding the fact that there were severe constraints of facilities and resources. It may be relevant to mention here that there is a very long list of Nobel laureates affiliated to the Academy of Sciences.

### Heritage of Literature, Drama, and Ballet

In the environment of a strong political fervour and global aspirations of proving the superiority of socialism, what was immensely soothing in the Soviet era was the seamless pursuit of cultural heritage, particularly in literature and music. During the course of our language studies we were introduced to the golden age of the Russian literature and sprinklings of the Russian classics. The works of the $19^{th}$ century stalwarts, namely Alexander Pushkin, Mikhail Lermontov, Nikolai Gogol, Ivan Turgenev, Fyodor Dostoevsky, and Leo Tolstoy, were so affectionately and reverently referred to and excerpts of their works presented to us by our language teachers and later by some of our well-read Russian friends that many of us were deeply moved. My attachment to the Russian literature grew to such an extent that later, when there were no classroom compulsions, I continued dabbling in the Russian classics and also in getting myself acquainted with some of the more famous $20^{th}$ century poets and novelists such as Anna Akhmatova, Sergei Yesenin, Vladimir Mayakovsky, Ivan Bunin, Maxim Gorky, etc., in whose works I could already feel the impact of the societal changes.

However, I was told by some of my friends that this period should be regarded only as the silver age of the Russian literature, compared to the previous golden era.

It is interesting to look at the list of the Nobel laureates in the Russian literature, which reveals how the literary works were influenced by the socio-political environment. Ivan Bunin, who had migrated to Paris and was awarded the Nobel Prize in 1933, focussed on crudity of the rural life and decline of the class of landlords in his works. The story of Boris Pasternak and his prize-winning novel 'Doctor Zhivago' in 1958 is well known, though under severe political pressure he had to decline the award. The Nobel Prize for Mikhail Sholokhov in 1965 was a landmark event, when we were just students in the Soviet Union. What a passionate writer he was! He took 14 years to complete 'Tikhii Don (And Quiet Flows the Don'. In fact his tales from the Don stay as a remarkable chronicle on World War I and the then Russian culture. The award to Alexandr Solzhenitsyn in 1970 and his work 'One Day in the Life of Ivan Denisovich' were topics of wide discussion as much in the free world as within the student circles in the Moscow University those days. The subsequent Nobel awardees, Joseph Brodsky in 1987 and Svetlana Alexievich in 2015 are also interesting case studies. Born and brought up in St Petersburg, Brodsky, the poet, was an émigré in the USA, when he was awarded the coveted prize for poetry. I found 'Chast' Rechi (A part of Speech)' was an engrossing one. Svetlana Alexievich was from Belarus and was known for her 'documentary' novels, a class by itself. The book 'Voices of Utopia' is a worthy example.

Thus, from the above short narration, it is not difficult to notice a very impressive tradition in the Russian literature from the pre-revolution period to the present times. The discourse on the creative culture will remain incomplete if I do not make a brief mention about the Russian drama, music and ballet. One day our language teacher in the Moscow State University, Valerya Vasilevna Dobrovolskaya, held a few tickets in her hand and announced that she would take us to Moscovsky Khudozhestvenny Teatr ( Moscow Art Theatre) on a given date to watch the famous Russian play 'Tre Sestri' (The Three Sisters) of Anton Chekhov, the playwright and short-story writer of the golden age. The announcement was a bolt from the blue as we had seen that for such plays scores of people used to queue up for tickets in front of the theatre halls several months in advance of the actual performance dates. How she could procure the tickets, we wondered. Later, we were given to understand that our tickets were a special dispensation for the foreign students. I reminisced about the event only to highlight the massive popularity of plays in the Soviet era, and the stage décor and performance were mind-boggling. This was equally so for the concerts and ballets, for which people waited for months. 'Lebedinoye Ozero' (The Swan Lake), composed by Pyotr Tchaikovsky, is a ballet that is talked about all over the world for decades. The infrastructure that was created for dramatics, opera and ballet in the imperial days was rejuvenated in the post-revolution Soviet era, and the legacy continues even today, notwithstanding the vicissitudes of time and changes in the political landscapes. Bolshoi theatre in Moscow (Picture 05-07) and Mariinsky theatre in St Petersburg (05-08) stand as witnesses to the soft creative culture of the country.

*The Bolshoi theatre in central Moscow (Picture 05-07)*

Both the theatres represent the imperial legacy. The Bolshoi theatre was conceived in 1776, and the first instance was built between 1821 and 1824. It is considered to be the oldest and the best known ballet and opera company in the world. The building has undergone several renovations during its history but its heritage flavour has not been lost at all. Similarly, the Mariinsky theatre in St. Petersburg (Picture 05-08) has a long history. It came up in 1860 and maintains its popularity even today, perhaps, as much as the Bolshoi theatre in Moscow. Though during the post-revolution period, the Mariinsky theatre was renamed as Kirov theatre to commemorate the assassination of the Leningrad Communist Party leader Sergei Kirov, the name Mariinsky theatre could not be obliterated.

*The Mariinsky theatre in St Petersburg (Coutesy: Nikolai Bulykin)*
*(Picture 05-08)*

## Changes in the State-Religion Relationship with Time

It is known widely that there were innumerable turns and twists in the history of religion from the times of Russian imperialism to the post-revolution Soviet era. Just a few instances are briefly illustrated here. According to the Church Tradition, Christianity was first brought to the territory of modern Belarus, Russia and Ukraine by Saint Andrews, the first Apostle of Jesus Christ. The spread of the religion had happened over two hundred years from the 8$^{th}$ to 10$^{th}$ centuries and the supremacy of the Church had gained ground over the next seven centuries and the Russian Orthodox Church eventually became the largest Eastern Orthodox Christian Church in the territory. Peter the Great, the founder of the Russian empire, however, had a low regard for church and had kept it under tight governmental control. He replaced the Patriarch with a Holy Synod, which he controlled and appointed all bishops. Politically the church was bereft of all power. Later in the 18$^{th}$ century Catherine the Great seized all properties of the Church and reduced the priests to be only the provider of services like baptism and marriage for fees.

Notwithstanding such changes, the religious establishment expanded. It is reported that in 1914 there were more than 55,000 churches and close to 30,000 chapels with more than 100,000 priests. In addition, there were about one thousand monasteries and convents accommodating about 100,000 monks and nuns. In 1918, the Bolshevik-controlled government of Soviet Russia enacted a decree to separate the Church from the State, and deprived the religious organisations of their right to property. The State proclaimed freedom to profess any religion or profess none. This approach led to serious confrontation between the Bolsheviks and believers in Petrograd, today's St. Petersburg.

The Soviet Union, formally created in December 1922, was perhaps the first country in the world to pursue an ideology of eliminating religion. Following this objective, the communist regime confiscated the church property, harassed the believers, and tried to propagate materialism and atheism instead. Many stories of persecution of priests were matters of private gossips. But it is interesting to recall that though the members of the Communist Party publicly displayed their distance from religion, the common people could not be persuaded to shun their belief and the aged persons in particular used to practise religion clandestinely. Swearing in the name of God ('*bozhe moi*' in *Russian*) was very common in person-to-person conversations. I had seen *babushkas* visiting churches in early hours of important holy days. In the last two decades there was progressive softening of views and practices of religion.

Let me close this section with the story of the 'Cathedral of Christ the Saviour' in Moscow. It was built in gratitude for the Lord's intercession in a critical moment of the Russian history. It was to commemorate the courage of the Russian people during the Napoleon's invasion in 1812. It is said that it took 44 years to build the Cathedral. In 1931 the Soviet regime intended to demolish the structure and build a grandiose palace of the Soviets there. However, the Cathedral could not be destroyed completely. Ultimately, in 1994 the liberalised Russia took up reconstruction of the Cathedral and in the course of time it regained its glory and has now turned into a wonderful tourist destination. The soaring white structure with gold plated domes is recognized as the tallest Orthodox Christian Church in the world and it dominates the city's skyline (Picture 05-09).

*Cathedral of Christ the Saviour in Moscow (Picture 05-09)*

## Role of Media in Shaping the Public Opinion

In our student days in the Soviet Union we used to read two newspapers: '*Pravda*' and '*Izvestia*'. Literally, the Russian word '*pravda*' means 'truth' and '*izvestia*' means 'news'. Most of my Russian friends used to joke that there was no truth in *Pravda* and no news in *Izvestia*. Broadly speaking, they were not wrong. From headlines to editorials, the newspapers carried stories and achievements of farming collectives and manufacturing units of Russia and other republics of the union. Political activities that took place at Kremlin and visits of the political leaders from only the friendly countries were always in focus. Small events and successes in the Central Asian states, pre-Baltic states, Ukraine, Moldova, Belarus, Far Eastern Region and Siberia were specially highlighted. The international news clips were presented very selectively in the form of snippets in the third or the fourth page, primarily to highlight the plight of the people in the non-communist states and countries. In effect, the entire population of the country suffered from severe paucity of real news, be it domestic or global. Glory of the Soviet regime was repeatedly hammered on to the citizens at large. The attempt was so blatant that our Russian friends and more particularly the friends from other republics hardly picked up the dailies from the university kiosks to read. But these newspapers had another value as they served well as toilet papers which were always in short supply in our hostel toilets. Hence, we seldom forgot to buy the dailies on our way to 'stolovayas' every day.

We, the Indian students, used to render a great service of news dissemination to our Russian friends. It was a routine with us to visit our embassy every week to collect our personal letters. Let me first explain why. The Soviet postal service those days was awfully slow and sluggish. Airmails posted in India by our parents and friends used to reach us after three or four weeks. We were extremely concerned with this delay. Hence, a very special dispensation was worked out by our embassy. Letters addressed to the Indian students and sent to a specific address in Delhi were forwarded to the Moscow embassy in the diplomatic bags on a regular basis. We used to collect our letters from the embassy once a week. With no communication channels of modern times being available then, this arrangement was a great boon for us. While collecting our letters, we used to pick up the Indian newspapers and bring them over to the University. These newspapers were a feast for the Russians and students from the other republics who could read English. For those who could not read English but were starving from paucity of global news, it was a task for many of us to translate the more important and relevant snippets to them.

The print media was the principal channel of information those days. The facility of television was available The number of channels was limited, and the channels used to telecast the agricultural and manufacturing achievements were publicised in the print media. We, however, had some entertainment through television as there was a great emphasis in the Soviet regime on sports, particularly football, athletics, skating, skiing, and ice hockey. The subjects pertaining to physical education received high importance. We could fill up some of our spare times by watching such programmes on TV.

**Political Messaging to the Students**

Were there any visible attempts to influence the political leaning or thinking of the foreign students or, for that matter, the students, coming to Russia from other republics of the Soviet Union in the Institutes of Higher Education ? I often pondered over this issue but could not recall any specific events. But I distinctly remember that in most of the big cities I visited, including Moscow, where I had spent long years, we came across huge hoardings portraying combined pictures of Marx, Engels and Lenin and hoardings displaying political slogans like 'Workers of the world - unite', or 'Peace to the World', 'Salute to CPSU' etc.. I do not remember to have seen anywhere any slogan such as 'Down with Americas', which I had seen permanently engraved on the wall of the lobby of a high-ranking hotel in Teheran in early nineties. The hoardings in the Soviet cities were so prominent and attractively done that they would make you interested in searching for the stories behind them. The miles-long queues of the Soviet citizens every day at the Lenin's mausoleum in the Red Square (Picture 05-10), the background view of the Kremlin, the huge departmental store standing in a heritage building on the Red Square, the grand museums on the square, and other conserved heritage structures swayed us to think more about Soviet history, although there was no forcing anywhere. The environment in the city and suburbs was already so different from the free world that one coming from outside was compelled to think about the reality and virtuality of the Soviet era.

*Visitors' queue in front of Lenin's Mausoleum (Picture 05-10)*

Quite often, the University used to organize special lectures on Marxist thoughts and theories. These lectures were open to all but not mandatory for any of the students and scholars. Renowned professors and political scientists used to deliver these lectures. Every time, I used to find the lecture halls quite full, a fact that made me curious. I started attending some of those lectures. I had no idea of what communism really meant. Right or wrong, it was here that I learnt that 'Communism was a specific stage of socioeconomic development predicted upon a superabundance of material wealth, which was postulated to arise from advances in production technology and the corresponding changes in the social relations of production.' Having failed to understand the later part, in one of the talks I ventured to seek a clarification from the speaker of what the 'social relations of production' meant. I was told that it meant the distribution of material wealth, based on needs of individuals who are freely present in the society that was classless, stateless, and free of exploitation. The communist society would be characterized by the common ownership of the means of production and free access to the articles of consumption. The concepts were ideally covetable in our world, I felt. How far had the Soviet Union progressed towards this goal, asked another friend. The speaker looked at him with a soft smile on her lips, and said that the country was on its march towards the 'magnificent' destination. The country, according to her, was at the initial steps, endeavouring to change the means and intensity of production. Hopefully, these changes would cause the ideology and culture of the people to change some day, profoundly influencing their interactions with one another.

While coming out from the lecture hall, I tumbled on Valya, a pretty Russian girl, who was studying Hindi language at the University. With a naughty face, she said '*Namaste*' and asked if I had already turned a Marxist. Why such a question I wondered. 'Simple, I want to start sharing your stock of Indian tea,' she said. We laughed and departed. While walking back to my hostel room along the long corridors, I was trying to figure out the extent of distribution of material wealth that I had witnessed in the Soviet Union by then.

I had experienced free pick up of bread and salad in the hostel canteens, no doubt, but I had also seen long queues of babushkas (old women) on the pavements, when fresh cucumber was on occasional sale in a makeshift kiosk. I had witnessed huge crowds wrestling with each other for entry to the departmental stores, whenever there were Polish or Bulgarian cosmetics and toiletry goods on sale. I had seen young girls jostling to buy fancy Czechoslovakian (one country then) crystal ornaments. I watched from a distance how my Russian friends used to rush to the shops, whenever they heard that 'Zenit' camera, the best indigenously made export product those days, was leaked into the domestic market so as not to deprive the country's population. As in our country, there was a craze among the Russians to acquire electronic goods from Japan and Germany or perfumes from France, to which they hardly had any access. There was a chain of dollar shops, called 'Berezka', where the Russian roubles could not be used as a legal tender. The population at large did not have access to these shops, although the Russian diplomats and some other high-ranking officials had special permits. The university students used to depend on friends like us, coming from other countries, to fulfil their dream purchases from the 'Berezka' shops.

Let me mention here one relevant incident. A Russian girl, who was employed somewhere, used to type the dissertations of some of our friends to augment her earnings. My friends recommended her to me, when I was finalizing my thesis, and I engaged her. As time passed, I found that her progress was quite unsatisfactory, although the quality of her work was very good. The deadline for submission of my thesis was drawing nearer and nearer and I could not find an alternative typist of her standard. A friend of mine then suggested that I should offer her an incentive of purchasing a selection of cosmetics and jewellery from the nearest Berezka as part payment. This incentive had worked like a magic.

Numerous examples of the gap between what the people wanted and what was available to them were observed in most of the social segments, barring those who were high-ups in the government or CPSU. This gap in the consumer goods demand and supply remained strikingly large after forty years of the revolution.

## Industrial Production and Planning

I had occasions to visit steel, cement, and refractory plants in the Soviet Union on various occasions. These visits were obviously ~~were~~ technical and professional, and not for tourism and publicity. It all started with my first visit in 1967 to the Lipetsk Steel Plant, situated about 450 km south of Moscow on an important north-south railway link of the country. This visit was for my industrial training that formed an essential part of my PhD programme. In the overnight train ride, I was accompanied with a senior faculty member of our department, who carried the necessary university documents for facilitating my entry into the plant and stay there. After handing me over, she returned and I had to manage myself inside the plant for the next few days with the help of the plant personnel. It was a rich and an unforgettable experience, which in its totality cannot be narrated here for brevity.

If my memory goes right, the plant even then was of a capacity exceeding three million tons of steel. The furnaces were huge and the layout was massive. I went through different sections of the plant and the operators there explained the processes as practised. They could not explain the theories and principles behind the practices. They knew the production targets but did not know the energy and utilities consumption norms. In the integrated plant, the unit operators were blissfully ignorant about the upstream and downstream processes and requirements.

The picture remained the same in many of my later visits to other plants. Since steel and cement were in the core sectors of the Soviet economy, the plants were large and massive. The production targets were rigidly enforced with year-on-year increments without any clear emphasis on the design capability, predictive maintenance, energy conservation, and consumption norms of utilities.

Pyatiletka i.e., the five-year planning was the motive force of industrial planning. Fulfilling the current plan in terms of industrial production was the watchword of the Soviet bureaucracy. Gosplan, i.e., the State Planning organization was a very powerful body. I had often heard that plans were drawn up, based on what was termed as the 'theory of productive forces that formed the foundation of the ideology of the Communist Party for development of the Soviet economy'. I hardly ever understood the concept and intricacy of this theory. What I found was the enormous power and influence of the state machinery and total compliance of industrial and manufacturing units without questioning the veracity or feasibility of targets. Many independent-minded academicians even then in informal discussions predicted about the collapsing health of plant and machinery, severe damage to industrial viability due to production at any cost, and unreliability of production statistics.

Notwithstanding what I have stated above,, there were some green seeds and shoots in the industrial sector. Decades back, I noticed that the concept of 'circular economy' was working in some industrial complexes, in which the waste of one plant was being used as the raw material of the other. A thrust for waste recycling and utilization was not, however, pursued then from the perspective of cost reduction and production economics. It was more of a scientific curiosity with a view to deriving unforeseen benefits of product quality or novelty. Another important developmental strategy that unfolded then in the industrial manufacturing arena was the adoption of 'product standardization'. The concept was in essence a beneficial one. But in reality, like 'Gosplan', another powerful arm of the State under the banner of 'Gosstandard' grasped the industry.

## Bond of the Constituent Republics

During the course of the long years of stay in the university I had numerous occasions of developing friendship with students coming from Baltic states, viz., Estonia, Latvia and Lithuania. Those whom I had come across were from the respective capital cities Talinn, Riga and Vilneus. These republics and particularly these cities were the most attractive holiday destinations for us, where we could feel and smell Scandinavia and North Europe without being there and, more importantly, without spending any hard currency. Our Baltic friends used to make the affordable stay arrangements, whenever we visited. The kind of implicit dislike of the peoples of these republics towards the Russians that I had observed during those travels was an eye-opener for me for the prevalent inter-republican bonds. Although they had their school education in Russian, they never liked the language. There was massive immigration of the Russians into those republics, which the Baltic population hated. The Baltics knew that they were the most productive republics within the Soviet Union and felt that they were being only exploited by the Soviet regime.

Such feelings in more pronounced manner were observed in the Ukrainian Republic. The Ukrainians thought that their historical and cultural heritage was many times superior to that of the Russians. In the post-war era the break-up of the larger Ukraine and the partial annexation with the Soviet Union always remained a sore point. The forceful settlement of the ethnic Russians in the Ukrainian territory was strongly decried in private. An Indian friend of mine was married to a Ukrainian girl in the city of Kiev, which I had attended. The wedding reception had several Ukrainian friends of the bride. After they were fully drunk by the midnight, the anti-Russian outburst that I had seen and heard stayed indelibly in my memory forever.

The stories of the Central Asian republics were not much different. I had visited only Tashkent and Samarkand in the republic of Uzbekistan. I had a roommate from Tashkent in my hostel in St Petersburg for several months. Predominance of the Russians, attempts to change the demography of the republics by 'russification', and subjugating the local language and culture to a second place were the complaints I had heard repeatedly.

Even in the 1960s, after the existence of the Soviet regime for almost four decades the bonds of the constituent republics were weak, cracked, and in some cases, fractured. I am sure that some prudent political scientists in that period might have predicted the likelihood of dismemberment of the Soviet Union that happened in the 1990s.

**Changes in the Political Landscape**

Let me now come to the closing remarks. The increasing authoritarian rule of the State machinery, weak feedback system, and failure of course correction measures in due course led to the disintegration of the country and to its disastrous economic conditions in the late 1980s. I could no longer recognize the country that was so dear to me, when I revisited during that period. The evidently loose bonds of the constituent republics due to, if I am permitted to say, expansionism of the Kremlin, was visible much earlier to cause such a disaster.

For me, however, it was a relief to see an economically stronger and politically more liberal face of Russia during my recent visits, though many other traits and features of the emerging Russia were perceptibly different from what I had observed and known in the previous decades. I certainly missed the familiar strains of the past. I tried to recollect the words and tune of the song 'Podmoskovnye Vechera', which was a very popular gramophone record we used to play so often. I still recollect the line, 'if you only knew how dear to me were those Moscow summer nights!' But the consolation was in the same song in the last few lines, which said,

"The dawn is bright and filled with light.
Just be patient, my dear. But do not forget those summer nights".

# CHAPTER 6

# Some Recalls from the Land of Plenitude – The North America

The United States and Canada have been at the center of attraction for peoples across the world for education, work, living and leisure. Having a landmass of about 13% of the Earth with less than 5% of world population, these two countries have been the destination for many, though the intents and interests are not always the same. These two countries differ from each other in many aspects, and more particularly, in population, but the economic affluence of both the countries is not significantly different. Between the two, the attraction is more for the United States for a variety of reasons. The young and the learning minds are first attracted by the academic atmosphere and innovation opportunities of the renowned universities and institutions. Having tasted the living and working comforts there and after discovering multifarious future opportunities, the majority of students prefer to stay back, unless compelled to leave the land of prosperity for other reasons. The opportunities for growth and prosperity in the country emerge from the large scale, broad scope and openness of research; size, wealth and technological sophistication of the market; the nation's capacity for spawning new technology-intensive products and services; and the global reach of the US high-tech industries. The military might and the space research have been the additional strengths of the country to attract the entire world. The net result has been the movement of a large number of immigrants into that country. It is tentatively estimated that around a million new entrants migrate into the United States every year, perhaps the largest number in the world.

Canada has also been the land of preference for some immigrants. Broadly speaking, in relation to population in 2021, the immigrants constitute about 14% in the United States and 23% in Canada. As a result, in both the countries one comes across noticeable ethnic diversity. In addition to the natives, there is a pleasure of encountering and interacting with whites, blacks, Asians, Pacific Islanders, Hispanics, Chinese, Japanese, Vietnamese, Koreans, Indians, and so on.

The business world looks towards the healthy, competitive, easy-to-do, and technologically advanced business environment in the country. Backed by a regulatory environment that is particularly conducive to start-ups, the US business culture encourages free enterprises, which attract a large number of entrepreneurs to search their pick. The commercial interests from different parts of the world result in plethora of business trips to these countries. In addition to the business trips, the volume of travelers has effectively grown due to the growth of the tourism industry in these countries. The count of tourists that come to the United States is only next to the numbers that visit France and Italy every year. The tourist attractions are essentially to see natural wonders, well known cities, historic landmarks and entertainment venues. Interestingly, the tourists apparently spend more money in the United States and Canada than anywhere else in the world.

This is understandable because a large number of cities across North America with distinctive landscape and populace are the most attractive destinations for the tourists. Furthermore, close to many of the cities, one may witness spectacular scenery, rarely seen anywhere else. In addition, some of the most recognizable icons on the planet can be visited in this part of the world.

### Spectacular Gifts of the Nature

Before we indulge into a selective narration of the natural beauties and landscapes of this continent, it may be helpful to make a brief recap of its physical geography. For the convenience of readers a physical map is reproduced here, which highlights the Canadian Shield in the north, the Rocky Mountains in the west, the Great Lakes Basin and the Appalachian Mountains on the east and Mexico with the Sierra Nevada Mountains in the south (see Picture 06-01). The narration that follows is broadly confined to this frame.

One of the Nature's picturesque presents to this land, to my mind, is the Yellowstone National Park, located in the upper western states, largely in the northwest corner of Wyoming and extending into Montana and Idaho. This is recognized as the largest nearly-intact ecosystem in the Northern temperate zone. The Continental Divide of North America, the Middle Rocky Mountains, runs diagonally through the southern part of the park, which spans an area of about 9000 square kilometer. In addition to the overlooking mountains, the area contains lakes, canyons, rivers, geysers, hot springs and waterfalls.

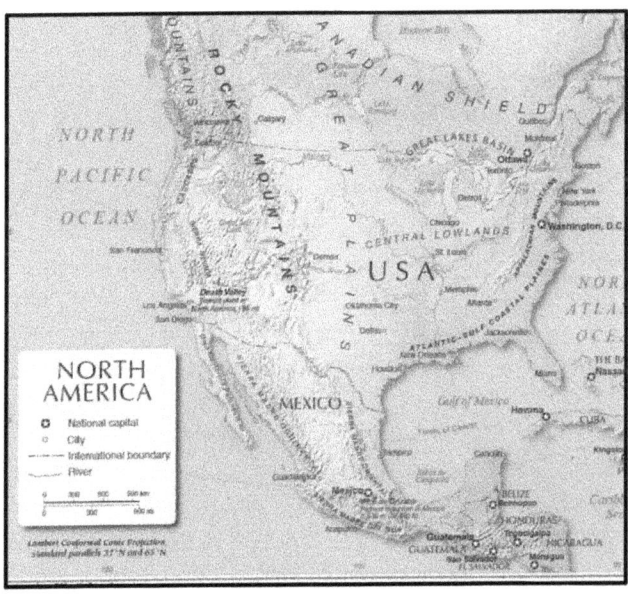

*Physical map of North America showing the mountain ranges and lake basins*
*(Picture 06-01)*

The Yellowstone Lake (Picture 06-02) is one of the largest water bodies, situated at a high altitude of about 2400 m, and is centered over the Yellowstone Caldera, the largest dormant super-volcano in the continent. The park has a rich spread of flora and fauna. Grizzly bears, wolves, bison, elks, etc. are some examples of the animal world here. No doubt that the Yellowstone National Park is a great attraction for the earth scientists, bio-scientists and nature lovers. In 1978 the park was recognized as the UNESCO World Heritage Site.

*Panorama of the West Thumb area of Yellowstone Lake in 2018 (Source: whoisjohngait website) (Picture 06-02)*

Another geological wonder, which is more widely known to the outside world, is the Great Lakes basin (Picture 06-03), in which five interconnected freshwater lakes (Superior, Michigan, Huron, Erie and Ontario) are situated in the upper mid-east region in the border area between Canada and the United States. The lakes connect to the Atlantic Ocean via the Saint Laurence River. The surface area of these lakes adds up to about 244100 square kilometer, which is comparable to the size of the United Kingdom. These lakes hold approximately 21% of the Earth's freshwater, which is only marginally lower than the freshwater volume of the Lake Baikal in Russia. Dispersed throughout the Great Lakes are approximately 35000 islands. The earth scientists have estimated that these lakes have been formed about 10000 to 12000 years ago, at the end of the last glacial period, when the Laurentide Ice Sheet had receded.

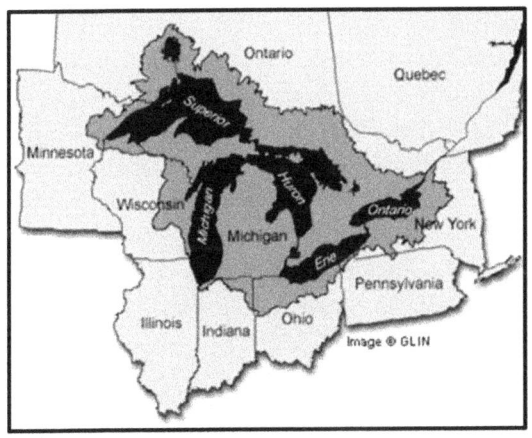

*Schematic diagram of the Great Lakes Basin with the encompassing provinces/states (Source: upload by Jean Brodeur) (Picture 06-03)*

In the context of describing this region, I have to mention about the Niagara Escarpment, a long steeply sloping geomorphological feature, running predominantly east-west from New York through Ontario, Michigan, Wisconsin and Illinois. The popularity and the name of this structure come from the world-famous Niagara Falls, created by the natural plunge of the Niagara River over the cliff. In 1990, the Niagara Escarpment was declared as a UNESCO World Biosphere Reserve.

*Three falls view of Niagara (Source: Saffron Blaze in Wikimedia Commons) (Picture 06-04)*

The Niagara River drains the water of Lake Erie into Lake Ontario and the three falls at the southern end of Niagara Gorge spanning the border between the province of Ontario in Canada and the State of New York are the famous Niagara Falls. The Horseshoe Falls at the Canadian side has the deepest drop of more than 60 m, while the American Falls and the Bridal Veil Falls, both in the US territory, are smaller, dropping about 30 m and 26 m respectively. The Horseshoe Falls is easily approached from Toronto city in Canada and the Falls on the US side are close to Buffalo city in New York.

Another mind-blowing geological feature in the United States is the Grand Canyon, curved out of the Colorado River, The Canyon cuts deep into the landscape, creating cliff walls and ridges. Visitors standing on the ridge of the Canyon can see down to the floor that is more than two kilometer deep. The ridges and cliffs run as far as one's eyes can see. The southern rim of Grand Canyon is close to Las Vegas city, only a drive of about five hours. The formation of this Canyon is a result of a gigantic geological event dating back to a few hundred million years. Scientists say that such horizontal uplifting of the Colorado plateau is a geological wonder, rarely seen in other parts of the world, and involved the deposition of thick layers of sedimentary rocks over a basement rock. In addition to being a venue for scientific studies, the place is a great attraction for tourists. The skywalk with a panoramic view of the canyon is a great attraction for visitors (Picture 06-05).

*The Grand Canyon skywalk (Picture 06-05)*

While describing some of the impressive natural geomorphological structures in this land, I felt it was important to mention about two valley regions in the United States: the Tennessee Valley and the Napa Valley. The Tennessee Valley is the drainage basin of the Tennessee River. Situated in the State of Tennessee, it stretches from the Southern Kentucky to North Alabama and from Northeast Mississippi to the mountains of Virginia and North Carolina. The Tennessee River Gorge is a long canyon, extending for more than 40 kilometer, and is known locally as Cash Canyon, perhaps due to the economic prosperity around the valley. Knoxville, the most popular metropolitan area in the valley, is at the confluence of the Tennessee River with two other rivers. Knoxville and the nearby Oak Ridge and Maryville Alcoa form a major research and manufacturing corridor, spearheaded by the University of Tennessee, the Oak Ridge National Laboratory, and the headquarters of the Tennessee Valley Authority (TVA), which is a multi-functional corporate body known for power generation, fertilizer manufacturing, navigation, etc. TVA is often referred to as an example of an economic development model of a region. An enchanting view of Norris Dam of TVA is presented in Picture 06-06.

*Norris Dam of TVA (Picture 06-06)*

Quite unlike the Tennessee Valley, the Napa Valley, located in Napa County in California, is known as one of the premier viticulture regions of the world. The combination of Mediterranean climate, geography and geology of the region are immensely conducive for grape culture suitable for wine production. The valley floor is flanked by the Mayacamas mountain range on the north and northwest, and the Vaca mountainous range on the east. Several valleys exist within these two mountain ranges. The valley floor has a gentle slope from the north to south. The geological history of this valley region is essentially volcanic. The Napa Valley with all its characteristic features has grown into a pleasant tourist destination. Some experience of touring in this valley has been narrated in Chapter 7.

**Cities and Icons: a Cursory Look**

The North America is regarded as the most urbanized continent in the world. While the average global urbanization is about fifty-six per cent, the urbanization of the North America touched eighty two percent in 2020. Hence, one finds umpteen choices of cities, at least fifty at any point of time, to visit or even to settle down. Ten cities in the United States have population in excess of a million with New York City topping the list with 8.6 million people, followed by Los Angeles in California on the Pacific coast with 4.0 million people and Chicago in Illinois with less than 3.0 million. Most cities have their characters by which they are often nicknamed. For example, New York is known as 'the city that never sleeps'; Los Angeles is called 'the city of angels'. Chicago is popularly named as 'the windy city'. Similarly, Houston in Texas is called 'the space city', while San Jose in California is known as 'the capital of Silicon Valley'. In terms of the footfall of tourists the preference list of the cities is somewhat different, though New York remains as the most visited city with about 60 million visitors per year. The other popular destinations in decreasing order of visitors per year are Chicago, Atlanta in

Georgia, Anaheim/Orange City in California, Orlando in Florida, Los Angeles, Las Vegas, Philadelphia, San Diego and San Francisco. It may, perhaps, be relevant to mention that many visitors club their itinerary for the east coast cities with visits to Washington DC to enjoy the sight of White House and other historical memorials.

In Canada, the visitors primarily prefer Toronto in Ontario Province in the east and Vancouver city in the Pacific coast. However, cities like Montreal, Quebec and Ottawa have also their specific attractions. I, for one, found that the Old Montreal with cobbled pavements (see Picture 06-07), the long promenade along the Saint Lawrence River in Quebec, the Rideau Canal in Ottawa are some of the impressive features that linger on in one's memory. Perhaps one may find a bit of Europe more easily in the Canadian cities than in the cities in the US.

*A cobbled road in Old Montreal (Source: getmyguide.com/montreal-l195)*
*(Picture 06-07)*

My hops and stops in the US were understandably many more than in Canada. I visited the country at frequent intervals between 1980 and 2016. The visits were mostly official and job-related, though a few visits had been undertaken particularly to meet friends and families. These visits enabled me to be acquainted with the country from Boston and New York in the east to San Francisco and Los Angeles in the west, as well as from the Great Lakes in the north to Florida in the south. As I said, the sightseeing was not generally my agenda but still I had numerous opportunities to witness many unforgettable landscapes and wonderful icons of the world.  Equally memorable were the professional visits and interactions. I have no intentions of writing a chronicle on my different missions, nor do I feel the urge of narrating our boat ride to the Statue of Liberty in New York or our afternoon walk along the Golden Gate Bridge in San Francisco. Instead, I felt that it would be interesting to share with my readers some special moments and feelings of awe and wonder that I had experienced during a few of my visits to different parts of the US and Canada. Some of these reminiscences are narrated in Chapters 7, 8, and 9.

# CHAPTER 7

# Unique Travel Instances in North America

### Reminiscing the Transpolar Flights

Though I am not an explorer or a pilot, the very idea of being flown over the poles of the Earth had always fascinated me since my young days, when I had read some stories about the attempts made by a few daring polar aviators. Before I indulge in narrating some of these stories, let us try to recollect the overall geographic orientation of the North Pole and the Arctic Circle from the map given below (Picture 07-01).

*Map of the arctic region (Picture 07-01)*

In all probability, the hot-air balloon expedition by Solomon Andree, a Swedish engineer, over the North Pole in 1897 was the event that marked the beginning of polar aviation. The story goes that he, accompanied by two crew members, flew out from Svalbard, an archipelago in North Atlantic Ocean. Just three days into the expedition the balloon had crashed into the polar ice cap around the $83^{rd}$ parallel. They wandered in the uninhabited, frozen icy land for months but could not be saved.

In 1926, however, from the same place, Lt. Commander Richard Byre of the US Navy successfully flew over the North Pole in a special Fokker aircraft, returning back to the starting airport in about 15 hours. Interestingly, Richard Byre is credited with the success of flying over the South Pole as well. The South Pole flight is certainly another historical event, and it was accomplished by Richard Byre from Ross Ice Shelf in about 18 hours. It may be interesting to recall that the Ross Ice Shelf is the largest ice shelf of Antarctica, which is several hundred meters thick with more than 600 km long nearly vertical ice front opening to the sea.

In the 1930s, there were several attempts by the Soviet aviators to undertake transpolar flights. The attempts made by Sigizmund Levanevsky between 1935 and 1937 are worth remembering. Levanevsky belonged to the Soviet Air Force and was bestowed with the title 'Hero of the Soviet Union'. His first attempt was in August 1935 to fly from Moscow to San Francisco over the North Pole in a prototype single engine long-range bomber aircraft. A thousand miles into the flight the oil tank developed a leak presumably due to overfilling and the mission had to be aborted. The following year Levanevsky along with his navigator Levchenko undertook a new mission of setting an air route between the erstwhile USSR and the US via the Bering Strait. They completed a multistage flight of more than 19000 km from Los Angeles to Moscow in a Vultee V-1A floatplane. For such an adventurous aviator, however, the end was tragic. On 13 August 1937, Levanevsky with a crew of six made another attempt to fly from Moscow to Fairbanks in the US pacific coast in a long-range bomber aircraft over the North Pole. After he crossed the North Pole the next day, his radio communication broke off, when the aircraft encountered an adverse weather condition and suffered an engine failure. It is reported that the Soviet authorities, even in those days had financed and organized two aerial searches with the help of Canadian and American experts. Unfortunately, the searches failed and in due course Levanevsky was declared dead along with his crew members. However, that was not the end of the Soviet attempts to overfly the North Pole. The transpolar flights of Valery Chkalov from Moscow to Vancouver and Mikhail Gromov from Moscow to San Jacinto, California are remembered as success stories. With the technologies of the 1940s another success was achieved, when a modified B-29 craft flew more than 15000 km nonstop over the North Poles from Hawaii to Cairo in less than 40 hours, firmly proving the capability of the aviation industry to undertake long-distance flights over the Arctic.

The polar aviation race between the Soviet Union and the western countries came to a halt during the Cold War years as the Arctic region acted as a buffer zone between them. The civilian flights from Europe to Far East in Asia were prohibited to overfly the Eastern Bloc countries, the Soviet Union and China. The flights were routed via the Middle East or across the Arctic North America and Greenland with a refueling stop at the Anchorage International Airport in Alaska. While talking about the Cold-War tracks, it is difficult to forget what happened with the Korean Airlines Flight 902. It was shot down by the Soviet Air Force fighter aircraft after the flight made a gross navigational error attempting to fly the polar route. Nevertheless, in the 1980s, several commercial airlines operated scheduled flights connecting the East with the West via Greenland and Alaska. Finnair was probably the first then to fly between Helsinki and Tokyo via the Arctic Ocean and Alaska without a technical stop. Needless to mention that after the Cold War a number of routes had opened up connecting many Asian cities with the Pacific coast cities in North America over the Black Sea, the Soviet Union and the Arctic Ocean. Many carriers take advantage of what is often called "Santa's short-cut", as these routes significantly cut the flying hours and fuel costs.

It may be relevant to mention that such concepts of short-cuts haven't worked out for the Antarctica and the South Pole. The main reasons for the South Pole not catching up with the North Pole are the following: the weather conditions in the South Pole region are far more treacherous than the North Pole; there are fewer airports to divert flights in case of emergency; and the commercial demand for scheduled civil flights is limited. On top of these, there are certain hassles of international laws. Thus, the Antarctica remains essentially free of commercial flights while the arctic polar flights continue to increase. This part of the story would remain incomplete if I do not touch upon the flight that flew around both the poles in a single effort. It was in 1966 that a Boeing 707 jet flight, the first of its kind, flew out of Honolulu and returned back there, after covering more than 45000 km and flying over both the poles in five legs in about 62 hours. It was, perhaps, only to affirm that the South Pole was not invincible but the relative level of experience and confidence was more for the North Pole.

**Technical Complexities Involved in Polar Flights**

The growth of the cost-saving transpolar commercial flights in the north also depended on understanding and overcoming several technical impediments. There are some special requirements for polar flights, which include a special communication facility, cold-weather suits for the crew members to face emergency, designation of diversion routes, recovery plans for stranded passengers, and so on. Beyond these requirements, a great disadvantage is that the geographic North Pole and the magnetic North Pole are more than 950 km apart. Get in between them and your compass behaves erratically. Hence, improvements in navigational practices were necessary. Another disadvantage of the polar flights is the solar radiation. As we all know, most solar radiation is reflected by the Earth's magnetic field. But at the poles the field converges into the Earth, allowing the solar radiation an opening into the atmosphere. However, as claimed by the aviation experts, no polar flights generally exceed the limits of polar radiation and passengers are safe. But due to repeated exposures the flight crews could face some risks, an issue that cannot be lost sight of in the commercial polar flights. Polar night is another phenomenon that may require attention. It occurs in the northernmost and southernmost regions of the Earth and lasts for 24 hours, emitting blue twilights. It may have to be reckoned with by the aviators. Another formidable aspect is the chance of fuel freezing. Generally, the freeze temperature is below minus 40 degree Celsius. These temperatures are frequently encountered at cruise altitudes but no freezing effects are experienced in normal flights all over the world as the fuel retains its heat from lower elevations. But in the case of polar flights the aircrafts encounter intense cold over extended durations, which may cause the fuel temperature to approach freezing points. Provision of suitable alerts is therefore essential in polar flights. It is also reported that pilots descend to altitudes 0f 3000-4000 m over the North Pole to prevent fuel freezing, which offers a lifetime opportunity to passengers to catch a glimpse of the white wilderness.

Although near-polar flights over Greenland were in operation in the 1980s, the start of strictly polar flights over the Russian air space continued to have problems of poor radar coverage and lack of English-speaking controllers. To solve these problems, a coordination body termed as RACGAT (Russian American Coordinating Group for Air Traffic) was formed in 1993 and by 1998 four cross-polar routes were opened. Perhaps, the Cathay Pacific flight from New York to Hongkong on 7 July 1998 was the first nonstop cross-polar flight. The projected route is shown in Picture 07-02. It is claimed that this flight crosses through the

North Pole at 85.6 degrees north (the North Pole being 90 degrees). Needless to mention that for modern airlines flying over the North Pole has become a relatively mundane affair. Many carriers now take advantage of this 'Santa's short-cut'.

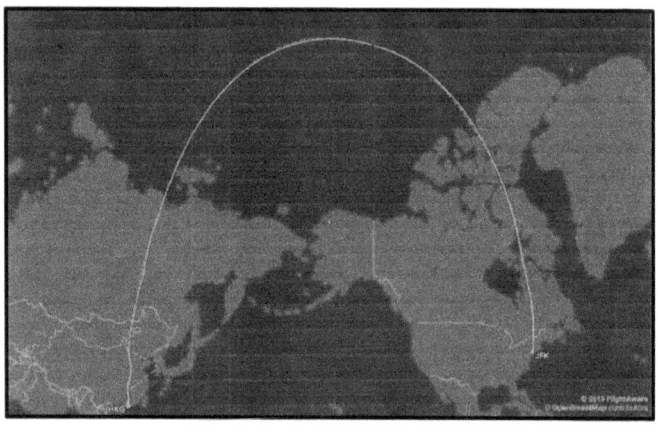

*The projected transpolar flight route connecting New York with Hong Kong*
*(Source: The Point Guy) (Picture 07-02)*

## Unforgettable Near-Polar Day Flight from Frankfurt to Vancouver

The long history of failure and success and the progressive overcoming of the technical impediments were behind my fascination with the transpolar flights. I looked for opportunities for flying over the poles and I was not disappointed in life. I had quite a few occasions to satisfy myself with near-polar flights in my journeys from India via Middle East and Europe. One such flight was from Frankfurt to Vancouver to deliver a keynote address at an international conference at the University of British Columbia. This flight left an indelible impression in my mind as I could see from my window seat in daylight a stretch of polar ice cap progressively merging into green mountains, rugged hills, steep-walled valleys and deep blue water bodies meandering through the valleys. Patches of landmass with pine trees extensively decorated the landscape away from the snow-covered surfaces. An aerial view is presented in Picture 07-03. I do not remember to have witnessed any comparable scenario anytime anywhere else. Why was I not a painter! I lamented all the way as I flew to Vancouver. I was totally unmindful of the pages laid on the small table in front of my seat in the aircraft for preparing the conference talk. Though the preparation for the lecture remained incomplete, I carried with me a grand treasure for the rest of my life.

*An aerial view of the landscape (Picture 07-03)*

**Remembering the Concorde Flight**

It was in the 1990s. I was on an official assignment to the United States. Those days as a company director, I had the perquisite of flying in the first class. My last stop was in the New York City, where I had checked in a hotel near the Central Park. In the evening before the day of my departure from New York to London a message was left by the British Airways, the airline on which I had my round ticket from India, to call them back urgently. After my return to the hotel from my work I called up the number and I had a pleasant surprise. I was told that for the New York – London sector my ticket was upgraded to the Concorde flight next day morning and I was asked if I would accept this upgrade. Who would miss this opportunity? I confirmed forthwith. Everything appeared so special the next day morning. I was going to be a supersonic flyer in the next few hours. I went through all the formalities at the JFK airport and even now I am left with the indelible impressions of the BA Terminal 7 of those days, spectacular Concorde lounge, proud walking with the Concorde passengers and a close look at the aircraft from close proximity (Picture 07-04).

*Concorde with front wheels up in air (Source: the British Airways files)*
*(Picture 07-04)*

When I came close to it for boarding, it looked more gorgeous. The overall appearance was far more elegant than the supersonic fighter planes like the Mirage, or Sukhoi or F-15 planes. It had a distinctive white coat of paint on its body, which, I was later explained, was applied so that the aircraft body could withstand the stresses due to expansion during its supersonic speed. Inside the craft the look was quite sober. We were 100 passengers in the flight, seated in two cabins in rows of four with an aisle at the middle. I occupied an aisle seat in the fourth row and could see a front panel that displayed the speed and altitude of the plane (refer Picture 07-05) as it took off, cruised, and landed. It was a unique experience to feel the take-off speed of over 400 kilometers per hour, to watch the progressive height gain above 15000 m, and to observe how the speed crossed 2 Mach to achieve double the speed of sound. Once the plane had reached its flying altitude, the passengers were treated with lobster, caviar and Champagne. The entire duration of the flight was so smooth that I felt as if I was floating in a clear blue sky with no clouds in the vicinity.

*Speed and altitude display inside the passenger cabin (Picture 07-05)*

Amongst the in-flight reading materials there was a leaflet giving a brief history of Concorde's development. It was interesting to learn that towards the end of 1962, Britain and France signed a treaty to share costs and risks in producing a supersonic transport aircraft. Apparently, this was the first major cooperative venture of two important countries in Europe to design and build an aircraft. It took about 5 years of extensive development work for the British Aerospace and the French Aerospatiale to build the airframe and for Britain's Rolls Royce and France's SNECMA to develop the jet engine. It is in record that the first flight of the Concorde took place on March 2, 1969. The 1970s saw the proliferation of Concorde flights.

I remember that the specific flight in which I had travelled had taken about three hours to reach London from New York. During my onward journey just a few days earlier, the subsonic flight had covered the same distance in about eight hours. Despite all the flying comforts, the Concorde flights are a memory now and the crafts have turned into museum exhibits. Both Air France and British Airways stopped their Concorde flights in 2003 apparently due to unviability and noise pollution. I do not know to what extent the fatal mishap of the French Concorde flight of July 25, 2000 en route from Paris to New York had influenced the closure of supersonic passenger flights.

While the creative spirit of the scientists and engineers took the Concorde project almost to the threshold of a long lasting success but ultimately it turned into a dismal failure. Whether the project will be revived by the innovative urge and perseverance of the creative community, it is difficult to forecast. Perhaps, only time will tell. As of now, to me, it is a dismal instance of failure of human endeavor of innovation and scientific competence.

**California State Highway One on the Pacific Coast**

A drive along Highway 1 in California is a dream for many foreigners and a coveted holidaying for many Americans. Since I had occasions to visit many places on the Pacific Coast stretching from Seattle to Los Angeles, I always longed for a drive along the Highway. My dream came true, not once, but twice, in two different stretches.

It is a major North-South Highway in California stretching over 1000 km (see Picture 07-06). Starting from the northern side, it runs from Mendocino County and connects San Francisco Bay

Area, Monterey Bay Area, the Big Sur, the Central Coast, Los Angeles and Ventura Counties, and ends at Orange County.

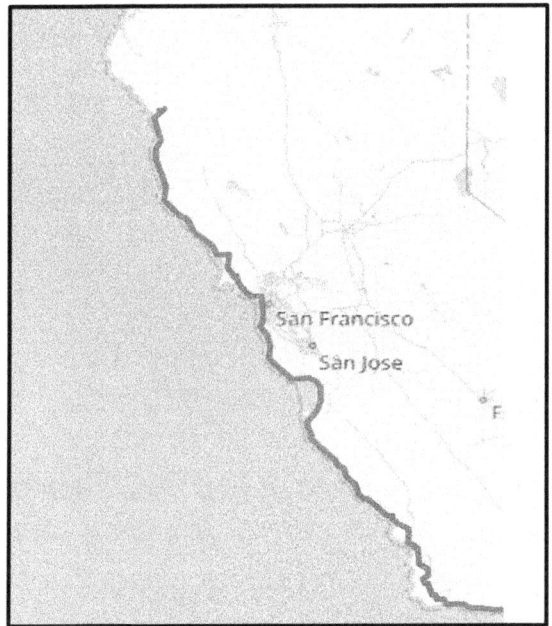

*The coastal stretch of the highway (Picture 07-06)*

Only a few stretches between Los Angeles and San Francisco have been officially recognized as 'scenic highway', where one may encounter memorable landscape with no visual obstruction or intrusions. Big Sur is located along the scenic highway approximately 250 km south of San Francisco. Historically, the name Big Sur was derived from 'El Sur Grande', meaning 'the Big South', an area that was apparently unexplored and uninhabited wilderness in the 1830s. Today, the stretch is a vibrant tourist attraction. In 1937 the present highway was completed after about 18 years of construction at a considerable expense, though, it is said that the convict labour was engaged in this project. The highway is flanked on one side by the majestic Santa Lucia Mountains and on the other, by the rocky Pacific coast. Imposing geography, rich vegetation, and the dramatic meetings of land and sea are the greatest attractions to the public. A coastal vista, shown in Picture 07-07 below, brings to the tourists a sublime feeling.

*An unobstructed view of the Central Californian coastline (Picture 07-07)*

The road briefly leaves the coast for some distance, passing through redwood forest in Big Sur River Valley, where one can come across a few historic bridges. A remarkable sight is that of the Bixby Creek Bridge, made of reinforced concrete with almost 100 m span over the gorge.

The redwood forest was of special interest to me as I had learnt that it grows in a very narrow strip along the coast, maybe 30 to 50 km, where there is a thick summer fog, moderate temperature round the year, and considerable winter rainfall. Redwood is a rapidly growing tree and some trees grow to heights beyond 100 m. It appears that the redwood trees are the tallest tree species on the earth (see Picture 07-08). While visiting the forest, we were told that at Peiffer Big Sur State Park, one of the tallest trees, nicknamed 'Pioneer tree', was hit by lightning strikes and the top was severed.

*Glimpses of the Redwood forest trees with green leaf groves on the left and tall woody stems on the right (Picture 07-08)*

**Napa Valley Wine Train Ride**

Another pleasant travel memory is the ride on the Wine Train in Napa Valley. The geological and geographical features of Napa Valley have been described in the previous chapter. We drove down from San Francisco to downtown Napa Valley for a round-trip Wine Train ride to St. Helena, which was about a 50-km journey. It was a vintage train with early 20$^{th}$ century Pullman cars that slowly but comfortably rolled through the well-known wineries in the region, stopping at some designated ones. With its Honduran mahogany paneling, brass accents, etched glass partitions and plush armchairs, the train ride provided a taste of luxury train travel of the early 1900s (see Picture 07-09).

*The Wine Train at the Napa Valley (Picture 07-09)*

As the train lugged on, we started enjoying the landscape that was distinctly different from what you see elsewhere, particularly when you are served with a four-course meal with local wines. The entire combination of gourmet food, wine tasting, landscape viewing, and all that on a heritage train made the journey profusely enjoyable (see Picture 07-10).

*A view from inside the train (Picture 07-10)*

It wouldn't be in order if I do not mention about the Love Lock Bridges (LLB), in the context of the wine train ride. If you have been to China and Korea, you must be aware of LLB, which is a small pedestrian foot bridge that connects a station to the boarding platform of the train. Over the bridge there is a sort of wire net fence, where lovers can fix a personalized padlock (see Picture 07-11), decorated with their names, lock it and toss the key into the abyss below the bridge. This is the way to lock your soul together, according to the Chinese practice. In certain sections of the Wine Train track in Napa Valley, one may find an opportunity to try out this practice.

*A Love Lock Bridge site (07-11)*

## Memories Abound

It is true that one may write a voluminous book only on travel reminiscences within the United States and Canada. Since my intentions were only to pick up a few unique travels from my large basket, I had to overcome the temptation of narrating my experience of the boat ride to the Statue of Liberty in New York, the drive through the Tennessee Valley, catching the beauty of the half dome trail in the Yosemite National Park, the windy boat ride to Alcatraz Island in the San Francisco Bay, a long walk on the Golden Gate Bridge and so on. Nevertheless, a few snapshots are shared below just for the purposes of highlighting that those destinations are no less unique and no less attractive (Pictures 07-12 to 07-15).

*Alcatraz Island with the prison museum in the San Francisco Bay (Picture 07-12)*

*A mind-blowing view inside the Yosemite National Park (Picture 07-13)*

*The Golden Gate Bridge – the Icon of San Francisco (Picture 07-14)*

*The Statue of Liberty – the Icon of New York (Picture 07-15)*

If you happen to visit these places, you must dive into their historical past. The stories and anecdotes are more engrossing than the sights.

# CHAPTER 8

# Enjoying Kebab at the Niagara Falls

To an Asian, African, European or American, the word 'kebab' (often spelt as 'kabab') is not new or unknown. It has long been a part of multinational cuisine. Personally speaking, an enticing encounter with kebab happened with me, when several decades back I was studying at the Moscow State University in the then Soviet Union, a story worth recalling, and I shall narrate it later. But the incident had propelled me to go back in time to find out the origin and history of kebab, though, to my surprise, I could not locate then any worthwhile information.

In the present age of the Internet, there is, of course, a Wikipedia on kebab, which mentions about the anthropological Grecian relics of stone skewers used before the 17$^{th}$ century BC (see Picture 08-01).

*The 17$^{th}$ century BC Grecian relict of stone support for skewers (Source: Museum of Prehistoric Thera, Greece) (Picture 08-01)*

It appears that in the Iliad and in some mythological stories of the Mahabharata, there are mentions about meat roasting. Much later, in the 10th century, Ibn Sayyar al-Warraq prepared a compendium of the culinary legacy of Mesopotamia, Persia and Arab land, in which there are descriptions of kebabs as cut-up meat either fried on a pan or grilled over a fire. There is also a Turkish claim that kebabs might have originated there when soldiers used to grill chunks of freshly hunted animals skewed on swords in open field fires. In fact, the name came from a Turkish script named 'Kyssa-I Yusuf' of the 14th century. It seems that the Turkish name was 'kebap', while the Arabic version was 'kabab', both apparently meaning 'to roast'. Essentially, it's a way of cooking a number of varieties of meat dishes together. Most often, they are cooked either on a skewer, as mentioned above, or on a spit.

Keeping the historical anecdotes aside, let me go back to my Moscow days in the 1960s, when I had made a beginning for tasting and appreciating kebabs. In the University hostel my next-door neighbour was a friend from Pakistan – Taki Mohamed Taki. He always sported a beard, had a serious but soft mien and meticulously observed all his religious rites, including month-long 'Ramzan', entailing fasting throughout the day, even when the outside temperature used to be below minus twenty degrees Celsius. But I always anxiously waited for him to end his monthly ritual as I was sure to get on the last day a treat with soft and juicy kebab on one side of the plate and sweet 'shemoi' preparation on the other. Taki was not much of a cook and like many of us, he used to dine regularly in the University cafeteria. Only on the closing day of Ramzan he used to indulge in preparing the above special dishes and share with the friends. The event always provided us with a fabulous change from the usual cafeteria menu.

Before I befriended Taki, I used to pronounce kebab as 'kaabaab' in a purely Bengali style. He only taught me how to stress which syllable, though he was not sure of the etymology. He presumed it was an Arabic word that came into the Urdu vocabulary. He did not have any idea of the Turkish or Persian connections of the cuisine. Being more ignorant about the subject, I used to enjoy the tidbits of his Urdu lessons without getting into any serious controversies. My mind was focused on the enticing, juicy kebab.

I got the sense of cosmopolitanism in kebab later in the 1980s, when I visited Sudan as a member of an official Indian delegation. All of us were invited to a formal dinner in the Presidential Palace in Khartoum on the banks of the Blue Nile. We were led to a huge well decorated dining hall with a large magnificent oval wooden table with presumably 70 chairs placed around the table. The Sudanese officials were already there to show us the designated seats. The table was already laid with countless dishes and, to my utter surprise, I found a lamb standing at the center of the table almost like a living species. I had never witnessed such a scene earlier. I asked in whisper one of the Sudanese hosts sitting close to me what it was and why it was displayed on the table. In reply, he asked, 'Are you a vegetarian?'. When I said 'No', he broke into laughter and told me, 'It is a 'Keyun Kebab', very tasty. When your turn comes, you cut out a piece and enjoy. 'That's okay, but how do you cook it?' I asked. 'Simple, a whole lamb is cleaned, prepared, stuffed, stitched and roasted in a covered pit', he said. Putting the roasted lamb erect on the dining table is an art of decoration. It appeared cruel to me. I was afraid that I might not be able to overcome the inhibition to chop off a piece from the roasted lamb for myself. I requested one of the hosts to do it for me. At the end, however, I discovered that the kebab was exquisite!

In some of the European countries, particularly in Germany and France, I got acquainted with another variety of kebab, called 'Döner', or simply, "rotating" kebab. In fact, more than a decade back, when I had put up in a hotel in the city of Avignon in France, it came to my notice. From the window of my room, I could see a small non-European eatery across the side lane, wherein a vertically spinning cone-shaped stuff was visible almost throughout the day (see Picture 08-02).

In order to explore the unknown, my wife and I went one evening to that joint for dining. It was a Turkish eatery and the owner explained in broken English what the stuff was.

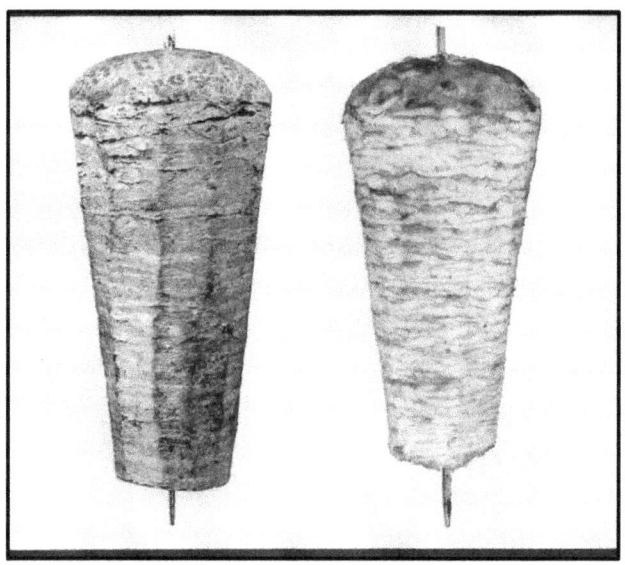

*Spinning view of Döner kebabs (Picture 08-02)*

The kebab is prepared by stacking layers of meat on to a large rotating spit. The outer surface is gradually cooked, sliced off, and served with flatbreads, topped with vegetables. A dish of that kind was served for our dinner, which we enjoyed to our heart's content.

I had more extensive encounter with kebabs when I visited Iran and Turkey. The most common variety, particularly in Turkey, was "şiş (shish) kebab" as in the Turkish language the skewer is called 'shish'. A properly garnished plate of şiş kebab with peeping metallic skewers is served on the table, and it looks elegant and tempting (Picture 08-03).

*A plate of şiş kebab as served in a restaurant (Source: goturkiye.com)*
*(Picture 08-03)*

There was another variant of shish kebab, in which the skewers were made of wood instead of metal but the kinds of marinades, meats and vegetables used remained the same. Since the meat cuts were smaller and vegetables fewer, the plate appeared lighter and is preferred as an appetizer. The dish is called " čop şiş kebab", meaning perhaps "throw away shish" (see Picture 08-04).

*A cop shish plate with wooden skewers (Source: goturkiye.com)*
*(Picture 08-04)*

Among numerous other varieties of kebabs, a special mention may be made of "Iskender kebab", which is incredibly popular in

Istanbul and Bursa, where, as I said earlier, kebab might have originated. Iskender is the Turkish version of 'Alexander', who was the 19th century chef from Bursa and said to be the inventor of döner kebab. Iskender kebab is to commemorate the inventive chef. It is one of the more filling kebabs and is truly delightful when cooked and served properly. It is prepared from the meat sliced from Döner kebab along with other ingredients (Picture 08-05).

*A plate of Iskender kebab (Source: goturkiye.com) (Picture 08-05)*

My most interesting encounter with kebab happened much later, perhaps in the 1990s, when I had revisited Niagara Falls in the United States along with my family. We stayed quite close to the falls in an inn standing on a lane leading to the viewing points. On the first day of our arrival there, we came out late in the evening for a stroll and dinner. To our surprise we discovered that all the eateries in close proximity were closed. As we were still looking around, to our amazement, we saw a kiosk at a distance, beaming a Punjabi Bhangra tune at full blast. We rushed to the kiosk to find that an Indian Sikh Sardar was busy taking orders for special "Peshawari" kebab dishes. The person behind him in the make-shift kitchen, visible to the customers, was a bearded tall middle-aged person, whom the Sikh Sardar was addressing as 'Khan Saheb". Apparently, "Khan Saheb" was from Peshawar in

Pakistan and was the Sarder's 'unique selling proposition' for kebab. The Peshawari Khan was the root of success, preparing the dish with his own recipe. Notwithstanding all these selling propositions, we were doubtful what the kebab would be like in such a place with all sorts of make-shift arrangements including the outdoor tables and chairs. With trepidation we ordered only one plate, which was reasonably sized as we saw, to be shared by three of us, my wife, my son, and me. As soon as the plate was served on our wayside table, we realized that the kebab was superb in taste and enticing in its aroma. My son was busy emptying the dish and my wife kept her wistful eyes on the rapidly disappearing kebabs. I remained as an onlooker with utmost despair.

Despite our momentary confusion, we realized that we needed to order some more dishes and we rushed to the kiosk to find that there was a queue in front of us, a Spanish-speaking couple apparently from the Latin America, a family of Indian-looking East Africans, and a Malaysian couple. Sardar politely told us not to stand in the queue as his raw material stock would be over by the time we reached him. With utter disappointment we left the queue and I looked at my son and said, "Could there be a better stuff from our part of the world for globalization and harmony? The salesman was from India, the producer was from Pakistan, and the eager customers were from different continents. Three cheers for kebab!"

The story did not end there. The Peshawari Khan Saheb saw some pain in my wife's eyes as we left the queue. He came out from the kitchen and caught up with us from behind and quietly told my wife, "Behenji, I kept away a small stock of raw materials for our own consumption. You come back after a brief stroll. By that time, I would have finished preparing and serving those customers who were in the queue. I would prepare a special dish of kebab for three of you. You need not despair."

It was almost like a midnight summer's dream for us. Being assured of the supper with kebab, we opened up our eyes to look at the Niagara River, its gorge and rushing down of water over the escarpment with a gigantic force but with beauty and rhythm. The night illumination of the falls was still continuing. The summer breeze was caressing us. The roaring call of the falls had a magnetic pull. We were absorbed in watching the play of water for some time (see Picture 08-06).

*The Niagara Falls at night (Picture 08-06)*

We loitered around the place and returned back to Peshawari Khan Saheb's kiosk. He indeed kept his words and gave no opportunity to lament. We left the place with a kebab-filled stomach and an utterly satisfied mind.

We once again realized that Nature is really bountiful. It creates an environment of its own that transgresses all boundaries, all barriers, all barricades often created artificially by the humans. No doubt, such an environment could bring together a Sikh and a Muslim to entertain peoples across the continents, from Asia to Latin America. The harmonizing kebab was a means perhaps to make us realize that if a four hundred meters wide gorge can find a rhythmic synergy with land and water, we the people of this planet, should find ways to circumvent our differences and coexist amiably and synergistically.

# CHAPTER 9

# The Hudson Riverfront at the Jersey City and Gathering of Slaves of a Different Genre

The name of Hudson River is widely known, not so much due its bigness or environmental impacts, as much due to its association with New York State and the City. The river is about 500 km long. It originates in the Adirondack Mountains of Upstate New York at Henderson Lake and flows southward through the Hudson Valley to the New York Harbor, situated between New York City and Jersey City. Eventually the River drains into the Atlantic Ocean at Upper New York Bay. The flow of the river is primarily through the eastern part of the New York State but it forms a physical boundary between the states of New York and New Jersey at its southern end. One may have a sketchy idea about the river's locational relation with the above two states from Picture 09-01, given below, showing the relevant portions of the Google map.

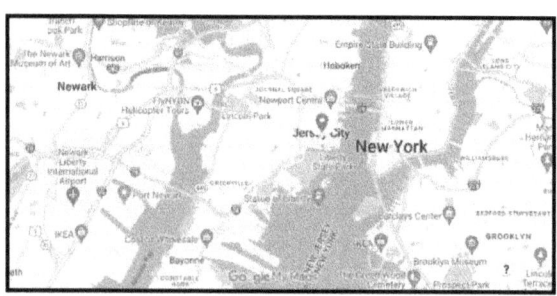

*Google map showing the Hudson River between New Jersey and New York (Picture 09-01)*

**Jersey City in the State of New Jersey**

It is the second most populous city with population of about 300,000, as of 2020, in the State after Newark. It also forms a part of the New York Metropolitan Area with frequent and regular mass transit connections to Manhattan. The Jersey City Waterfront, which will be narrated later in the chapter, has made it one of the largest centers of banking and financial services in the United States. The Hudson River is a picturesque bond between Jersey City and Manhattan (Picture 09-02).

*The Hudson River between New Jersey (left) and Manhattan (right) (Picture 09-02: Source: Beyond My Ken website)*

For those who haven't been to the Jersey City, I must say that it is a place for all moods. Geographically it is the seat of Hudson County in New Jersey. Given its proximity to Manhattan, Jersey City and Hudson County are often referred to as New York's sixth borough.

From the information given in the Wikimedia it appears that the history of Jersey City dates back to about 400 years. In 1609 the land was inhabited by the Lenope, a collection of tribes (later called Delaware Indians). Henry Hudson, looking for an alternate route to East Asia, anchored his small vessel at many places along the water way, which was first named as North River and later rechristened as Hudson River. In 1623 it became a Dutch Colony, named as New Netherland. In the next few years, a person called Michael Reyniersz Pauw received a land grant and choose the west bank of the Hudson River to develop as Hoboken and Jersey City. During the American Revolution for a brief period the area was under the British control. With several hundred years of history, the place acquired certain attributes of openness, tranquility and attractiveness. It is so near to Manhattan, yet so different in its character (see Picture 09-03).

*A recreational area surrounded by residential towers in Jersey City (Picture 09-03)*

Jersey City is one of the most ethnically diverse cities in the world. It happens to be a major port of entry for immigrants from different parts of the globe. About 28% of the population in the city is of Asian origin and another 25% is Hispanic or Latino. In fact, the New Jersey State, on the whole, has a very large community of immigrants. It is said that nearly 25% of the population of the state was born in other countries.

It is quite pertinent to mention here that over the time an Indian American enclave has grown in the Jersey City, which is called by various names such as India Square or Little India or even Little Bombay, not far away from the popular Journal Square (see Picture 09-04). In fact, there is a large South Asian market on the periphery of Journal Square, which is an interesting place to visit.

*A view of India Square (Source: Jim henderson own work uploaded in website)*
*(Picture 09-04)*

**The Hudson River Waterfront Walkway**

It is a spectacular pathway on the western shore of the Hudson River. The basic plan is to lay the pathway continuously for approximately 30 km length through nine municipalities. Though certain sections of this walkway have been built, the project, as far as I know, is still a work in progress. My focus, however, for the present, is on the stretch of the walkway in the Jersey City, which is about 5 km long, starting from the Hoboken Terminal in the north and ending at Colgate Clock in the south. A segment of the walkway is presented in Picture 09-05.

*A segment of the Jersey City Waterfront Walkway (Source: pexels.com)*
*(Picture 09-05)*

It is no exaggeration to say that the best view of New York City skyline is from the Jersey City waterfront. As you walk southwards along the walkway, you enjoy the NYC views of Empire State Building at midtown to One World Trade Center at the southern tip of Manhattan. While strolling along the walkway, you come across interesting neighborhoods of Jersey City. We enjoyed seeing a small sand beach at Newport with chairs and umbrellas overlooking the Hudson River. We enamored to see the bright white tall sculpture of a woman's face placing a finger on her lips with closed eyes (see Picture 09-06). The sculpture is the creation of Jaume Plensa, a famous Spanish artist, reminding us of the essentiality of silence to enjoy the music of water splashes.

*The sculpture of Water's Soul on the Jersey City waterfront (Picture 09-06)*

Most of the days we used to sit in Marina Park on the bank of the Riverfront, watching the children running on the walking paths laid through the flowering plants. Sometimes we walked all the way to the southern end where there is a gigantic 50-ft diameter octagonal Colgate clock (Picture 09-07). The clock was so named because it was in the close vicinity of the previous headquarters of Colgate.

Be it in the morning, or afternoon or evening or be it in the late night, I had never found the waterfront desolate. It had a charm of its own and those, who had experienced the pleasure of strolling there, will always carry many sweet memories. Let me recall one such unforgettable incident here – an interaction with Mr. Sridharan, whom we had encountered during one such aimless relaxing walk on a summer evening.

*The Colgate Clock at the south end of Jersey City Waterfront Walkway*
*(Source: Wikimedia Commons) (Picture 09-07)*

**The Anecdote of Sridharan**

I do not remember to have ever faced earlier the question if slavery has been abolished from our planet. For the first time, my wife and I faced this question from Mr. Sridharan during our accidental meeting on the Waterfront Walkway. It was a sunlit evening my wife and I, after some walk, decided to rest for a while on a comfortable wayside bench overlooking the river and the new 'One World Tower' on the opposite bank. We were quite absorbed in enjoying the landscape around. We watched the boats of various types and dimensions plying in different directions, rare water-bird species floating and cooling themselves in the flowing water, small waves splashing on the shore signaling the arrival of the high tides, joggers of all descriptions and attires running along the walkway, fast-moving youngsters returning from their work places, old Asian couples strolling with variety of expressions on their faces. Suddenly, a gentleman wearing shorts, T-shirt and sport shoes appeared in front of us with folded hands, smilingly looking at my *sari*-clad wife more than me.

'May I introduce myself', he asked, and without waiting for our consent continued, 'I am Sridharan from *Tamil Nadu*. I saw both of you from the other bench and felt like talking to you'.

We smiled and he in an encouraged mood went on appraising us that he had come all the way from Chennai to attend the first birthday celebration of his granddaughter. He had to come alone as his wife had to look after their son's baby somewhere else in this planet. We reciprocated by posting him that we were there for more or less a similar purpose to be with our son, daughter-in-law and two-year old granddaughter. Finding situational commonalities, we continued our conversations. All on a sudden Mr. Sridharan threw a question towards us with a pinch of emotion: 'Do you believe that slavery has been wiped off from this planet? Aren't we continuing to be slaves? Aren't we the slaves of affection? I don't think that you like to travel fifteen thousand miles at this age for nothing; I am sure you do not enjoy the same level of freedom here that you enjoy back at home. Yet you are here to be dictated by your children, to compromise with de facto 'home confinement', to strive hard to find ways of filling up your infinite leisure time. Isn't it slavery? Are we not slaves of affection?'

We did not have an answer. On our way back from the stroll we kept on churning the expression over and over again, trying to assess how precise Mr. Sridharan was to describe our state of pleasurable predicament. Next day morning, sitting in the easy chair, designated by my granddaughter as "*Dadu's* chair" where nobody else was permitted to sit, I could not concentrate on

Gurucharan Das's book entitled "The Difficulties of Being Good", as the expression of Mr. Sridharan kept on haunting me. I pondered and pondered to understand "what affection was." No doubt it is a disposition of mind, it is restricted to our emotional states but is it not quite distinctly different from any form of passion, I asked myself, "How does the affectionate behavior drive us? Why does our new friend think that it is enslaving us?"

The day went by and the glitter of the Sun was fading. We came out on our routine walk on the Waterfront Walkway. The scenario was almost the same as of the previous day. Some of the Indian parents were pushing perambulators of their grandchildren; some were rushing to take care of agile toddlers, and some others were trying their best to stop babies from crying, while at a distance in a quiet corner there were old couples seated on benches with stony silence and gazing far across the Hudson Bay. What were they searching for? Pleasure, relaxation, excitement or avenues to overcome displeasure and depression, we wondered. Looking around different dispositions of Indian parents in particular, I was reminded of the theory of personality that Henry Murray, the American psychologist, had developed. He had identified primarily four affection needs: affiliation, meaning spending time with other people; nurturance, meaning taking care of other persons; enjoyment, having fun with others; and succoring, to be helped or protected by others. Perhaps some of these affection drivers might explain why plane-loads of Indian parents arrive in the United States round the year. You derive a pleasure of finding some commonality of aimless but enjoyable existence. Encountering Sridharan is not a rare phenomenon there, though the exchange of thoughts might not be the same every time. The provocation of Mr. Sridharan that evening was an inducement to ponder and ponder.

Next day morning I heard some soft knocks on my door with a softer call, "*Dadu* , wake up" I rushed out to see the engrossingly smiling face, waiting to take me to my designated chair, where tea would be served to me. She brought her toy utensils. In her own style she prepared tea from nothing and I had to drink from her empty toy spoon and exclaim that it was the best of tea I ever drank. She trusted. She trusted me with everything. She would leave all her prized possessions with me, when she would go to the bathroom. She would cuddle in my lap and all around me. Sometimes she would bring all her musical toys to me and repeat the same rhymes innumerable times. Can there be a better expression of affection than what I was experiencing? It attracts and attracts so intensely that no distance would appear as distance to crave for her intimacy, no strain would tire you, no loss of freedom would be felt, and no thought of confinement would dare engulf you.

Where is the slavery then, Mr. Sridharan? Slaves are held against their will. But here is a different situation, where you would love to surrender on your own to the affection of your children and grandchildren. It is like a pool of intoxication. The more you dip into it, the deeper you would like to dive. I therefore, earnestly request you, Mr. Sridharan, to modify the expression. Do not call us slaves. Call us instead "honeybees of affection".

# CHAPTER 10

# St. Moritz – an Enchanting Winter Destination in the Swiss Alps

In Western Europe, Switzerland has always been a great attraction for tourists, both in summer and winter. It is reported that in 2019 the number of tourists touched 12 million and in terms of international tourism receipts, Switzerland stood at the 5th position in Western Europe and at the 21$^{st}$ position in the world. It is known widely that tourism has been contributing significantly to GDP (Gross Domestic Product) of the country. This has been possible due to the remarkable travel-friendly infrastructure built up there for international tourism. I am particularly fascinated by the ease with which one can travel through the Alps there in peak winter and enjoy the wonders of snow-wrapped surroundings (see Picture 10-01).

*The train service through snow-capped Swiss Alps at Zermatt with Matterhorn peak in the background (Courtesy: Victor He) (Picture 10-01)*

There is hardly any nature-loving person on our planet, who fails to be attracted by the gorgeousness of the mountain ranges. Coming from the land of the Himalayas, I have always been bewitched by its enormity and picturesqueness. At the same time, I heard so much about the beauty and splendor of the Alps that I looked for the right opportunity to enjoy the Alps from close vicinity and to make a mental comparison of the two famous mountain ranges. An exquisite view of the eastern Himalayas is shown in Picture (10-02).

*A view of the eastern Himalayas (Picture 10-02)*

## The Himalayas and the Alps – Do They Have Anything in Common?

The current physical map of the world does not show that the above two mountain ranges are connected in any way but, geologically speaking, both the ranges have formed from the same orogenic movements (mountain-forming crustal upheavals) due to the closing of the Tethys Ocean that existed in the geologic past between the two supercontinents, Laurasia and Gondwanaland. It is estimated by the geo-scientists that the structural reorganization of the earth's crust took place around 152 Ma (Mega annum or million years ago). The mountain-forming movements started from around 65 Ma (a period known as the Alpide Orogeny). At about 50-40 Ma the Himalayas started forming, when the Indian plate collided with the Eurasia plate, and the Alps started building up around 35-25 Ma with the African plate colliding with the Eurasia plate. Even the formation of the Hindukush, the Zagros and other ranges in between are also related to the same orogenic period.

The stretch of the Alps is about 1200 km, about a half of that of the Himalayas, from Austria and Slovenia in the east through Italy, Switzerland, Lichtenstein, and Germany to France in the west. Unlike the Himalayas having four parallel belts from the south to the north with scores of very high and steep cliffs and peaks, spreading over north-east Pakistan, northern India, southern Tibet, Nepal ,Sikkim, and Bhutan, the Alps is limited to only Europe and is divided into eastern, central and western segments. Further, the geo-scientists say that while the Himalayas are still growing vertically due to tectonic activities at a rate greater than 1.0 cm per year due to convergence of India-Eurasia plates moving at a rate of more than 6.0 cm per year, the Alps are no longer growing. Thus, the Alps are a quieter and a more stable and predictable mountain system than the Himalayas for promoting tourism and creating safe infrastructure for all kinds of winter sports. In reality, one finds that the Alps are more accessible than the Himalayas, and you may sip a cup of coffee in a quant café at the bottom of Mont Blanc, the highest peak, while watching the mountain climbers on the slopes. Experiencing the Alps in Europe, therefore, is a safe and coveted goal for all mountain-lovers, particularly if they are not trekkers or sports adventurists.

### The Alps from Engadin - St. Moritz Valley

Since most of my trips to Switzerland were work-related, I was primarily familiar with the western part of the country from Zurich to Basel in the north, Bern in the west center, and Lausanne to Geneva in the south-west. My glimpse of the Swiss Alps was only through the most popular sightseeing tours from

Zurich to Lucerne and then to places like Jungfraujoch and Mount Titlis. The ropeway rides over the green valleys to snow-covered mountain slopes in summer days were as enchanting as visiting the Zurich and Geneva lakes with distant view of the mountains. Such summer tours on week-ends made me more fascinated to explore the Alps specifically in winter. When I got the first opportunity to spend a short holiday in Switzerland in December 2013, I decided to rush to St. Moritz in the Engadin Valley along with my family. The valley lies at the southeastern end of the country and is connected by several passes and the Vereina tunnel to the northern part of Switzerland and the adjacent European countries. The highest peak in this part of the Alps is Piz Bernina (4049 m), which is situated at a distance of 15 km southeast of St Moritz, the hill resort we headed to. A summer view of the valley (Picture 10-03) and the approach map (Picture 10-04) are presented below. This valley region has long been renowned for winter tourism with St. Moritz as the largest hill resort there.

*A summer view of the Engadin Valley (Picture 10-03)*

Readers might be more familiar with the city named Davos located in this valley, which is famous globally for holding the annual conferences of World Economic Forum. But for winter tourism it appeared to me that St. Moritz was better equipped and organized. From the Swiss capital Zurich, the distance of St Moritz is about 200 km and the resort can be reached either by road or rail. There is an airport at Engadin, which is the highest-altitude airport in Europe. There are no regular and scheduled flights to this airport as it services, as far as I know, private and charter flights.

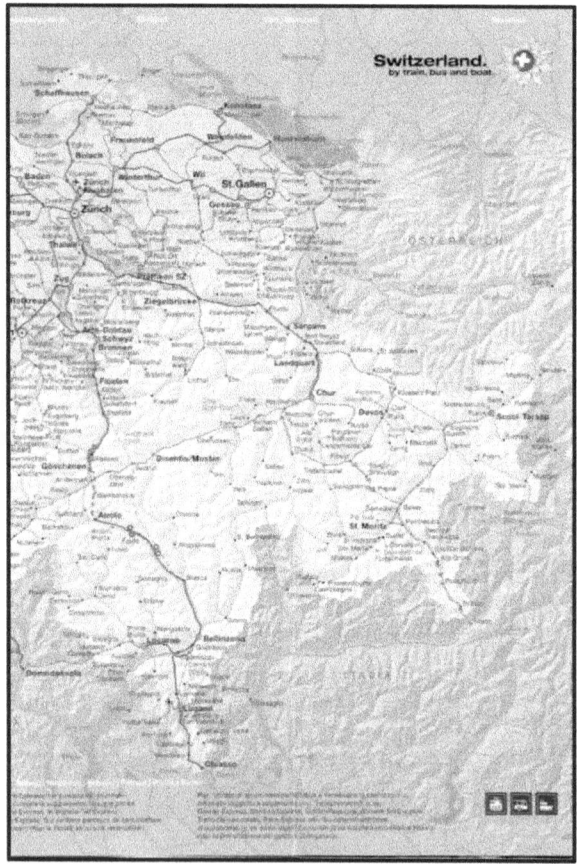

*Route map of the eastern part of Switzerland (Picture 10-04)*

We had travelled with the Swiss Federal Railways (SBB) from Zurich to Chur, as shown in the map, and then continued our journey with the Rhaetian Railway (RhB) to St. Moritz through the Albula Valley into the Engadin region. The journey was one of the most picturesque train rides we ever had. It is reported that the Albula – Bernina line is the first railway line in the world to be photographed and put on Google Street view.

## The Rhaetian Railway and the UNESCO World Heritage Recognition

The setting up of the Swiss Rhaetian Railway is an immensely interesting story of infrastructural development of a country. Though I have no intentions of narrating the full story here, I could not overcome the temptation of highlighting a few pertinent features. The initiation of the venture of laying a mountain railway in the Swiss Alps could be traced back to 1886, the Rhaetian Railway, as it is called now, took shape perhaps in the early decades of the 20th century. The network, as existing in August 2018, is shown schematically in the figure below (Picture 10-05).

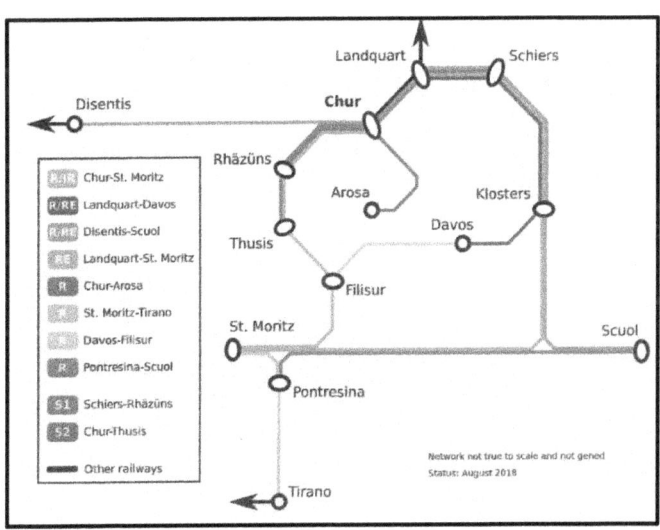

*The RhB network (Picture 10-05)*

The above network covers a distance of 385 km with operating speed of 100 km/h, though in certain high-altitude sections the speed is reduced to about 30 km/h. The highest elevation that the network touches is 2254 m at Bernina Pass. About 12 million passengers make use of this network, primarily for tourism. But at the same time the network connects the remotely located isolated villages in the mountainous terrain, helping in their livelihood.

In 2008, the section from Thusis to Tirano including St. Moritz was declared as the UNESCO World Heritage Site due to its unique construction features and socio-economic impact. It features an impressive set of structures that include perhaps 80 tunnels and galleries and about 200 viaducts and bridges in two sections of the railway meeting at St Moritz. The marvelous engineering features can be appreciated from Pictures (10-06 and 10.07) presented below.

*The engineering marvel of the mountainous railway track (Picture 10-06)*

*A view near the Albula Pass (Picture 10-07)*

When the train moves uphill slowly through the spiral tunnels and over snaky viaducts, one cannot but feel proud of human innovation and ingenuity. From the large glass windows of the train one can enjoy white mountainous terrains fenced with long green trees that seem to ignore the white winter and remind us that they are eternal and cannot be vanquished. In some places we noticed sprinklings of ice on the green leaves and grey branches, looking like winter blossom. The green seems to tell the white: "You stay in my lap but don't obliterate me". In the midst of the play of the white and the green, water bodies and rivers also seemed to assert their rights to exist and flow. But it didn't last long. As we moved further up along the mountain, they are found defeated. They yielded to the supremacy of the white brilliance. Pictures (10-08 to 10-10) shown below are witness to some of those visuals.

*The green and white landscape as observed from the train window (Picture 10-08)*

*Moving further up towards St Moritz (Picture 10-09)*

*Snow patches on the green trees (Picture 10-10)*

## St. Moritz – a Closer Look

On arrival at the St. Moritz railway station, we realized how far away we were from the maddening crowd and the hustle-bustle of busy cities. It was cool, calm and quiet all around us. We were picked up from the railway platform by a representative of the hotel. When the hotel was in sight, the view was a captivating one with snow-capped mountains in the background and bright snow-laid patches all around (see Picture 10-11). In fact, the entire resort is an enchanting combination of nature and sparsely distributed human abodes, where they do not appear to be in conflict at all.

*The hotel building with snow-clad mountain in the backdrop (Picture 10-11)*

St. Moritz is a holiday resort that had shaped up as the birthplace of winter Alpine tourism and winter sports way back in the 19$^{th}$ century. It had been the venue for two Olympic Winter Games in the 20$^{th}$ century (1928 and 1948) and numerous skiing and bobsleigh world championships. During the winter months, the enjoyable climate, the delightful landscape and the white wilderness in the surrounding valleys and mountains take you to a different world.

St. Moritz is famous worldwide for its "champagne climate", which is as sparkling and invigorating as the drink itself. Further, the summer temperature doesn't rise above 12⁰ Celsius, though in winter the night temperature often goes 10⁰ C below zero but the day temperature maintains at 2⁰-4⁰ C with bright sunlight. If you are dressed properly, a walk through the city is a great pleasure. In 2015, St. Moritz had celebrated 150 years of winter tourism, when there was a huge congregation of tourists from all corners of the world.

The city center looked so different at night and during the day. The nights were cold but dazzlingly illuminated and the days were sunlit, calm and soothing (see the night view of the city in Picture 10-12). There was a visible rush of tourists on the streets, hotels and restaurants in the evenings but the streets looked forlorn during the forenoons. But the small hilly city had scores of decorated shopping malls where there were no crowds, no jostling, and no hurries (Picture 10-13). To walk around in such an environment and to do window shopping, if you liked it, was simply a source of ethereal pleasure.

*St Moritz city at night (Picture 10-12)*

*St Moritz Street lined with shops in the winter morning (Picture 10-13)*

St. Moritz and its adjacent areas are home to strikingly rich gastronomic options. The restaurants bore a rustic but stylish charm and their menus featured delicious local specialties such as capuns (chard-wrapped dumplings), pizikels (buckwheat pasta), plain in pigna (baked potato hash browns with ham and bacon), maluns (fried potatoes served with mountain cheese and fresh apple puree, Zuos cabbage soup, and so on, in addition to the traditional Swiss delicacies such as the cheese fondu, rosti, raclette, etc. We were told that, if one could afford, one shouldn't miss the "mountain dining" at the Romantik Hotel Muottas Muragi at an altitude of 2456 m, overlooking the Engadin lake.

One bright morning, we decided to stroll along the street lined with a number of nicely decorated boutique and souvenir shops. The stroll ultimately turned into a shopping adventure when we turned into small side allays with genuine local products. We succumbed to some temptations and survived some others. After acquiring a few odd items, we were back on the main street. It was downhill all the way and led us to an exquisite lake. Water there was flowing with transparent ice flakes and sheets floating on it. These ice pieces were not coming from a distance. The nature, on her sweet will, had frozen the water in contact with the hill slopes and the ice sheets were slipping into the flowing lake from time to time. It was a marvelous scene and we stood on the bank to watch the caprices of nature (see Picture 10-14). Suddenly, our eyes went to the opposite bank. We saw at some altitude long white snow patches strewn on the gentle and greenish grey hill slopes. We noticed that people were moving around on these patches and after a careful look we could make out that they were sports lovers, enjoying their preferred forms of games. Some were playing ice-cricket, some were on their ski, and others were trying simply to slide down. It was an altogether a different world of merry-making.

*Floating ice sheets on the lake in St Moritz (Picture 10-14)*

The vista was so engrossing that we did not realize that the lunch time in the restaurants would soon be over. When we came back to our senses, we rushed to a nearby restaurant inside a skating complex (see Picture 10-15). Hurriedly, we ordered the Alpine draft beer and the local dishes.

*The restaurant premises at the far end (Picture 10-15)*

By the time we had finished our lunch, we saw through the window a distinctly different scenario. The twilight was setting in. The sky had streaks of faint rosy color just below the dusky white cloud. The brightly reflecting snow peaks seemed to be making the last-ditch efforts to penetrate the colorful sky. I was reminded of the beautiful poem "Twilight in the Alps" by Henry Van Dyke:

> "I love the hour that comes with dusky hair
> And dewy feet, along the Alpine dells
> To lead the cattle forth,
> A thousand bells chiming after her across the fair
> And flowery uplands,
> While the rosy flare
> Of sunset on the snowy mountain dwells,
> And valleys darken, and the drowsy spells
> Of peace are woven through the purple air.
> Dear is the magic of the hour: she seems
> To walk before the dark by falling rills,
> And lend a sweeter song to hidden stream
> She opens all the doors to light, and fills
> With moving bells the music of my dreams,
> That wander far among the sleeping hills."

While remembering these lines, it flashed in my mind that the Climate Experts are predicting that permafrost in the Alps is thawing and transforming what used to be sturdy slopes into loose screes. Disappearance of glaciers as water reservoirs is already posing a major threat to life and living. Farmers in Engadin who have been using melt water for irrigation for centuries are already facing water shortages. We heard the story that in summer they had to rely on helicopters to transport water to their herds in the Grison Alps. All in all, scary future is staring at the Alps as in many other places in our planet. The future planning off the beaten track is essential for saving the Alps. Let the Alps live both in poetry and in reality.

# CHAPTER 11

# The Baltic Sea and the Land of Vikings

The Baltic Sea Region encircled by several North European countries and having prominent estuaries, gulfs, fjords and bays is a unique geographical entity. Before we go into the narratives, let us have a quick recap of the regional geography with the help of a map prepared by Gabriel Zeigler in recent years and reproduced below from the internet (Picture 11-01). Broadly speaking, the Baltic Sea is the northern arm of the Atlantic Ocean. It looks like an inland sea encircled by Germany and Poland in the south, Russia and Finland on the east, and Sweden, Norway, and Denmark in the west.

*Map of the Baltic region (Picture 11-01)*

The Gulf of Finland and the Gulf of Bothnia are connected with the Baltic Sea on the eastern and the northern edges. The Baltic Sea is also connected to the White Sea in the north via the White Sea - Baltic Sea Canal and it is connected in the south to the German Bight of the North Sea via the Kiel Canal. The coastline of the entire water body in dotted with cities having great attractions for tourists. To name a few large cities are St. Petersburg in Russia, Helsinki in Finland, Stockholm in Sweden, Copenhagen in Denmark, Oslo in Norway – the ones that I had visited. In addition, I still carry excellent memories of visiting smaller cities like Riga in Latvia, Tallinn in Estonia, Malmo and Gutenberg in Denmark.

My first acquaintance with the Gulf of Finland was about five decades back, when I was a student in Leningrad, now known as St. Petersburg. The picturesque Neva River flowing in front of my University building merged into the gulf and the estuary was not far away from the University campus. The vista there was a feast for the eyes – both in the summer and winter seasons. The transparent blue water of the gulf in summer and the icy frozen white surface in peak winter days (see Pictures 11-02 and 11-03) created lasting impressions in me and my fellow students. We used to pester our language teacher to narrate the history of the Baltic region and to enrich us with the Russian poems and literature on this region. Obviously we could not absorb all that we were told then but some of the unusual bits of information remained somewhere in my memories. The topmost recall is the poem Parus (The Sail) by the Russian poet Mikhail Lermontov – a poem that many Russians can recite from memory. It was first published in 1841 and it depicted the tranquil view of the sail gliding in the blue of the Baltic Sea in the imagery of an approaching storm. The poem is a short one and consists of only three stanzas but with deep philosophical contemplation of a wanderer striving for peace of mind and moral renewal. The poem seems to have influenced the later Soviet authors, an example of which is the novel published in 1936 by Valentin Katayev that borrowed the first line of the poem "Beleet Parus Odinokiy" as the title of the book.

My affection with the Baltic Region deepened during those days not only due to the literary attractions but also due to its historical past. In the early middle ages Norse, more commonly known as the Scandinavian, merchants built a trade empire all around the Baltic Sea. It is believed that in the $13^{th}$ to $16^{th}$ centuries the strongest economic force in Northern Europe was the Hanseatic League, a federation of merchant cities around the Baltic Sea and the North Sea. There was a lot of power struggle among the coastal countries to dominate the sea. It was Sweden that encompassed the Baltic Sea in the $17^{th}$ century. The defeat of Sweden in the Great Northern War brought the Russian empire as a dominating power in the Baltic. Peter the Great saw the strategic importance of the Baltic and decided to establish his new capital St Petersburg at the mouth of the Neva River.

During the Crimean War (October 1853 to February 1856) between Russia and the alliance of the Ottoman Empire, France, UK and Sardinia there was decline of the Ottoman Empire and expansion of the Russian Empire. The Baltic Region has been a witness to both World War I and World War II. In World War II the Baltic Sea became a mass grave for the retreating soldiers and refugees as the troop transports were torpedoed. The sinking of MV Wilhelm Gustloff, the German transport ship, by the Russian submarine in 1945, is recorded as the worst maritime disaster in history killing about 9000 people. In 2005, a group of Russian scientists found over five thousand airplane wrecks, sunken ship and other materials from World War II on the sea bottom. Another war related aspect worth mentioning is the disposal of chemical weapons by various nations in the Baltic Sea after the end of World War II, raising concerns of environmental contamination. Over one thousand kilogram of catches of such materials between 2003 and 2005 were reported.

Despite such a war-torn history of the Baltic Region, it is now a peaceful haven primarily because it is dissociated from both the opposing military blocks of NATO and Warsaw Pact.

*The summer view of the Gulf of Finland (Picture 11-02)*

*A winter view of the Gulf of Finland (Picture 11-03)*

## Cruising in the Baltic Sea - the Changing Perspectives with Time

Looking back and forth, I find it enormously interesting to compare my cruising experience in the Baltic Sea five decades back and now. When we were students in the Soviet land, during the summer holidays we either used to join our University summer camp at Sochi on the Black Sea coast or travel to different European destinations. Once I along with two other Indian classmates had decided to undertake a boat journey from Leningrad to London. The journey time was about four days and route had stopovers at Helsinki and Hamburg before reaching Harwich Port in Essex. The very idea of cruising on the Gulf of Finland, the Baltic Sea and the North Sea in one go was enchanting to us. Without any second thoughts we plunged into it.

We reached the Leningrad Port in the afternoon of the day of our journey and saw from some distance our carrier standing on the jetty. Coming closer to the ship (Picture 11-04), we were able to decipher that it had five levels, which appeared then too grandiose to the eyes of the inexperienced seafarers like us.

*A cruise ship on the Baltic Sea in 1960s (Picture 11-04)*

We entered into the ship after completing the travel formalities. In order to reach our designated cabins in the tourist class category we had to go down into the belly of the ship but the steps and corridors were pretty nicely done up. From the ports in our cabins we could see the mildly waving blue sea surface. After keeping our luggage in the cabins, we rushed up to familiarize ourselves with the ship, had some enjoyable moments on the open corridors and the top deck (refer Pictures 11-05 and 11-06). The passenger count appeared to be a couple of hundreds, which, we felt, was a large crowd for a boat. Exploring further, we were enormously pleased to locate the bar, the lounge and the restaurant – all with wide glass windows offering glimpses of the vast sea.

*The corridor leading to the top deck (Picture 11-05)*

*Passengers enjoying the afternoon breeze on the top deck (Picture 11-06)*

Though the above cruise and its varied memories are indelibly embedded in my mind, I was flabbergasted to find the unimaginable changes that have taken place in the modern cruise ship. When I undertook a boat ride in the same Baltic Region a few years back from Copenhagen to Oslo, an overnight journey of just eighteen hours, I realized how seafaring has changed itself in a span of the last few decades. When I first looked at the ship from a distance (Picture 11-07), I was surprised and impressed with its size and appearance.

*The modern cruise ship in the Baltic Sea (Picture 11-07)*

I had considered a ship with five decks as colossal then. I did not have words to narrate the ship with eleven decks in front of me now. It was the time for me to realize that the modern cruise ship was no more a boat but had turned into a boutique hotel. I was convinced about the evolution, when I entered the ship and familiarized myself with its interior. It had perhaps one thousand cabins, fully furnished with essential furniture, attached bathrooms, television and other facilities. In different decks of the ship there were different types of lounges and kid's rooms. There were grand buffet arrangements for breakfast and dinner. In addition, if a passenger desired, there were a few restaurants with different global cuisines. One of the decks was equipped as duty-free market (see Picture 11-08). All in all, it was like a five-star hotel that we are familiar with on land.

*Inside view of the ship at the deck with duty-free shops at the far end*
*(Picture 11-08)*

## The Land of Vikings – a Unique Blend of History, Nature and Mythology

It is said that the Vikings, also known as Norsemen, lived in what is more popularly called the Scandinavian countries, primarily consisting of present-day Denmark, Norway and Sweden. The anthropologists and historians say that the Viking era was spread over three centuries from 740 to 1030 AD. The fierce bands of Viking men sailed across the North Sea to raid the coasts of Britain, Ireland and France. Many of the Norsemen moved further westwards to Iceland and Greenland. Erik the Red, who was evicted from Norway and later from Iceland, is known to have discovered Greenland and settled there with a few shiploads of goods and people around 981 AD. His second son Leif Eriksson is credited to be the first European to have visited the North American mainland around 1000 AD.

Much of what we know about the Viking era is from the sagas of Iceland that were written hundreds of years after the events took place. Hence, the accuracy of the dates and narratives are often doubted. However, the raids on the Christian monasteries in the British Isles in 791 AD, the Norse settlers occupying Dublin in Ireland in 840 AD, and founding of Normandy in France by the Viking Chief Rollo are some of the landmark events in the initial history of the Viking era that are often talked about. Raids, conquests, and settlements by the Vikings far and wide in a sense paved the way towards shaping the Europe of today.

The city of Oslo has created a unique museum to capture the seafaring of the Vikings. The museum is based on the ruins salvaged from the two ships that sank near Gokstad and Oseberg perhaps in 834 AD and 900 AD respectively, as estimated on the basis of historical findings. Skeletons of two females were also recovered from the sunken Oseberg ship. Efforts have been made to reconstruct the ships and other articles found in the ships (refer Pictures 11-09 and 11-10). The museum has a rare collection of articles of the Viking era and a storehouse of information regarding the ship-building capabilities of the Viking men. An unusual piece of information that I gathered there was the use of ship for burying the wealthy and influential men and women of the community. While burying them, precious gift items were placed in the buried ship, some of which have been salvaged and are on display at the museum.

*The display of a reconstructed Viking ship (Picture 11-09)*

*Wood carvings on a ship mast (Picture 11-10)*

Nature is overgenerous to the land of Vikings with mountains and fjords, which are a great attraction to the international tourists today. One may spend days floating in the slowly cruising boats with all modern facilities on the waterways through the fjords. The blue water, the profile of the mountains against the occasionally sunny and mostly cloudy sky, the tiny valleys sprinkled with picturesque villages take you to an ethereal world. Perhaps, Pictures (11-11 and 11-12), presented below, will help readers to get a feel of what I tried to narrate above.

*Vista from a boat passing through the fjords (Picture 11-11)*

*A picturesque village on the lap of the mountain as viewed from the boat*
*(Picture 11-12)*

While narrating the natural beauty of the terrain, it is imperative for me to mention about Oslo-Bergen train journey. Bergen is a coastal city situated WNW of Oslo and the travel time is about seven hours. The journey takes you through the most beautiful landscapes of Norway, a sense of which can be obtained from Picture (11-13) below. The train has multiple stops with hop-on-hop-off facilities. One of the stops is at a place called Myrdal, from where one may take a branch line to the Flam Valley and enjoy a river cruise. It has been a very popular tourist destination. One of the highlights is the Kjosfoss waterfalls along the Flamsbana railway track (Refer picture(no.)).

*The Oslo-Bergen railway and the landscape en route (Picture 11-13)*

*Waterfalls along the railway track (Picture 11-14)*

My narration would remain incomplete if I do not describe the Bergen City, albeit briefly. It is the second largest city in Norway after Oslo. It is known as the city of seven mountains that surround it. The city is known to have been founded by King Olav Kyrre in 1070 AD after the Viking Age in England came to an end with the Battle of Stamford Bridge. It served as the capital of the country for many centuries before the capital was shifted to Oslo perhaps in the 17$^{th}$ century. Disasters, damages and renovations are spread over the history of the city. Only a few buildings survived the ravages of time, one of which is St. Mary's Church that was constructed in the 12$^{th}$ century (Picture 11-15).

*St Mary's church at the far end of the street in Bergen (Picture 11-15)*

The oldest part of Bergen is the area around the Bay of Vagen in the city center. Here stands a huge food court, where you can select sea food of your choice that will be cooked and served to you, while you wait and sip your preferred drink. A view of a shop and a salesgirl in action is in the image presented below (Picture 11-16).

*A salesgirl in a restaurant in the food court (Picture 11-16)*

## Tales galore in Scandinavia

There is a prevalent hypothesis that the name of the region emanated from two German words 'Skadin' and 'Awfo', meaning 'danger' or 'injury' and 'land next to water' respectively. The treacherous waters and sandbanks in the southern Scandinavia made the region a 'dangerous island' and consequently, I guess, the name "Scandinavia" finally evolved.

But many others believe in a different theory. They say that the name of the region is connected with the Norse god Skadi. For the ancient Norse, every cold and harsh winter was brought on by Skadi, a beautiful but dangerous giantess who lived up the mountains in a hall called Thrymheim, the thunder home. The mythology goes that Skadi was mother of Freyr (Lord) and Freyja (the Lady), the twin brother and sister. Freyr was a widely worshipped god associated with kingship, fertility, peace, prosperity, fair weather and good harvest, while Freyja was the goddess associated with love, beauty, sex, war, gold, and the magic of forecasting and influencing the future. She was imagined to be the owner of necklace Brisingamen - perhaps an amber ornament, wore a cloak of falcon feather, rode a chariot pulled by two cats, and was accompanied by a boar called Hildisvini (battle swine). As it happens with most mythologies, there are many variants of these deities and their genealogy. Many literary works in Iceland and other Scandinavian countries published in the historical past are based on various mythological stories.

Drawing from the Norse mythology and the Scandinavian culture, the Nordic folklore is a vast collection of fables, epics, legends and fairy stories. An important reference for those interested in the topic is the publication of "Asgard Stories: Tales from Norse Mythology". While on the subject, I must recall some of the most beloved fairy tales that many of us might have read in our childhood days. Tales entitled "The Emperor's New Clothes", "Fir Tree", "The Little Mermaid", and "The Little Match Girl", are perhaps more popular.

Among the children's storybook writers, the most outstanding, to my mind, is the Nordic author Hans Christian Anderson, who made the children's world alive with lively description of earth, sea, icy winter and flowery spring along with the spirit of adventures that the young minds pine for. A bronze statue of the Little Mermaid, becoming human, was installed on a rock at the Langelinie promenade in Copenhagen in 1913. The statue, only 1.25 m tall, is quite unimposing but it is an icon of Copenhagen that attracts the tourists from all over the world (see Picture 11-17).

*Statue of the Little Mermaid (Picture 11-17)*

Let me now briefly recall the tale of Holgar Danske, the national hero of Denmark, who is said to be fast asleep in the underground passages of Kronborg Castle. The tourists visiting Kronborg castle now-a-days can see a statue of Holgar below the castle (refer Picture 11-18), which is a cast of the original statue made by the sculptor Petersen-Dan in 1907. The fairytale of Holgar is also a creation of Hans Christian Andersen presumably in 1846. The story goes that he was taken to Avalon, a mythical island that had featured in the Arthurian legends, by the enchantress Morgan Le Fay to rescue France from certain calamity. Later, he travelled to Kronborg Castle to sleep. According to the legend, he will wake up if the country is threatened.

*Statue of Holgar Danske in Kronborg Castle (Picture 11-18)*

*Path leading to Kronborg Castle (Picture 11-19)*

The above mythology leads us to recalling the historical and cultural relevance of Kronborg Castle (refer Picture 11-19). Located at a strategically important site commanding the Sund, the stretch of water between Denmark and Sweden, the Royal Castle at Helsingor (more popularly known as Elsinore) is of immense symbolic value to the Danish people as it played a key role in the history of Northern Europe during the $16^{th}$ to the $18^{th}$ century. Keeping aside the historical nitty-gritty, let me recap its literary heritage.

The famous drama Hamlet was written by William Shakespeare in the backdrop of Kronborg Castle. It is said that Shakespeare was inspired by Frederik II and his impressive royal banquets. His marriage with Queen Sophie in 1572 was a memorable event and was known as one of the happiest royal weddings in Europe. Hamlet was performed in the Castle for the first time to mark the $200^{th}$ anniversary of Shakespeare's death with casting of soldiers from the Castle garrison. The play has since been performed several times in the Castle's courtyard. The later performances of the play saw the appearance of world famous actors like Laurence Olivier there. At the Flag Bastion, in the Queen's chamber and in the chapel you can walk in Hamlet's footsteps. Today, Kronborg Castle is a UNESCO World Heritage Site.

All in all, travelling in the Baltic Sea region and the Scandinavian countries I felt that the tune and tenor of the human history are immeasurable. It is spread in different corners of the globe with their own peculiarities and specificities. Mythologies and fairytales bear the mark of different regions, no doubt, but a universal appeal remains behind the folklore of all countries and regions.

# CHAPTER 12

# China – a Land with Stunning Landscapes

In about 510 million square km of the Earth's total surface area, all the countries of the world occupy only one third land area. Keeping aside the Antarctica as the unclaimed territory of about 1.61 million square km, China as a country, spread over an area of about 9.6 million square km, ranks third in size after Russia and Canada, the United States of America being in a very close fourth position in dimension. It is also widely known that China is the most populous country of the world with 1.44 billion people in 2021. Geographically, China borders with 14 countries including Mongolia, Russia and North Korea. Administratively, it is divided into 33 units, consisting of 22 provinces, 5 autonomous regions, 4 municipal areas and 2 special administrative regions.

In this vast country there are significantly different regional climates, geomorphology, demography and habitat, which have resulted into unthinkable and spectacular variety of landscapes. It is not that such landscape patterns do not occur in other countries and regions of our planet but what makes the Chinese landscapes unique are the scales of occurrence and the human efforts made to preserve them. From the icy city of Harbin in Heilongjiang in the northeast of the country to the continental dry land in Xinjiang in the west, Gobi Desert in the central part, the Tibetan platform in the south west, and the tropical south extending to the rainforests in Hainan, the country is steeped in starkly different landscapes to which the tourists are attracted.

Personally and professionally, my involvement with China started in the 1990s, when there was a perceivable thrust in the country towards purposefully upgrading the industrial and environmental infrastructure with pre-set performance targets, both in the rural and urban segments. It may be relevant to mention that, like many other manufacturing fields, China continues to be the largest producer of cement in the world. Being in such a position, the country felt the need for commissioning a detailed study to find ways of implementing cleaner production methods and energy conservation techniques. The study was conducted by leading international organizations which called for my help and association sometimes for months on stretch. Consequently, I had opportunities galore to be acquainted with the land and its people.

Sometimes I had to undertake extensive road travels mostly in the southern and south eastern provinces such as Guangxi, Yunnan, Jiangxi, Hunan, Anhui, Henan, Hubei and Shandong (see the sketch map in Picture 12-01). Of course, for many of the official meets and also for international travels, visits to Kunming, Guangdong, Shanghai and Beijing could not be avoided. The net result of such travels was my exposure to some magnificent and iconic landscapes of the country, though I had missed the opportunities of visiting many others. To name a few that remain in my wish list are Lhasa, claimed by many to be the most beautiful city in the world; the Four Maiden Mountains in Sichuan region of the Tibetan Plateau; the ice and snow world of Harbin, where the annual Ice Sculpture Festival is held; the ancient oasis town of Dunhuang on the western edge of Gobi Desert on the famous Silk Road, where there are hundreds of caves with the Buddhist wall paintings; the Rain forests of Hainan Island with spectacular flora and fauna; and so on. Keeping aside the unfulfilled wishes, let me proceed follows hereafter with a brief narration of a few landscapes that I had witnessed and the prints of which are embedded in my memory.

*A sketch map showing the provinces in China (Picture 12-01)*

## The Li River Basin and the Reed Flute Cave

The Li River basin, or Li Jiang as it is called locally, is a spectacle of colors with green and blue water flowing through verdant mountains in Guangxi region in Southern China. The river originates in the Mao'ershan (Mountain) and flows southwards through the villages of Guilin, Yangshuo and Pingle. Other streams join the river as it continues and is renamed as the Gui River. Though the total length of both the river is more than 435 km, the most popular section for the tourists is a stretch of 83 km from Guilin to Yangshuo for boat ride and enjoying the view of mountain ranges along the banks (see Picture 12-02)).

*A view of the Li River with mountains on either bank (Picture 12-02)*

Geologically it is a limestone region belonging to the Devonian and Carboniferous age and having underground streams and cavities, often called the karst terrain. The landscape near Guilin, as shown in the picture, appeared as groups of hillocks with a common base and one could notice deep depressions between the peaks. Hundreds of caves and cavities were visible in the terrain. This kind of geomorphology, I was informed, is locally named "fengcong". But when we moved down the river towards the south of Guilin and closer to Yangshuo, the landscape perceptibly changed to isolated limestone hills with flat surface in between often covered with loose sediments. This type of landscape is known as "fenglin".

Another interesting site we observed in the course of one of the cruises was that of cormorant fishermen (see Picture 12-03). The cormorant fishing is one of the ancient fishing techniques, perhaps not of any commercial significance today. In this technique the fishermen train their diving birds, called cormorants, to catch fish for them with a special command that the birds could understand. In the shallow part of the river the fishermen waited in their bamboo rafts along with their trained bird till they noticed the movement of fish. On receiving the signal from the fisherman, the birds dived into the water and brought back the catch of fish for the master. It was immensely surprising that the birds did not swallow the fish and kept the catch in their protruding peaks for delivering to their master back on the raft.

*The cormorant fisherman on the Li River (Picture 12-03)*

I have already mentioned about the abundance of caves and caverns in this region. I had the opportunity of visiting one such cavern, called Reed Flute Cave, occurring on the south side of Guangming Hill in the northwest suburb of Guilin. The cave got its name from the reeds growing immediately outside its main entrance. It was a U-shaped cave with a roundabout path of about 500 m. The maximum height and width of the cave were 18 m and 93 m respectively. The size, color and variety of rock formations inside the cave were genuinely spectacular. The cave was full of stalactites and stalagmites, stone curtains, stone pillars and various other aesthetic formations. The formation of these scenic shapes and particularly of the stalactites and stalagmites happened over thousands of years by water ingress through the cracks in the rocks and dissolving calcium carbonate in limestone (see Picture 12-04).

*An illuminated panoramic view inside the cave (Picture 12-04)*

The tour guide told us that the cave was opened to visiting tourists in 1962 and the interior décor was progressively upgraded to make the cave look like a palace of Nature's art. There were some corners for capturing your visit against the backdrop of stalactites. As an illustration, a snapshot of the author and his Chinese associates inside the cave against the background of stalactites is presented in the picture below (Picture 12-05).

*A souvenir of my visit to the Reed Flute Cave (Picture 12-05)*

Let us now move away from Li Jiang to another location with an impressive landscape there.

## West Lake near Hangzhou City in Zhejiang Province

The West Lake area is about 200 km away from Shanghai City, the commercial hub of China. The lake and its surrounding scenic spots are spread over 49 square km, in which the water body itself occupies an area of 6.38 square km. The lake is surrounded on three sides by cloud-capped hills and on the fourth side is the city of Hangzhou. It is a fresh water lake, the natural beauty of which has been celebrated by writers and artists since the times of the Tang Dynasty (AD 618-907). It is said that the Tang Emperors and later the Song Dynasty (up to AD 1279) made outstanding contributions to beautify the lake and its surroundings by blending the natural splendor with human aesthetics. The artificial elements in the lake consist of two causeways constructed by repeated dredging in the 13$^{th}$ century. Three islands were also artificially created, though two other natural islands were there in the lake. The lower slopes of the hills were made more attractive with a large number of temples, pagodas, pavilions, gardens, and ornamental trees. A panoramic view given below may offer a partial impression of the lake beautified with human efforts (see Picture 12-06).

*An attempt to blend human aesthetics with nature (Picture 12-06)*

There is a legendary story about the creation of the lake. Once upon a time the Jade Dragon and the Golden Phoenix found a gigantic brilliant white jade stone. They were so amazed to find this rare stone that they started polishing it every day so that no speck of dust could diminish its brilliance. With their persistent efforts the polished stone became a stunning white ball, and wherever its light could reach, beautiful flowers would spring from the ground. The news in due course reached the heaven, when the Empress in Heaven insisted on possessing the stone ball. She dispatched her army to fight with the Jade Dragon and the Golden Phoenix in order to take possession of the ball. A bitter and prolonged fight ensued. One day accidentally the ball dropped from a great height. When it hit the ground, the impact created the West Lake and the surrounding Phoenix Mountains. It is believed that the Phoenix Mountains are keeping a watchful eye over the West Lake, protecting it from the agents of Heaven.

When we visited Leifeng Pagoda on the southern bank of West Lake, a more appealing folklore was narrated to us. Before I venture to narrate the story in brief, let me recap the history of the pagoda. It is perhaps the oldest pagoda in China. It was constructed in AD 975 but with ravages of time it collapsed in 1924. It was reconstructed at the same place with more or less similar layout in 2002 but primarily with modern materials including bronze. It is a five-storied tall tower with eight faces, surrounded with flower plants (see Picture 12-07).

*Leifeng Pagoda on the southern bank of West Lake (Picture 12-07)*

With this historical backdrop, let me now narrate the interesting the story "The Legend of the White Snake", one of the four great folktales of China, as it had unfolded in the region around the West Lake and this Pagoda. The story goes that Lu Dongbin, one of the eight immortals in China, once disguised himself as a food vendor at the Broken Bridge on the West Lake. He was selling magic pills mixed with *tangyuan*, a Chinese rice-based preparation. A boy called Xu Xian bought a portion and ate but could not digest. After three days he came back to the vendor and told him about his problem. The vendor immediately put the boy upside down and made him to throw up. The *tangyuan* fell into the lake water. A White Snake, living there, ate the pills and gained 500 years' worth of magical power to survive and transform into human body at her will. Evidently she felt grateful to Xu Xian for providing this opportunity, and thus, unknowingly, their destinies had converged in a way. A Tortoise in the Lake, however, did not have access to the stuff and could not consume the pills, which made him jealous of the White Snake.

Later the White Snake saw a beggar on the same bridge. He was carrying a Green Snake and wanted to dig out the gall of the snake to sell. The White Snake transformed herself into a woman, approached the beggar, bought the snake and saved her life. Thus the White Snake and the Green Snake became friendly like two sisters. In the meantime, the Tortoise practised Taoism and accumulated enough magical power. After eighteen years, the scene changed to a nearby popular festival, where the two sisterly snakes and the tortoise transform themselves into humans. The snakes turned into two beautiful ladies – the white Snake carried the name Bai Suzhen and the Green Snake was called Xiaoqing. The Tortoise turned into a powerful but jealous monk named Fahai. The snake ladies there met Xu Xian, because of whom the White Snake could swallow the pills and amass powers to become Bai Suzhen. Xu and Bai fell in love, got married, set up their own business of medicinal herbs, and started leading a happy conjugal life. Fahai, the Monk, however, was so envious of Bai Suzhen that he tricked Xu Xian to reveal that his wife was not a human but a snake. The revelation was so shocking that Xu died.

The story does not end there. Bai Suzhen was determined to revive her beloved husband and she as the White Snake managed to steal some heavenly plants to revive her husband after overcoming several obstacles on the way. By that time, Bai was already carrying the child of Xu in her womb. She managed to revive her husband Xu and confessed to him that she was not a human but a snake. Xu, however, said, "Human or not, I will love you always". Their reunion was very short-lived. Fahai continued with his conspiratorial plans with divine assistance. Bai declared war against Fahai with the help of Dragon King of the East Sea but she could not defeat the Monk, perhaps due to her pregnancy. She delivered her baby boy and tried to escape along with the

Green Snake on a lotus leaf. But all attempts failed. Ultimately, Xu was kept under captivity in the Jinshan Temple and Bai, the White Snake, was imprisoned under the Leifeng Pagoda.

In the final turn of the story, after twenty years, Xu Mengjiao, the son of Bai and Xu, joined hands with the Green Snake, after amassing lots of power and resources, rescued both Xu and Bai from captivity and reunited them. Fahai, the Monk, on the other hand fled and hid in the stomach of a crab.

The folktale that immortalizes the invincibility of genuine love and ultimate destruction of evil forces is so popular In China that it has been adopted in different versions in various regions of the country and even converted into opera and TV serials. In addition to promoting such legendary stories, the West Lake has influenced over the centuries poets and painters in their creative pursuits. It has also been a very popular destination for cultural and religious tourism. Over and above, the place is known to have influenced garden design in other parts of China as well as in Japan and Korean peninsula. In recognition of these attributes, the West Lake of Hangzhou was declared by UNESCO World Heritage Site in 2011. The picture of lotus blossoms presented below always reminds me of the poetic touch of the landscape (Picture 12-08).

*Cluster of lotus leaf and flower in the West Lake (Picture 12-08)*

## The Great Wall of China and its Historical Anecdotes

It is hard to believe that the iconic Great Wall of China is not known to the readers of this article. Yet I thought it would be unfair to talk about the Chinese landscapes and not to touch upon these iconic fortifications that were built over a time span of about 2700 years, starting from the $7^{th}$ Century BC to the $19^{th}$ Century AD. The Great Wall of China is certainly a unique feat of human engineering. As built over centuries, it stretched over a length of 21,198.18 km, which is almost a half of the equatorial circumference of our planet. But with ravages of time one third of the Great Wall has disappeared. The today's wall is primarily the relics from the Ming Dynasty (1368-1644 AD), measuring about 8,851 km. The wall sections near Mutianyu and Badaling, about 60 km from central Beijing, were restored and provided with cable cars, shopping and dining facilities, etc., and opened to tourists in the 1990s. I am told that more than 50 million tourists visit the Great Wall every year. A few glimpses of the Mutianyu section are presented below (Pictures 12-09, 12-10, and 12-11).

*Standing at a view point with the Great Wall in the background (Picture 12-09)*

*A distant view of the wall with a tower (Picture 12-10)*

*Walking up and down the walkway on the Great Wall (Picture 12-11)*

It is interesting to note that the construction of the Great Wall is intimately associated with the country's geography and history. It crosses 15 regions in the northern part of China from Heilongjiang in the northeast to Xinjiang in the northwest via Jilin, Liaoning, Heibei, Inner Mongolia, Beijing, Gansu, Shandong and many other places. Though Emperor Qin Shi Huang (220-205 BC) is often credited to initiate the construction of the Great Wall during his reign, many historians believe that the construction started much earlier in the 7$^{th}$ Century BC by the Chu State. Actually Qin Shi Huang first attempted to link the disjointed separate sections built by different States, after unifying the Central China and establishing the Qin Dynasty.

There is a story that Emperor Qin wanted to rule for ever but did not know how to attain immortality. So he engaged Lu Sheng, a necromancer, to find out the path towards his goal. After countless empty-handed returns, Lu finally brought back a rumor that Qin would be overthrown by the northern nomads. Emperor Qin was so frightened that he immediately issued an order to connect the walls and build new ramparts to guard the northern border. This was perhaps the beginning of constructing the gigantic defence infrastructure. It is said that more than twenty dynasties and states added to the construction of the wall over 2700 years. The protecting capability of the Great Wall was enhanced by constructing watch towers, troop barracks, signaling facilities with smoke and fire.

It is obvious that with change in construction periods the materials technology and building practices also changed, which can be observed in the following photographs of relics reproduced from the website of TravelChinaGuide (Pictures 12-12 and 12-13). Since everywhere the construction was massive in nature, the builders usually took recourse to local materials. In the rocky areas stone was the major material of construction, while rammed earth blocks were used in the plains. In desert, even the branches of reeds and red willows were layered with sand. Wooden planks were also used in some sections. In all probability, the brick-making techniques came into practice during the Tang Dynasty (618-907 AD) and became popular in the later periods. The bricks and blocks required mortars for jointing. It seems that unlike the present-day cement-sand mixes, the mortars then used glutinous rice flour as an adhesive along with lime.

There is an interesting story about lime-making in the ancient China. During the Warring States Period (770-221 BC), the King of Yan State employed farmers during their off-seasons to build a high wall of mud to prevent the incursion of enemies. Serendipitously, some farmers discovered lime which could make the wall stiffer and stronger. Later, when the Emperor Qin Shi Huang initiated the project of the Great Wall, he specifically asked the people of the original Yan State to make lime as they used to produce good quality lime with longer shelf-life. Later, in order to reward the Yan people, Emperor Qin ordered to construct a separate town for them, which was named Yanjing, now known as Beijing.

*Relics of sand-and-earth wall (left) and wall with layers of sand-and-reed branches (right) (Picture 12-12)*

*The Great Wall relics in Gansu (left) and in Inner Mongolia (right) (Picture 12-13)*

In addition to the historical relations of the Great Wall, some of which are briefly narrated above, there is a plethora of anecdotes involving the Wall and its Passes. The stories mostly relate to successes and failures of protectors and invaders, loyalty and treason of the warring people, ambitions of the royalty and suffering of the common masses. Perhaps it might be relevant to recount briefly the fall of the Ming Dynasty and beginning of the Qing Dynasty (1644-1911). Towards the end of the Ming Dynasty, when the last Ming Emperor committed suicide, there was a peasants uprising led by Li Zicheng on one hand and invasion from the northeast by the Manchu army on the other. At that time, Wu Sangui, a notorious army officer of the Ming Empire, with his army was present at the Shanhaiguan Pass. Li realized the threat of Wu and kidnapped Wu's family to force him to surrender. In order to save his family Wu pretended to surrender to Li and in the meantime contacted Dorgon, the General of the Manchu army, for help in lieu of some territories in the Shanhaiguan region. Both Li and Wu did not catch the trap laid by Dorgon. When Li arrived at Shanhaiguan, Dorgon came with his troop, defeated Li first and then forced Wu to surrender without keeping any escape routes for him. Wu handed over the Shanhaiguan Pass to Dorgon, who then entered the central plain with his army, occupied Beijing and established the Qing Dynasty.

There is also a sad image of the Great Wall. It is called the longest cemetery of the world. It is not known for certain how many construction workers had been deployed over the three millennia in building and renovating the Great Wall; Perhaps, a million or more? It is also conjectured that about half of the workers might have perished or might have been buried there, though no physical evidence of such burials are available.

All in all, the Great Wall is still a witness to an outstanding human endeavor. It continues to be one of the most visited tourist destinations of the world. In 1987, it was recognized by the UNESCO as a World Heritage Site.

At the conclusion, I wonder if the readers are now charged with enhanced curiosity and inquisitiveness to learn about many more destinations in China, where human imprints have combined with natural landscapes to create marvels. I could not write about many such destinations as I did not have the opportunity for visiting them. I still wish if I could walk along the Silk Road and be at Dunhuang, the ancient oasis town in Gansu Province, and visit hundreds of caves with Buddhist wall paintings; I wish to ride the train from Beijing to Lhasa in Tibet, crossing eight provinces and riding through Tanggula Pass at an altitude of 5072 m. I want to enjoy the Wuzhishan Tropical Rainforest traversed by the Shuiman River and enjoy the Nature's bounty near the Wuzhi Mountain in the Hainan Island, and many such unique locations in China and elsewhere.

# CHAPTER 13

# The Story of Diamonds and a Revelatory Visit to an Australian Mine

Diamond, a naturally occurring mineral, is known from the ancient times, particularly due to its use by kings and emperors as the sign of their superlative affluence and wealth in possession. Who hasn't heard the name of Kohinoor Diamond? It is a gem with a very long history, partly attested and partly anecdotal, and one may see it displayed in the Tower of London even now. A fairly representative replica of Kohinoor can be seen at the Prince of Wales Museum in Mumbai (Picture 13-01). Unfortunately, the replica has a defect in having a black facet, which is not there in the original, but still it conveys an impression of the original stone.

*Replica of the Kohinoor Diamond at the Prince of Wales Museum, Mumbai (Picture 13-01)*

The Kohinoor stone on display in London is hardly four centimeters long but it is one of the largest cut-and-polished diamonds in the world, weighing 105.6 carats (21.12 g) and truly justifies its Persian name, which means a mountain of light. It exists as a part of the Crown Jewel in the United Kingdom. Though the information about Kohinoor is meager and imperfect prior to 1740 AD, still it is interesting to trace how the gemstone landed in the British Empire.

Apparently, there are no differences in views among the scholars about the original source of the gemstone. In the ancient times, the gravel of the Krishna River, flowing through the southern Indian state, now known as Andhra Pradesh, used to carry raw diamond pieces of large dimensions. Some of the pieces recovered from the gravel by a technique called the placer mining are now of legendary fame. One of them is Kohinoor. It is believed that till about 1726, when diamonds were first discovered in Brazil, the Indian subcontinent was the major, if not the only, source of diamonds in the world. Some of the old publications indicated that the original weight of Kohinoor after cutting and polishing was 191 carat (38.2 g), which reduced to its present weight because of further cutting and polishing of its faces for a second time during its long history to bring out its brilliance. In fact Golconda in the same southern region in India was in those days the diamond processing center, where the world used to converge for diamond processing. From the stories available, it appears that Kohinoor changed hands several times from the Kakatiyas to Moghul kings. Finally, it landed in the treasury of Emperor Shah Jahan, which already had abundance of many other jewels and gemstones of natural origin. When the Emperor made the Peacock Throne in 1635 AD, Kohinoor found the most prominent position in the stone settings.

The Peacock Throne was so well known to the royal world at large that the Iranian Emperor Nader Shah, when he conquered Delhi in the course of his invasion of the Northern India in 1740, plundered it. Then again the diamond started changing hands until it was given to British Queen Victoria, when the East India Company annexed the Punjab State in 1849, by the minor ruler of the Sikh Empire Maharaja Duleep Singh. It is said that Queen Victoria used to wear the diamond in a broach. After she died in 1901, Kohinoor was set in the crown of Queen Alexandra. It was then transferred to Queen Mary in 1911 and finally to Queen Elizabeth (the Queen Mother) in 1937 for her coronation. It is known that India had repeatedly claimed the ownership of the diamond. There have been other Asian claimants as well. Since there are evidences of legal transfer of the diamond to the then British Empire, the priceless gemstone continues to be on public display in London.

This is the long and the short of the Kohinoor story. But the Krishna River gravel mining had yielded quite a few other legendary diamonds, one of which is called the Orlov Diamond. It also has an interesting story behind it. As common, there are many versions and some versions have overlaps with the diamond known as the Great Mogul Diamond of Shah Jahan, which perhaps ultimately became famous as Kohinoor as narrated above, and not the Orlov Diamond.

The story of Orlov stone started with its discovery in Golconda in the 17$^{th}$ century. It is now publicly displayed in the Kremlin's armory in Moscow. Cut and polished, the diamond looks transparent, tinged with a faint bluish color. In shape it appears like one-half of an egg, weighing about 190 carat. It is said that originally it was set as the third eye of Lord Vishnu at the sanctum sanctorum of a temple at Srirangam near Mysuru in South India. A French deserter during the Carnatic War at Srirangam disguised himself as a Hindu convert and stole the diamond in 1747. The gemstone did not carry any name then but was highly valued and passed hands from merchant to merchant and eventually appeared in Amsterdam for sale by an Iranian millionaire. The transaction of the diamond to Count Gregory Gregorievich Orlov apparently took place here via his agent

Hovhannes Lazarian supposedly against a payment of 1.4 million Dutch florins.

Count Orlov was romantically involved with the Russian Empress Catherine the Great. He is said to have masterminded the coup d'etat to dethrone Peter III, the husband of Catherine, and elevate her to power. Though later Catherine forsook Count Orlov and embraced Gregory Alexandrovich Potemkin, she had a soft corner for Orlov, who made an attempt to rekindle her romance by gifting the diamond, as she had coveted it earlier. Catherine then named the gemstone as the Orlov Diamond and commissioned her jeweler to design a scepter with the diamond placed in it. The task was accomplished in 1774 (see Picture 13-02)) and the scepter is now on display in Kremlin as mentioned above.

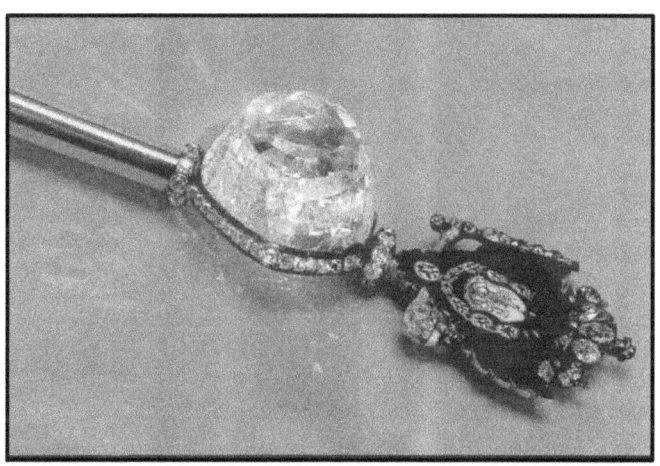

*The scepter of Catherine the Great with the inset of Orlov Diamond*
*(Picture 13-02)*

The penchant for diamonds hasn't died with waning of imperialism in the world. Notwithstanding its preciousness and problems of affordability, it continues to be the most coveted gemstone even today in the affluent society. An overwhelming rationale for all lovers of natural diamonds, then and now, is its timelessness. They are in vogue for ever, transcending ephemeral fashion trends. The diamonds has always been the ideal heirloom and legacy to pass on to future generations. I still remember that during my sacred threat ceremony, a milestone event in the life of a young Hindu Brahman, I was insisted upon to wear a diamond ring that was in possession of my forefathers as a family tradition. Sporting a piece of jewelry with diamond insets that has been part of your family for generations is not considered an empty luxury but a symbol of infinite continuity. An obvious question then springs up in mind. Why is a diamond, unlike many other gifts of Nature from the planet Earth, is so rare, precious, mind-boggling and long-lasting?

## Creation and Journey of Diamonds

In our school-days a teacher had explained that the stuff that makes coal and graphite also makes diamond. His statement was in the context that some, among us, were as brilliant as diamond and some were as dull as coal (see Picture 13-04 below). I must add that though the picture presents a physical comparison of the two carbon products, our teacher never hinted at our physical differences. He was comparing our mental reflects in differentiating our brilliance or dullness. But the ultimate message was that the environmental impacts go a long way in forming and shaping an entity. Diamond and coal, both originating from the element carbon (C) is probably a unique example of Nature.

*Carbon in two contrasting forms (Picture 13-03)*

Carbon as charcoal or soot was known from ancient times but the fact that diamond is made of carbon was experimentally proven in 1772 by the French scientist Antoine Lavoisier by heating diamond and charcoal and measuring the released carbon dioxide gas per gram of material. If carbon is the mother of diamond, then why is diamond so rare? This is a question that baffles us all the time. But the reality is that diamond is created deep inside planet Earth. It is known that the Earth's structure is a layered one and if one could penetrate the planet from the surface to its core, one would have encountered progressively layers of crust, upper mantle, lower mantle, upper core and inner core as shown in the diagram below in a very simplified manner (Picture 13-04).

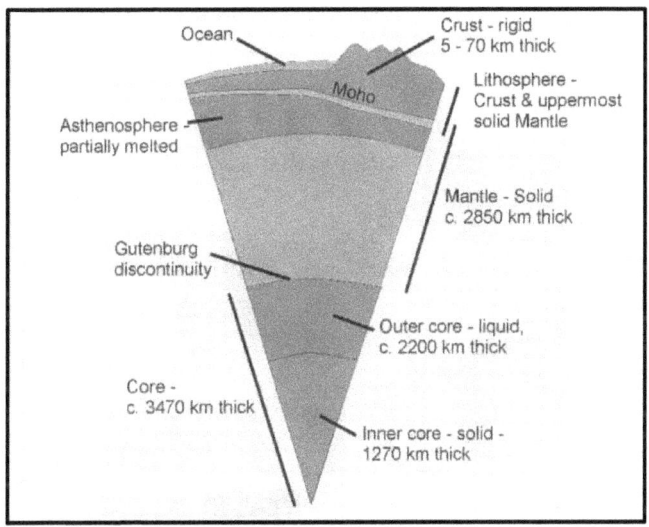

*The structure of the Earth (Picture 13-04)*

As the diagram shows, the crust appearing below both the land and the ocean is of variable thickness up to about 70 km. Much less understood are the layers down below the solid crust. There is a partially melted layer, geologically called asthenosphere, is a part of the upper mantle and the boundary between the crust and the asthenosphere is named the Mohorovicic Discontinuity. Below the mantle, which is about 3000 km thick, there is an outer fluid core of more than 2000 km, leading down below to a metallic solid inner core. In this complex structure of the Earth the temperature and pressure increase with depth and act upon the primordial carbon or the carbon that existed from the time of the planet's creation. The temperature is about $1000^0$ C below the crust, around $3500^0$C at the base of the mantle and about $5000^0$C at the core. These are indicative numbers and the pressure conditions also vary along with temperature due to various geological conditions and activities. Though it is estimated that about 0.025 percent carbon is present in the crust, no formation of diamond has taken place there. The incubation of diamond has happened in the upper mantle and that too much below the continental crust only at specific locations, called Cratons, only where the temperature, pressure and hosting conditions were favorable. The geological dating studies have indicated that these phenomena had taken place 1-4 billion years ago at depths of more than 120 km.

The forming conditions resulted in a natural mineral with pure and perfect crystals having carbon-carbon bond, and making it the hardest of all known natural substances. A diamond can be cut by using only another diamond and no other material. Physically the diamonds vary from being colorless to black and they can be transparent, translucent or even opaque to transmission of light. Diamonds used as gems are mostly transparent and colorless, and sometimes faintly tinged, and occasionally having distinct pink, red and yellow coloration. Because of its unusual hardness, deeply colored impure diamonds and diamond dust find various industrial applications.

**Occurrence and Accessibility of Gem-quality Diamonds**

If the diamonds originated deep inside the planet Earth, how did it come up to the surface and that too in certain sparsely located regions of the world? Though India was the major source of diamonds in the ancient times, it is not so now. In the present millennium, the countries like Australia, Congo, Russia, South

Africa and Botswana are the first five producers of diamond. The rarity of gem-quality diamond may be understood from the fact that in 2006, according to the data of the US Department of Interior, the world production of this class of diamond was only 85 million carats and Australia topped the list with production of 25 million carats. But the question remains how the diamond found its way to the surface in these regions of our planet. To understand this mystery one has to go back to the geological history again. Diamonds are known to be carried to the Earth's surface by what the geologists call 'magma', a very hot fluid or semi-fluid material under the Earth's crust, from which igneous rock is formed by cooling. Due to various geological disturbances the magma carrying diamond forced its way up to the surface, perhaps 100 million years ago, through inverted carrot-like pipes and formed essentially three types of rocks called kimberlite, lamproite and lamprophyre. Of these three rocks, kimberlites are the most abundant carrier of diamond and several hundred kimberlite pipes have been located in various regions of the planet. However, the contents of diamond in all the pipes are not large enough to justify mining. Hence, the diamond mines are so rare and location-specific. From the specific locations of the diamond-bearing pipes, diamonds in many places were released in the form of sand and gravels through the natural processes of fluvial or glacial erosion into river beds, from where diamonds are also recovered through appropriate placer mining techniques.

**Diamond Mining in Australia – a Glimpse**

As discussed above, in modern times Australia has been a major source of diamond, particularly of the gem quality. I had a rare opportunity of visiting the Argyle Diamond Mine, when it was in the peak of its mining and lapidary activities. A snappy recall of this visit is topmost in my mind.

The mine is situated in the northeastern part of Western Australia, 540 km southwest of Darwin and 2200 km northeast of Perth, the State capital (refer the sketch map below). A team of company executives including me was on a business trip to Australia and we had our first set of official engagements in Melbourne, from where we flew to Perth with a specific plan of undertaking a short tour of the Argyle mine of Rio Tinto Group, a diversified mining company. The generalized sketch map (Picture 13-05) shows the location of diamond occurrences in the Kimberley craton region of Western Australia. The Argyle mine is situated east of the craton near the northeastern boundary of the Halls creek mobile zone. The nearest town is Kununurra, about 125 km away from the mine.

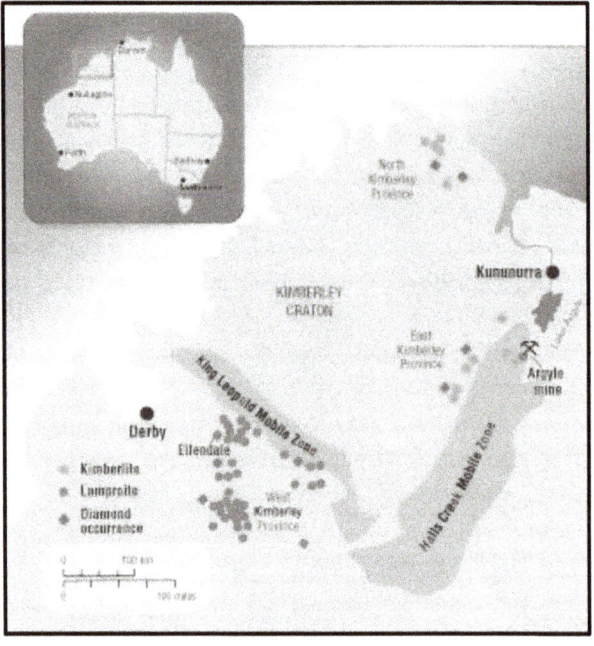

*A sketch map of the Argyle mine region (Picture 13-05)*

We were flown by a small chartered plane with a seating capacity of twenty persons from Perth to the mine. The most surprising feature of the flight was that it was entirely a one-man show. The pilot performed as the host and also as the navigator. The duration of the flight was about three hours. It was summer time in

Australia then and the clear aerial view along the long flight path gave us the impression of an awfully desolate rugged terrain over which we flew the entire distance. The aerial view of the mines area presented a different landscape (refer Picture 13-06). The open-pit mine benches were visible along with the dumps of overburden rocks removed during the course of developing the mine. The vegetation cover over the landscape was sparse, consisting mostly of small trees, bushes and grass, as normally seen in the tropical Savannah region.

*An aerial view of the Argyle mining site (Picture 13-06)*

The mine had a landing strip of its own, where our plane landed. After we reached the mine office, we were given an elaborate briefing on the developmental history, technology of mining and extraction, social and environmental issues, and so on. Though much of it was of technical nature, some information was of general interest and uncommon in nature. Let me narrate a few of them here.

Traditionally, the entire Western Australia has been the habitat of aboriginal tribes of various descents and within the State different regions had different groups of tribes. We learnt that the presence of aboriginal inhabitants has been traced back to fifty-to-seventy thousand years prior to the European settlements there, though the documented history is available from external sources only after the Europeans settled in the city of Perth. Like other tribal groups, the aboriginal inhabitants in the Kimberley region, where the Argyle mine was situated, spoke in a variety of languages and started interacting with settlers from outside over centuries in different ways. Apparently, there was exploitation and not much of social development. As a result, when the Argyle mine came into existence, there was severe crunch of technically and managerially skilled manpower, though the mine encouraged local employment. Ultimately the company found a novel solution for the manpower problem. Several hundred workers and employees commuted from Perth for alternating two-week shifts at the mine. During their two-week shift, the workers stayed at a permanent village located in the vicinity of the mine site, where there were both living and recreational facilities. Our stay for a couple of days there at the mine site was organized in the same village.

The other surprising information was the unusually long gestation period of a large diamond mine starting from the phase of finding out the primary source of diamonds through complicated geological prospecting activities in desolate and rugged terrains to the stage of extracting and processing of mined ores in sophisticated plants. The history of the Argyle mine was an eye-opener to us. Small quantities of alluvial diamonds were known in the region since the late $19^{th}$ century, first found by prospectors searching for gold. However, no source in the form of a diamond-bearing pipe, as discussed in the earlier pages, could be located. After years of intense prospecting in late 1979 the Argyle pipe was discovered. During the subsequent three years the deposit was assessed for economic viability. The decision to mine was taken in 1983 and it took another couple of years to start the open-pit mine. With continuing operations in due course it was established that the Argyle mine was the fourth largest mine by volume, averaging annual production of 8 million carats. Ore processing and diamond sorting facilities were created on site. Separating diamonds from the mined ore required a primarily mechanical multi-stage process. Once diamonds were physically removed without damage from the ore and washed with acid, they were sorted and shipped to Perth for further sorting and sale. It was interesting to learn that a significant quantity of uncut diamonds was dispatched to India for processing as the small-sized diamonds could be cut and polished more economically there.

An impression of how large the ore processing operation at the Argyle mine site was can be gathered from the aerial view of the plant given below (Picture 13-07). Perhaps, it is also relevant to mention here that the plant we visited employed contemporary technology. An interesting technology was the use of X-ray Luminescence, in which X-rays were used to make the diamonds luminesce. An optical sensor triggered a blast of air to remove each diamond from the concentrate. We were told that these X-ray sorters were developed specially for use at the Argyle mine, which could detect approximately 200 diamonds per second at peak sorting rates. Quite in sync with such technological developments, the entire processing operation was mechanized and automated with all the machines being monitored and managed from a central control room.

*An aerial view of the ore dressing and diamond sorting plant (Picture 13-07)*

No doubt that there were multiple challenges in running the operation of the mine and the plant, the most critical being the protection and rehabilitation of the local environment. Protection of local vegetation, water conservation, ensuring water quality standards in the streams and in the groundwater, periodic consultation with traditional aboriginal land owners, and holding on to many other regular management practices for energy, environment, occupational health and safety made the entire operation arduous and formidable. Yet the Argyle diamond production has continued for about four decades. It saw the peak production of 42 million carats in 1994. In the initial two decades the mine was operated as an open pit and in 2005 it expanded to underground operation. But after producing 865 million carats of diamond in its lifetime, the mine ceased its operation in 2020, initiating a detailed and lengthy closure procedure. The decommissioning of the mine and rehabilitation of the site may stretch over five years or so.

Let me close the story of Argyle diamonds with a gossip that I had picked up about the first sales of Argyle diamonds in Antwerp in Belgium, the world's marketing hub for diamonds. The Belgian Customs Office in Antwerp was used to receiving diamond shipments from the producing countries in small parcels or perhaps in satchels for relatively large deliveries. When the diamond shipments started from the Argyle mine, the quantum of consignments received at Antwerp increased suddenly by several orders. The Customs Office there did not have adequate storage and handling facilities. With trucks waiting before the office, the Customs officials called the Manager of the local Argyle sales outfit, situated nearby, to take away the consignments immediately. The Sales Manager of Argyle rushed to the Customs Office but he was also not prepared to transport the consignments. Because of the insistence of the Customs Officer, he had to use trolleys to push millions of dollars' worth of diamonds through the streets. But soon the Sales office safe was filled up with diamonds, leaving no further space for the new consignments in transit. The Argyle Manager had to find out an innovative way to sell diamonds in stock. He decided for the first time the mode of bulk sale of diamonds. On the first day of bulk sale, to the utter surprise of the Manager, the Indian diamond merchants trading in Antwerp bought out the entire lot, which was equal to the Argyle's sales planned for three months. While the process of bulk sale of diamond was continued to be pursued by the Argyle Manager, the first day's sale was the breaking news then, reaching even The New York Times, and the Indian merchants were in the spotlight as the bulk buyers.

**Concluding Thoughts**

From the above discourse it is evident that there are multifarious reasons to justify why diamonds are the most coveted and the most expensive jewelry to possess as an heirloom. But what has not been delved upon is its immense value for studying the origin and evolution of our planet. Diamond has a unique position as one of the Earth's oldest preserved minerals. Understanding the formation and crystal chemistry of diamond shows the way to trace the origin and evolution of the Earth. The advances in the scientific research tools during the last two decades have led to new conclusions about how diamonds crystallize and remain stored in the mantle below the Earth's crust. Now we know that they form from carbon dioxide-rich fluids that flow through deep mantle rocks. These fluids cause rocks to transform under high temperature and pressure, precipitating diamonds. Since we have recognized diamonds as deriving from a mobile carbon-bearing fluid, it assumes new importance in tracking carbon mobility in deep mantle and tracing the carbon cycle more comprehensively. The study of diamonds also provides a way to study the convection process in deep mantle, which relates to the phenomena of plate tectonics, which, as we know, is the basic cause of continental drifts.

What we are yet to understand is the nature of carbon in diamond. Is it primordial or recycled? How has carbon accreted into the Earth and stored inside the planet since the earliest times? How potentially widespread is the occurrence of diamond in the mantle as opposed to their scarcity in diamond pipes explored and mined on the surface? Has the process of diamond formation ended a billion years ago in the mantle or has the process continued in more recent geological times? Is the process occurring even now? There are scores of questions in the minds of researchers. New studies will reveal new facts about diamonds, the most endearing and enchanting gemstone.

# CHAPTER 14

# Africa – a Variegated Continent with Surprises Galore

In our school days we read or learnt very little about Africa to know what the continent was really like, but it was enough to raise curiosity and bewilderment in us about the land and the peoples. Our scanty knowledge then was limited to the ancient civilization of Egypt and pyramids in North Africa; the Nile River as one of the longest rivers in the world, flowing from the Lake Victoria region in east central Africa to the Mediterranean Sea in the north; wildlife sanctuaries and national parks in Tanzania, Kenya and the surrounding region; and, perhaps, apartheid prevailing those days in South Africa. My scribbling in this chapter is not on these widely known features of the continent. My penchant is to narrate lesser known facts, features and bizarre incidents I came across during my multiple travels to different parts of the continent.

For this, let us first recap the broad features of the continent with the help of the map that follows (Picture 14-01). Africa is the second largest and the second-most populous continent in the world after Asia. As given in the Wikipedia, with a little over thirty million square kilometer area, the African continent covers about 20% of the landmass and 9% of the total surface area of the Earth. The continent includes Madagascar and several other archipelagos. Interestingly, the whole continent has a population of 1.4 billion, which is almost the same as of India as a single country. Regarding the population, the other interesting statistics is that the median age profile of the continent is the youngest in the world, it being about 20 years. Politically, it is reported that in 2021 Africa had 54 fully recognized countries, eight territories and two de-facto independent states with limited or no recognitions. Geographically, the most interesting feature is that both the equator and the prime meridian pass through the continent.

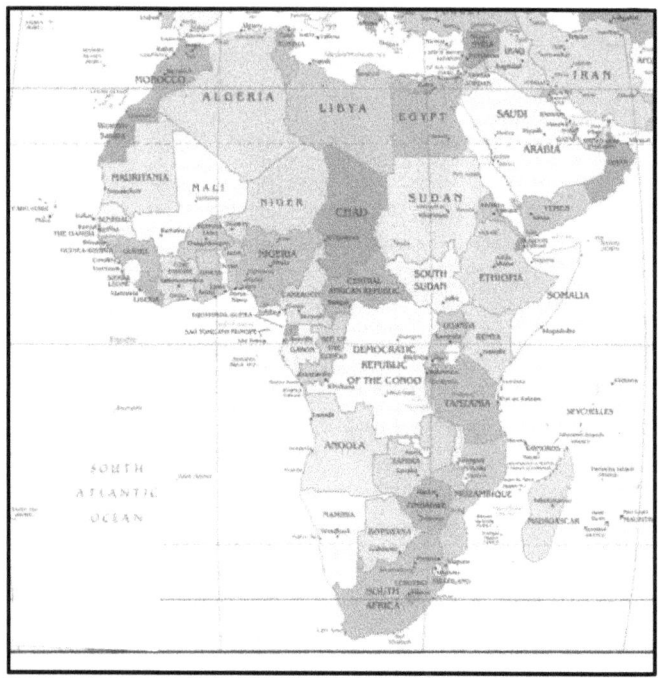

*Map of Africa showing the boundary of different countries (Picture 14-01)*

Though I had occasions of visiting several countries in the continent at different points of time, I thought of limiting my narration in this chapter to three countries – Algeria, the largest country in the continent by area; Sudan, wherein the capital city Khartoum happens to be the meeting point of both the White Nile and the Blue Nile; and Nigeria, the largest country by population in the continent. Another attraction for me towards these three countries was a peep into the Sahara desert from different locations.

**The Algerian Narrative**

The southern fringe of the Mediterranean Sea is surrounded by four North African countries - Morocco, Algeria, Libya and Egypt - from the Atlantic coast in the west to the Red Sea coast in the east (see the map above). As already stated, Algeria happens to be the largest country but more than 80% of it is covered by the inhospitable Sahara desert. Consequently, the vast majority of people, maybe about 90%, live in the temperate hilly north-eastern part and the fertile coastal planes along the Mediterranean Sea. The northern region of Algeria is dominated by two parallel mountains – the Tell Atlas and the Sahara Atlas, which form a natural barrier between the Mediterranean Sea and the Sahara desert. Several major cities of Algeria are located at the foothills of the Tell Atlas.

Algiers, the capital and the main seaport of Algeria, is the political, economic and cultural center of the country. It is built on the slopes of the Sahel Hills, which run parallel to the Mediterranean Sea, extending for more than 15 km along the Bay of Algiers. The location and disposition of the city make it a picturesque place to visit. To my mind, one of the modern landmark architectural monuments of Algiers is the Martyrs' Memorial erected in 1982 to commemorate the twentieth anniversary of the Algerian war of independence. It is designed in the shape of three standing palm leaves, sheltering the eternal flame within it (Picture 14-02).

*The Martyr's Memorial in Algiers (Picture 14-02)*

Though the Algerian struggle for independence is a part of the modern history of the Mediterranean region, the city's founding dates back to 3rd century or even earlier. It is said to have been founded by the Phoenicians as one of the numerous North African colonies. It was known to the Carthaginians and the Romans as Icosium, meaning "seagull's island", but the city really prospered under the Berber dynasties beginning in the 10th century. In the early 16th century many of the Muslims and Jews expelled from Spain took asylum in Algiers. During World War II, Algiers served as the headquarters of the Allied forces, and for some time, it housed the French capital. In 1962 it became an independent nation.

Because of the historical past, one may observe impressive architectural diversity in the city. Broadly speaking, the upper reaches of the hill slope are dominated by the Muslim and Turkish features with high-walled houses and narrow winding lanes, while the lower reaches look more French in character. The

Qasbah Fortress in the Muslim section was recognized as a UNESCO Heritage Site in 1992

The Algiers 1 University, which I had to visit once, is located in the modern part of the city in a sprawling heritage building (Picture 14-03). The University was established in 1909 by amalgamating different academic institutions and it was an active centre during the years of Algerian struggle for independence. In due course later Algiers 2 and 3 Universities were established.

*The heritage building of the Algiers 1 University [reproduced from a postcard preserved in an institution (Picture 14-03)]*

## Acquainting with Albert Camus' Life

Along with my specific assignments there, I took the opportunity to know the basic contours of the life and philosophy of one of my favorite authors Albert Camus, who was born to a poor farmer's family in war torn Algeria and had graduated from the above University. My curiosity about Camus was due to several reasons. I found that he was the second youngest Nobel laureate after Rudyard Kipling at the age of 44. Though he had a short life due to a car accident in France within two years of his becoming a Nobel laureate, his concepts of existentialism and philosophy of "absurd-ism" made him a famous novelist, essayist and philosopher who is read and remembered even today; politically, he was a liberal socialist and was a severe critic of the Soviet socialism.

Though I did not find much additional information and snippet about Camus in the University, my brief chats with some lovers of literature there were rewarding. I learned how a deaf and illiterate widow mother brought up Camus and his brother. Despite the deprivation of his childhood, Camus won a scholarship to a prestigious High School in Algiers and went on to study philosophy at the University during 1933-1936. His thesis was on Plotinus, a Hellenistic Platonic philosopher who was born and raised in the Roman Egypt (204-270 CE). He began his writing career as a journalist for the newspaper *Alger Republicain*. After moving to Paris, he became involved in Resistance Movement, editing the clandestine paper *Combat*. The memories of the World War II and experiences under the Nazi occupation permeated the philosophy and writings of Camus. The novel entitled "The Stranger" and his essay "The Myth of Sisyphus" catapulted him to fame and brought him closer to Jean-Paul Sartre. He was also influenced by Frantz Kafka and many other literati and philosophers of that era.

The most bewildering to me was his philosophy of "absurd-ism". He believed in the fact that life is devoid of meaning or man's inability to know that meaning if it were to exist. He expanded this philosophy in his essay "The Myth of Sisyphus", in which the human longing for order and meaning of life was compared with the rolling of a huge boulder up a mountain by the Greek mythological hero Sisyphus, who was condemned by gods to do so for eternity. Camus was in admiration for Sisyphus, who experienced the pointlessness of pushing up the boulder that was rolling down but still kept trying. Perhaps the author endeavoured to convey that we, the humans, first accept absurdity and meaninglessness in our existence and then take on the purpose of creating value and meaning in life. Somewhere else, he also distinguished between revolution and rebellion and wrote that "the only way to deal with an un-free world is to become so absolutely free that your very existence is an act of rebellion." He apparently did not believe in both Nazism and the Soviet Revolution as there was a specter of totalitarianism in both the systems.

## From Albert Camus to Desert Rose

The work schedule did not permit me to continue in the dream world of literature and philosophy in the University. I had to return to stark reality from that sombre world. The following day I found myself in a small oasis town called Tamanrasset in southern Algeria in the Ahaggar Mountains in the heart of the Sahara. It is the capital of the Algerian province of the same name, approximately 2000 km south of Algiers, the national capital. Though a small town, it is connected by air and has resort facilities. I visited the oasis town as a part of the team that was invited to explore the possibilities of setting up manufacturing plants for cement and other building materials as the entire region was totally dependent on supplies from the north.

The visit was rewarding as it gave us a splendid opportunity to realize the vastness of the Sahara and its changing geomorphology and landscape. We had seen at the north western part of Algeria closer to the coast of the Mediterranean, particularly between the Tell Atlas and the Sahara Atlas, hilly steppe like planes. The stretches of sand dunes appeared to the south of the Sahara Atlas, which, we were told, are called Grand Erg Occidental in the center of Algeria and Grand erg Oriental on the eastern flank. But a totally different landscape of the Sahara was noticed closer to Tamanrasset, situated in the Ahaggar Plateau. The Plateau has an elevation of more than 900 m and over it stands a mountain chain (Picture 14-04). In the heart of this chain is the Atakor range. Relicts of extinct volcanic activities in the shape of spires and needles created an unbelievable scenario. In some places, the congealed lava flows gave rise to unique features that looked like gigantic mushrooms standing on stalks on a vastly stretching sand bed (Picture 14-05).

*The basaltic spires and cones in the Ahaggar Mountain region (Picture 14-04)*

*A mushroom like feature in the Atakor region (Picture 14-05)*

It is worth mentioning here that Tamanrasset is not a new city. It was established in ancient times by the Tuareg community of the Berber tribe as oasis for the camel-borne traders passing along the north-south trans-Sahara route. The Tuareg community, which dominated this region, is an interesting tribe having their own dialect and rituals. The name, I was explained, means "abandoned by God", as they were late in accepting the Muslim religion. In 1905, Charles Engene de Foucauld, the French Explorer and an Ascetic, built his hermitage in Tamanrasset, where he compiled a Tuareg language grammer and dictionary. With this kind of legacy, Tamanrasset has now become a tourist attraction in Sahara combining the vista of yellow sand, Ahaggar Mountains, and about 3000-m high Tahat peak, the highest point in the Sahara.

The camel trade route is now the well-engineered Trans-Sahara Highway, often called the African Unity Road that connects Algiers, the Algerian capital with Lagos, the de-facto capital of Nigeria, a distance of 4500 km or so. Almost one-half of the highway runs through Algeria, and Tamanrasset happens to be the south station of the Algerian part of the highway as in the olden days (Picture 14-06). We had occasions to drive along the highway. The drive on the asphalt road piercing through the undulating brownish yellow stretches of sand with no habitats gave us a pleasure of its own kind.

*A glimpse of the Trans-Sahara Highway (Picture 14-06)*

What we enjoyed more than anything else was the discovery of desert roses (Picture 14-07), a rosette of mineral gypsum grown naturally on the bed of sand. While driving along the highway, we noticed the roses at a distance. We stopped, walked through the sand surface and discovered the stunning creation of the nature. The rose petals were the flattened crystals of the mineral gypsum fanning open in radiating clusters.

*A close-up view of the desert roses (Picture 14-07)*

## Sudan and the Niles

Roaming in the Sudanese land had a distinctly different flavor from that of the Algerian travels. The journeys to the two countries were not in continuity, nor at the same time, but that did not matter in understanding their intrinsic differences, not influenced by time.

Prior to 2011, Sudan was the largest country in the African continent but with the separation of South Sudan it is now reckoned as the second largest country. The location of the major cities and the courses of the Niles within the state are shown in the map presented below (Picture 14-08). The most interesting and distinctive feature of the place was the coexistence of the desert-like planes and the rivers, particularly the Niles, flowing through them. The banks of the Niles looked thriving with life and habitat, while some distance away in the desert planes there was isolation and emptiness. Before coming to Sudan, I had little idea about what in the Arabic language meant by "Wadi". I realized primarily in the western part of Sudan that, though the word traditionally referred to a river valley, here it essentially described   ephemeral riverbeds that contained water only when heavy rain occurred. One of such wadi-like features was called Yellow Nile – a surprise to me.

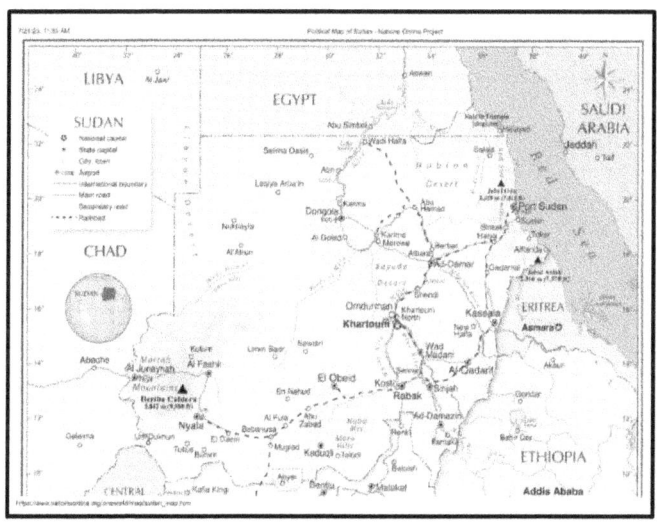

*Map of Sudan with the location of the major cities (Picture 14-08)*

Staying at Khartoum, the capital of the country, and interacting with the corporate world there on one hand, and travelling to Port Sudan on the Red Sea coast and the cities like Atbara to the northeast of Khartoum and Rabak to the south of the country, on the other, provided me with immense opportunities to acquire a lot of friends and to understand the culture and practices of the country.

Khartoum, however, being the confluence or *al Muqran* as popularly called in the Arabic, attracted me more to the Niles. The White Nile and the Blue Nile join in Khartoum to form the bottom of the slanting S-shape of the main Nile as it flows through the Northern Sudan into Egypt at Lake Nasser (see the map in Picture 14-09). What was initially puzzling to me to understand why the Blue Nile is blue, different from the colour of the main Nile River. As I tried to resolve this mystery, I made an attempt to learn about the Blue Nile from its origin.

*Confluence of the Blue Nile with the main stream at Khartoum*
*(Picture 14-09)*

As shown in the map, the main stream of the Nile starts its journey from Lake Victoria through Uganda on to Sudan. The much shorter Blue Nile, which flows out from the mountains of Ethiopia over the Tis Issat Falls that feed Lake Tana (Picture 14-10), takes a north-westerly turn in Sudan to join the White Nile at Khartoum. The White Nile that flows on for hundreds of kilometers thereafter effectively depends on the volume of water that it receives from the Blue Nile and the Blue Nile is nourished by the heavy precipitation in the Ethiopian mountains. During flood times the water content in the Nile goes so high that its colour changes to deep blue or even black, from which the name of the river is derived. Though short, the Blue Nile is gorgeous. In fact, in 2004, Pasquale Scaturro, a geologist, and Gordon Brown, a documentary film maker, became the pioneers to navigate the Blue Nile and chronicled their adventure in the form of a film and also in a book entitled "Mystery of the Nile". It is also worth remembering that the might of the river is utilized in meeting almost 80% electricity demand in Sudan.

*Tis Issat Falls in Ethiopia, feeding Lake Tana, the source of the Blue Nile*
*(Picture 14-10)*

Steps away from the Blue Nile, was the Grand hotel, a colonial-era property and the first hotel built in Sudan, where we had the opportunity to stay in Khartoum. We also had occasions to visit the University of Khartoum (Picture 14-11), which was initially founded as Gordon Memorial College in 1902 in memory of Charles Gordon, a British Army Officer and Governor-General of Sudan, who was killed inside his palace in 1885 during the Mahdist uprising. In fact, the Khartoum city is replete with centuries of history. It is a strange place that was founded as part of Egypt, that was ruled by the Anglo-Egyptian forces, that has a root in African culture and bears a strong Arabic influence in its culture and language. In the recent times, there has been imperceptible seepage of the Russian culture due to expanding education of the young Sudanese students in that country. Despite all such diverse influence in the socio-cultural frame and notwithstanding the autocracy and military dominance in the country's governance, a strong undercurrent of nationalism can be felt in the country.

*University of Khartoum – main entrance area (Picture 14-11)*

The University of Khartoum has been the primary centre for creating national talents in politics, literature, science, medicine and agriculture. It has also been the centre for students' uprising for democracy from time to time.

Another very interesting nationalistic trait of the country has been the women's dress code. In place of "burqa", the Sudanese ladies prefer to use "toub", a long thin colourful fabric wrap worn on top of the dress like an Indian "sari" (Picture 14-12).

*The Sudanese women in toub, the national dress code (Picture 14-12)*

The Sudanese literature is predominantly in the Arabic language, though the works of some of the writers have been translated in English. Tayeb Salih, an alumnus of the University of Khartoum, is one such acclaimed novelist in the country, some translated works of whose are available in English. A brief mention may be made of Bushra Elfadil, who had completed his higher education in the Russian language and literature in the then Soviet Union and worked as a faculty member in the University of Khartoum, was awarded in 2017 the Caine Prize for African writing, often considered an equivalent of the Booker Prize, for his short English story entitled "The story of the girl whose birds flew away". But the author had a prior history of being expelled from the country in 1990s for his participation in political movements in the University and had to settle down in Saudi Arabia later on.

There are many other memories of Sudan including my driver's losing the truck tyre marks in the desert land while returning from Atbara and his persistent efforts to track the unpaved desert road with the help of stars in the clear sky almost at midnight. I was lucky enough to finally return to my hotel in Khartoum in the early morning hours, when the Indian Embassy officials had already started their search mission. This incident and all the above narratives are my Sudanese treasures.

## Knowing Nigeria

In the present article, my third and final stop is Nigeria, situated in West Africa on the Gulf of Guinea. It is not only the most populous country in the African continent but it also happens to be the country with the largest economy among the African nations. It is a federation of 36 states and one Federal Capital Territory, within which the capital city of Abuja is situated (Picture 14-13). The country is known more by its largest city Lagos on the Gulf coast. The economy of the country is dependent on oil. It ranks as the 15th largest oil producer, having the 9th largest proven reserves of oil.

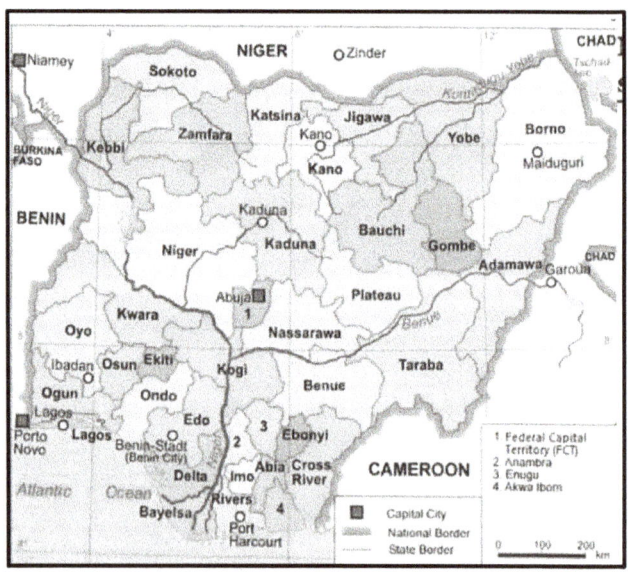

*Map of Nigeria with state boundaries (Picture 14-13)*

The modern state originated with British colonization in the 19th century and Nigeria became formally an independent federation in 1960. However, the country continued to be politically disturbed with successive military dictatorship interspersed with democratic elections right up to the end of the 20th century. By coincidence, my work took me to Nigeria within the disturbed period. Notwithstanding the problems, my long stays in cities like Sokoto, Kano, and Lagos provided me with a great learning stint to understand the socio-cultural framework of the country.

I had a taste of the factory environment in Sokoto. I had to attend the daily management meetings in the morning hours, which were chaired by the Operations Head of the factory. Interestingly, the meetings used to start and end with religious prayers. If on a day the meeting started with a Muslim prayer, it used to end with a Christian prayer. Next day the prayer sequence was reversed with a Christian prayer at the beginning and the Muslim prayer at the end. The religious freedom is guaranteed in the constitution in many countries of the world but the peaceful co-existence those days of the Christians and the Muslims in the sub-Saharan Nigerian city was an eye-opener to me. In my residence there, I had a Christian driver, a Muslim servant and another Christian guy as a cook. I never saw them in conflicting postures due to their religious differences. I heard then that the northern half of Nigeria was Muslim dominated, while the Christian community was more concentrated in the south. Yet I noticed the extensive mobility and employability of people with different faiths. With such comfortable feeling of the past, I now feel deeply aggrieved when I read about the recent Boko Haram incidents.

My extensive interactions with the labor force and management of several manufacturing plants revealed the existence of different native ethnic groups in the population, who had widely differing cultural practices and languages. Notable among, say, 250 ethnic groups in the country were the Hausa in the north, Yoruba in the west and Igbo in the southeast. I was given to understand that more than 500 distinctly different languages and dialects were spoken in the country. Coming from India, I was aware of what the diversity of culture and language means in a country, but I could not imagine the magnitude of the diversity that I found in Nigeria. No doubt that the country, like India, adopted English as the lingua franca, though they recognized the three major ethnic languages, Hausa, Yoruba and Igbo, as the national languages.

One of the notable infrastructural features of the country is the network of highways, which were built, avoiding the villages and habitats, but without any emergency facilities. The problem that I had once faced on the highway from Sokoto to Kano is worth remembering. I was reading a book in the back of the car which was being driven at a high speed. My brief case containing monies and essential travel documents, was lying by my side. All of a sudden the driver halted the car. I looked up and noticed a car overtaking our car from the left and blocking the road. Immediately two masked fellows came out, one holding a revolver in his hand and pointing at me. By that time my driver fled away from the car. I soon realized that I was facing the highway robbers. The robbers managed to open my door and snatched my brief case. I was perplexed for a moment but didn't lose my nerve. I asked them what they were looking for. In their typical intonation they shouted "monies, monies". I mastered enough courage to shout, "How can the small brief case contain monies? They are in my suitcase that is lying in the boot of the car". The robbers sharply reacted, threw the small brief case back to me, opened the boot, and took away my large suitcase that contained all my daily needs and dresses but no money. Since I got back my brief case, I could resume my journey to Kano for travelling to Lagos as soon as my driver came back to the car after noticing from a distance that the robbers had fled away. In my heart of hearts, I thanked the robbers for their foolishness. Had they not returned my brief case, I would have lost my passport and several other valuable things. The loss of the suitcase was much simpler for me to make up. Later on I learnt that theft, burglary, robbery and many other social disruptions were rampant those days. In fact, the prime reasons were the high disparity between the rich and the poor and low HDI (Human Development Index) in the society. I must add here that such problems of social disparity are not specific to only Nigeria, They are there in all developing economies but may not be so glaring as I had encountered in Nigeria.

But surprisingly this social disparity did not pose much of a barrier to the steady growth of education and literature in Nigeria. When I visited the University of Ibadan (Picture 14-14), I was impressed to learn that it was the oldest institution to award degrees, which started functioning as an associate college of the University of London in 1948 and became an independent University in 1962, immediately after the independence of the country.

Wole Soliyanka, the Nigerian novelist, playwright, poet and essayist, was the first sub-Saharan African Nobel laureate, who received this honour in 1986. He was born into a Yoruba family and was educated in the University of Ibadan first and then in the University of Leeds. Chinua Achebe, who won the 2007 Man Booker International Prize, belonged to the Igbo community and was an alumnus of the University of Ibadan. His first novel "Things Fall Apart" occupies a pivotal role in African literature. It would be an act of impertinence on my part if I do not mention the name of Ben Okri in this context. Though he was not an alumnus of the University of Ibadan, he had a part of his schooling in Ibadan and was the youngest winner of Booker Prize at the age of 32 for his novel "The Famished Road". Though Ben Okri was born in central Nigeria, he is now a British national and received the knighthood in the 2023 Birthday Honors in the UK.

*University of Ibadan – the main entrance (Picture 14-14)*

The story of Nigeria cannot be completed if I do not touch upon the Nok civilization, about which I heard a lot while visiting Koduna. Nok is a modern town situated midway between Koduna and Abuja (see the map in Picture 14-13). Around this place, spread over almost 78,000 square kilometer area, unique archaeological artifacts, made of clay and iron, were found. In 1943, when the occurrence of such objects was brought to the notice of a well-known archaeologist Bernard Fogg, he determined that they belonged to an unknown culture existing in that area in the period that dated back to 500 BCE or even earlier. This unknown civilization was named after the town of Nok. According to the historians and archaeologists, this civilization perished in 200 CE. Nothing much is known about the Nok civilization, except the terracotta sculptures and the iron tool relicts. The terracotta sculptures were of human bodies and faces and also of animals. The human sculptures were characterized by the triangular or oval eyes and elaborate hairstyles (see the images in Pictures 14-15 and 14-16). It is claimed that tens of iron-smelting furnaces were located near a village called Taruga. Surprisingly, the transition from clay to iron, which happened in other places via the Bronze Age, was not noticed in the Nok archaeological relicts. There are, thus, many unknowns about this civilization.

*Nok sculpture: clay bas-relief (Picture 14-15)*

*Relict of terracotta horse-rider of Nok civilization (Picture 14-16)*

**Closing Comments**

The present chapter has not dealt with the sub-equatorial countries of the continent as, I am afraid, justice could not have been done through brief narratives of their geological and archaeological histories and natural wealth. This part of the continent has the largest number of mega-fauna species as it was least affected by the phenomenon of the Pleistocene extinction. Further, Eastern Africa is widely accepted as the place of origin of hominids, perhaps seven million years ago. The earliest remains of the homo-sapiens, i.e., the modern humans, were found in Ethiopia and South Africa, which approximately date back to three million years. Because of long and complex history of civilization, migration and trade, Africa hosts a large diversity of ethnicities, cultures and languages. From the late 19th century to the early 20th century, the Europeans colonized all of Africa, excluding perhaps Ethiopia and Liberia. The emergence of new Africa due to progressive decolonization was seen after the World War II. Africa is no more a dark continent. It is a variegated continent for endless learning.

# CHAPTER 15

# Seychelles Archipelago – The Nature's Bounty

The Republic of Seychelles, an archipelagic state in the Indian Ocean, is perhaps not so popular as a tourist destination as Mauritius, though both of them are situated in the Indian Ocean at a distance of about 1800 km from each other on the east coast of Africa as shown in the following sketch map (Picture 15-01).

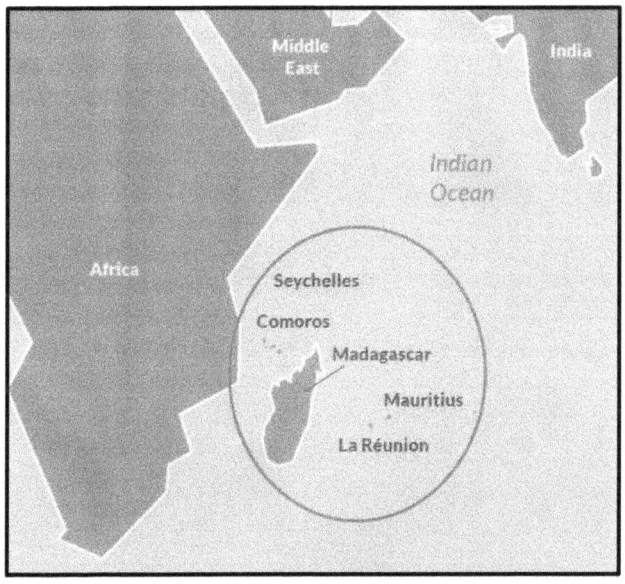

*A sketch map showing the islands near the east coast of Africa (Picture 15-01)*

Though both the island nations have a lot of similarity, for the nature lovers, to my mind, Seychelles has something more to offer. We had chosen this destination for holding our corporate strategy meeting spread over a few days in pristine surroundings so that we would not be disturbed by business calls and urban compulsions during our sessions. We, however, hardly imagined then that the beckoning of the verdant hills and call of the splashing waves in Seychelles could turn out to be far greater distracters. The narratives in this chapter are thus to familiarize my readers with little known details of this island nation gifted with enchanting nature.

## Historical Outline of the Island Nation

As I gathered from different sources, this group of islands remained unknown and uninhabited till Vasco da Gama and his $4^{th}$ Portuguese India Armada discovered it on 15 March 1503. It is a matter of conjecture that the boats of Vasco da Gama went close enough to some of the islands, and as the story goes, could map in all seven islands, which they named as "The Seven Sisters". However, the earliest recorded landing there was in January 1609 by the crew of the "Ascension Voyage" under the command of Captain Alexander Sharpeigh during the $4^{th}$ voyage of the British East India Company. It is said that much later in 1756 a stone of possession was laid by the French on Mahé Island and the entire group of islands was named after Jean Moreau de Séchelles, a Minister of Louis XV. Apparently, this event led to inevitable clashes of interests of both France and the Great Britain. Finally, after a war between the two countries, the archipelago was surrendered to the British by the Treaty of Paris in 1814. Named then as Seychelles, the archipelago was administered as a dependency of Mauritius. It is interesting to note from the historical anecdotes that following the abolition of slavery in England in 1835, the Royal Navy was seriously engaged in intercepting the Arab dhows in order to curb trading of the East African slaves. They had set free almost 2500 slaves in the Mahé Island between 1860 and 1870, perhaps giving birth to a nation in some sense. In 1903, Seychelles was given the status of a separate British crown colony. In 1975, Seychelles obtained a new constitution and independence within the framework of Commonwealth of Nations. It was quite surprising that in 1979 a new constitution was drafted by the government then to transform the archipelago into a one-party socialist state. This political format, though not very popular in the nation, continued for a few decades, and the change towards a multi-party democracy took place in early 1990s. Today, it is an independent country with an elected democratic government. With an international airport at Mahé Island, it is now a coveted destination for many tourists.

## Stepping into Mahé Island – the Life Centre of the Archipelago

We reached Mahé, the biggest island in Seychelles, by a five-hour flight from Dubai. We were over the island in the early morning hours. As we were landing, the very glance of the light olive green sea spotted with widely spread islands was a delightful greeting to us. The glittering sun rays were dancing on the moving waves. Closer to landing, the hunch-back rocky coastline came in view that was so enchanting with its partly bushy and partly bare surface against the blue seawater merging into the distant horizon (see Picture 15-02).

*The hunch-back rocky coastline in the Mahé Island (Picture 15-02)*

From the airport we transferred to a seaside resort with a private beach and having rooms overlooking the sea. We checked in, freshened up and rested a while before going to the dining hall for a fabulously laid buffet lunch. It was an unusual coincidence when you have a grand feast for your stomach and an equally grand feast for your eyes at the same place and at the same time. The white sand beach, the lush green trees, and a colorful sea within a close proximity made an awful combination with multinational dishes laid on the tables. The vista was simply an éclat (see Picture 15-03).

*An afternoon view from the dining hall of the resort (Picture 15-03)*

**Victoria - the Smallest Capital City in the World**

We sneaked out from the scheduled programs to look around the island and Victoria, the capital city of the archipelago, situated in the same island. It is about 20 square kilometer in area and is considered the smallest state capital of the world. We drove to the city center through well maintained narrow hilly roads in about 20 minutes from our resort. The capital city area was flat, plane and picturesque with a clock tower in the pattern of Little Ben in London (see the picture 15-04). As the picture shows, the city center had all the features of a metropolitan city but in a miniature scale. The city had a small population of about 26,000 only. Historically, it was first established as the seat of the British colonial government. In subsequent periods it turned into the capital of the entire archipelago and also into the main business center of the state. The Greater Victoria grew up into an extended city with added amenities and social comforts. On the slopes of the surrounding hills one may enjoy the sights of small tea plantations. The Mont Fleuri campus of University of Seychelles is located in Victoria. If you are a religious person, you may find your place of worship in the city. Some of us visited the Cathedral and a Hindu temple in the capital city (see Pictures 15-05 and 15-06).

*The clock Tower area in Victoria (Picture 15-04)*

*The Cathedral in Victoria (Picture 15-05)*

*The Hindu temple in Victoria (Picture 15-06)*

The small capital city gave the impression of a cosmopolitan society with a market-oriented diversified economy with traits of a rapidly rising services sector and tourism promotion activities. Though French and English are the official languages, Creole, a French-based native language, is widely spoken in the archipelago and appeared to be the de facto national language. We learnt that the business in the National Assembly is carried out in Creole, though laws are passed and published in English. We were given to understand that as per the 2010 census more than 85% people are Christians. The followers of the Hindu religion, numbering 2.6% of population, constitute the second largest group, followed by 1.6% believers of the Islamic faith.

## Unraveling the Scattered Islands

The constitution of Seychelles lists 155 named islands and seven other reclaimed islands. As already mentioned, the majority of islands are uninhabited. Some islands are designated as nature reserves. Geologically two types of islands are distinguished there: granitic and coralline. The granitic Seychelles consists of 42 islands, made up of the granitic rock, and they lie in the central position on the Seychelles Bank (see the schematic map in Picture 15-07). These granitic islands plus two coral islands along the rim of the Seychelles Bank are together called "inner islands". The granitic islands are fragments of the ancient supercontinent, geologically known as "Gondwana", and age wise they were separated from other continents probably 75 million years ago.

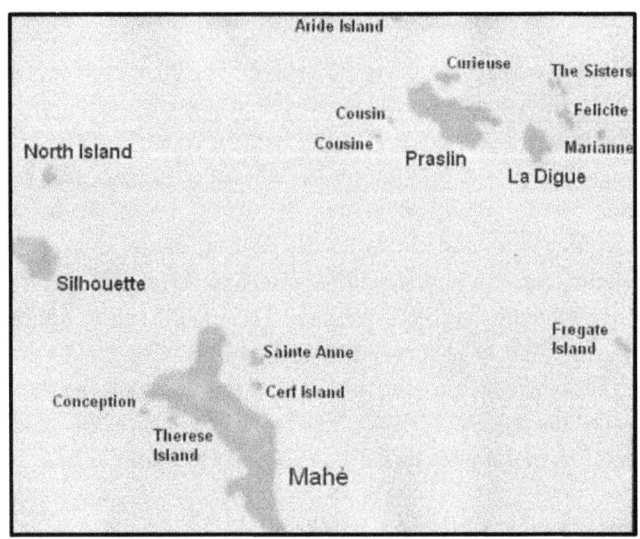

*Map showing the scatter of the inner islands (Picture 15-07)*

As far as the coral islands are considered, only two, known as Bird Island and Denis Island, occur within the spread of the inner islands. The remaining vast majority are situated as "outer islands" to the west and south of Mahé.

There is, of course, a general curiosity regarding the formation of coral islands. Corals are basically marine living organisms that secrete calcium carbonate to form a hard crust. They typically form compact colonies mostly of identical polyps. They grow under favorable conditions in tropical oceans. A part of the Western Pacific lying between Australia, New Guinea and Vanuatu is called the Coral Sea, though here the discussion is of coral reefs in a part of the Indian Ocean, where the conditions so far have been favorable for the growth of corals.

Coral reefs begin to form when free-swimming coral larvae attach to submerged rocks or other hard surfaces along the edges of islands and continents.. As the corals grow and expand, the reefs take on one of the three major characteristic structures – fringing, barrier or atoll (see the diagram in Picture 15-08).

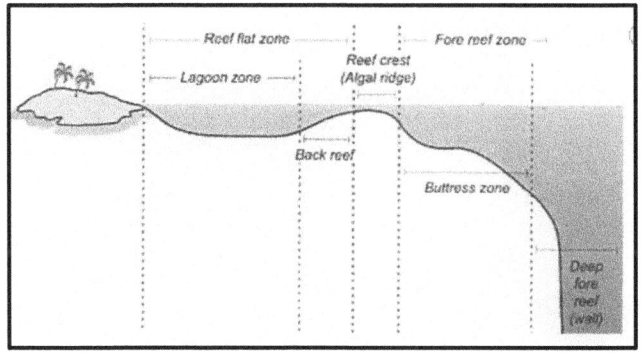

*A general and not universal illustration of the coral reef profile (Picture 15-08)*

In Seychelles various types of coral islands including atolls are available and may be of great interest to the specialists.

Though Mahé Island itself is charming, the real beauty of Seychelles lies in the scattered islands. The best way to unravel the nature's bounty there is through island hopping. For the more popular islands there are well-connected ferries and air shuttle services. Private cruises are also organized, if desired. Other than Mahé, the relatively big islands like Silhouette, Praslin, and La Digue are better equipped with touristic facilities. You may make it a point not to miss a ride in a glass-bottomed boat to a marine park, where one could see rich deposits of corals. As you float in the boat, you can see a variety of fish species playing hide-and-seek in the chunks of coral. In some designated parts of the marine parks you can throw pieces of bread provided by the boat master into the water to enjoy how the fish population is enlivened to float up to the surface to catch the food pieces.

The islands are home to many rare bird species. We learnt that "black parrot" has been given the status of national bird of the state. But the most charming bird is the paradise flycatcher sometimes spotted in La Digue Island (see the picture 15-09).

*The paradise flycatcher spotted in La Digue Island (15-09)*

It is important to mention here that the Bird Island, which can be reached in about 30 minutes by a light aircraft from Mahé, is the gateway to a unique bird sanctuary and a nature reserve in Seychelles. It is a sandy coral island having a circumference of about five kilometer, the east and south sides of which are surrounded by a protective barrier reef. A magnificent view of flocks of birds there is a feast to the eyes of tourists (see Picture 15-10).

*Birds galore in the Birds Island (15-10)*

While discussing about the living organisms on the islands, a mention has to be made of lizards, reptiles and giant tortoise. We did not have much opportunities of encountering the first two but we had a look at the giant tortoise (see Picture 15-11). Several extinct species of tortoise are being protected in the atoll of Aldabra, which is declared a UNESCO World Heritage Site.

*The giant tortoise (Picture 15-11)*

Aldabra is the world's second-largest coral atoll situated in the 'outer islands' of Seychelles. We came to learn that a healthy population of 150,000 tortoises live today solely in the Aldabra atoll, which is also declared a UNESCO World Heritage Site.

Apart from the zoological uniqueness, the emphasis on development on agroforestry in the island nation was noteworthy. The common agricultural products that we came across included coconuts, cinnamon, vanilla, sweet potatoes, cassava and tuna. The forests of palm trees were quite frequent in occurrence. However, the Vallée de Mai on the Praslin Island is the largest palm forest and has been declared another UNESCO World Heritage Site.

## Bidding Adieu to the Archipelago

All good things, as they say, come to an end and our stay on the island state could not be an exception. The day came to leave behind the pristine nature. But the previous evening we made it a point to sit on the beach to watch the play of the Sun with the cloud before it loses its glitter at the distant horizon into the darkening sea (see Picture 15-12).

*The farewell evening at Seychelles (Picture 15-12)*

While looking at the setting Sun, I wondered if I got the answer to the eternal question that the poet Henry Van Dyke posed in the following lines:

> "Through many a land your journey ran,
> And showed me the best the world can boast.
> Now tell me, traveler, if you can,
> The place that pleased you most."

Perhaps, I got the answer at Seychelles that evening.

# CHAPTER 16

# Dubai – a Microcosmic Urban Wonder in a Desert Land

There is hardly any literate person who would not have heard about the city of Dubai, leave aside the international travelers who would not have passed through the airports of this city. For the peoples of the Indian subcontinent, for all practical purposes, Dubai is the gateway to the west. Compared to many other metropolitan cities of the world, it is rather small in area, about 35 square kilometers, having a population of 3.49 million as of 2021. But for business and tourism purposes the city exerts a gravitating pull to the world at large.

For the initial orientation purposes, let me recap that the city is situated in the eastern Arabian Peninsula on the coast of the Persian Gulf as indicated in the map (Picture 16-01).

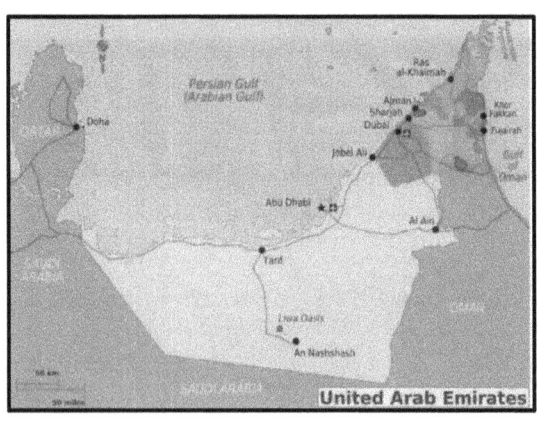

*Sketch map of the United Arab Emirates showing the location of Dubai*
*(Picture 16-01)*

Dubai is one of seven emirates that constitute the federation of the United Arab Emirates (UAE) with its capital at Abu Dhabi, though the city of Dubai, the capital of the Dubai Emirate, happens to be the largest city. The UAE region in general and Dubai in particular have a long history of human settlement and trade, an impressive growth trajectory during the last couple of decades, a fascinating urban outlook at present and a promising future, notwithstanding the barriers of demography and geography. My focus in this chapter is on some of these aspects, more as a story-teller than an authentic historian.

**Round-up of the Past**

The history of human settlement and trading activities in the region, now defined by the borders of the UAE, dates back to the Ubaid period (c.5500-3700 BC). Generally speaking, it is a prehistoric time that owes its name to the place in Mesopotamia where the archeological artifacts of this period were first discovered. The archeological findings in the UAE region indicate convincingly that there were trade links through this land between the Indus Valley civilization and Mesopotamia in the prehistoric times. These ancient trade links have been traced right up to the Iron Age (700-1BCE) from multiple locations of archeological excavations in this region. The Hill Archeological Park, a UNESCO World Heritage Site in Abu Dhabi, dates back to Bronze Age (2300-700 BCE). A notable structure in the Park is the Grand Tomb with ancient engravings of humans and animals (see Picture 16-02).

*A part of the Grand Tomb wall in Abu Dhabi (Picture 16-02)*

The Jumeirah Archeological Site in Dubai revealed remnants and artifacts of much later period, perhaps, ranging from the 9th to 11th century. The site was excavated in the late 1960s and revealed remnants of structures of a mosque, caravan *sarai* (motels of those days), residential houses, pottery articles like jars and plates, bronze coins, etc.. The excavation was over 8 ha area along a caravan route that indicated links between India, Oman, Dubai and Iraq. The Al Fahidi Fort in Dubai is the popular museum in Dubai that has galleries preserving the archeological artifacts. The renovated entrance to Al Fahidi Fort is shown in Picture (16-03). The Museum with large courtyards and multiple galleries is an interesting repository of evidences regarding the life and living in Dubai in the past, which are in stark contrast with the present-day Dubai. It may be pertinent to mention here that I had learnt from a scholarly person that the name of Dubai had appeared in the "Book of Geography" published probably in

1095 by an Arab geographer Abu Abdullah al-Bakri of Andalusia.

*Renovated entrance to Al Fahidi Fort (Picture 16-03)*

The recent historical narratives on Dubai indicate that it was established as a fishing village in early 18$^{th}$ century close to the creek. In this context, it is interesting to note that geographically Dubai is an extension of the Arabian Desert with no water bodies or rivers, except the marine incursion, known as the Dubai Creek with shallow water. It is said that by 1822 about 1000 members of the Bani Yas tribe had settled there as subjects of the ruler of Abu Dhabi. After the power struggle, in 1836 Maktoum bin Butti established the Maktoum Dynasty of Dubai. The British Naval Survey in the Persian Gulf caught sight of the settlement. In due course, Dubai along with some other states signed the General Maritime Treaty with the British Government. The signatory states came to be known as Trucial States, which stayed as a British Protectorate under the banner of Persian Gulf Residency from 1820 to 1892. Eventually, there was formation of the UAE which became an independent federation of seven states on 2 December 1971.

## Pre-Oil Days of Dubai

The proximity of Iran helped Dubai to grow as a trading hub. Initially, apart from being a transit route of goods from India and China to Middle East countries, the natural pearl industry grew up in Dubai. One may visit the Dubai Museum to see the gallery with mannequins of pearl sellers (Picture 16-04), which looks almost real-life to an onlooker. In fact, Dubai in 1930s was widely known for its pearl exports. But the Great Depression of that era and, later, the innovation of cultured pearls brought an end to the pearl trade business of Dubai. However, the tradesmen switched over gradually to gold trade with the support of the state policies. The gold trade flourished so much in the Emirate that an ornaments industry prospered there as a proposition of value addition and convenience of exports. The gold ornaments business continues with a firm footing in the Emirate even today. It may be pertinent to mention here that the Maktoum rulers started making investments into the development of the country's infrastructure from the trade revenues. In parallel, they also examined the possibilities for off-shore oil exploration in 1937. However, the efforts did not succeed then due to World War II but finally yielded results in 1966. Obviously the oil revenues substantially added to the prosperity of the Emirate and of the Dubai Metropolis.

*A gallery depicting the pearl trade in Dubai Museum (Picture 16-04)*

**Sprucing up of Dubai into a Wonder Metropolis**

There is a chorus that one cannot miss in Dubai giving out an important message that Sheikh Mohammed bin Rashid Al Maktoum, Vice President and Prime Minister of UAE and Ruler of Dubai, is the real force behind the transformation of Dubai in many ways, though his predecessors laid the foundation and the cardinal directions. It is interesting to recall that the city's first master plan was created way back in 1959 with the help of John Harris from Halcrow Group, a British architecture firm. In the subsequent periods, further contemporary plans and targets were set and executed. For example, there is a current target to make the city smart by 2030. The project aims to integrate the private and public services, enabling the citizens to access these services through their smart phones. Some of the initiatives include the Dubai Autonomous Transportation Strategies to achieve driverless transits, providing thousands of hotspots, smart cards to pay for all transportation services such as metro, road buses, water buses, taxis, etc., assigning QR code to each building for citizens to obtain locational information, and so on. The Smart City Index 2021 ranked Dubai and Abu Dhabi as the smartest cities in the Middle East and North African region, holding worldwide ranks of 28 and 29.

Further, Dubai Internet City, which was established in 1999, now houses a large number of global ICT companies and the city has succeeded in promoting itself as an unmatched hub of international financial services. Airports in Dubai serve as one of the best international travel hubs in the world. The Dubai Metro can make you feel the rare pleasure of unmanned stations. Burj Al Arab, Burj Khalifa and Emirates Palace are the hotels of exuberant pomp and luxury. In addition, the development of real estates with architectural excellence and road networks of efficient and safe connectivity is phenomenal. A solar park of 5000 MW capacity, set up in 2017, is perhaps one of the biggest in the world. The above examples are only to illustrate how much emphasis the Emirate has laid on the development of world class infrastructure.

All this progress has taken place and continues to happen in a country, which is really cosmopolitan in character. They say that close to 200 nationalities reside in Dubai and possibly 90% of its present population is born in other countries. As per the 2015 statistics, the largest ethnic group in the Emirate is that of the Indians, constituting about 38%. In a manner of speaking it is a microcosm of a kind.

### Queer and Unique Landmarks of the Emirate

It goes without saying that Dubai is famous globally for its high-rise buildings. It is claimed that compared to any other country, the count of buildings having heights of 250-650 m is more in Dubai. Sheikh Zayed road in the city appears to be in an unceasing competition for an expanding skyline up and up. The biggest tourist attraction, however, continues to be the Burj Khalifa Tower, almost 830 m high, built on an abstracted version of the flowering plant called hymenocallis with unusually long strappy leaves. Most often the visitors, when given an introduction to the tower, are told that it has 163 levels or floors and 2909 stairs. It took about six years to complete the construction of this tower and it became operational in 2010. The world's highest restaurant is situated on the $122^{nd}$ floor of this tower. Two observation decks, made of transparent glass, are available on the $124^{th}$ and $148^{th}$ floors. Numerous tourists rush every day to these observation decks through a very organized entry system and using super-fast elevators that operate at a speed of 10 m/s. The 360-degree aerial views of Dubai from the decks are awesome. Some of the views captured by us are presented in Pictures (16-05 to 16-07). When we saw the setting sun from the deck of the tower with the view of the city and the creek down below becoming obscure and obscure, it was simply poetic and unforgettable.

When we got down from the deck, it was dark outside but the courtyard of the tower along with its adjacent artificial lake was brightly illuminated. The lake could be easily approached from the Dubai Mall side as we did and found that hundreds of visitors had already assembled there to watch the captivating display of illuminated water jets from a submerged fountain in the lake, swaying rhythmically with known and unknown tunes and bands (see Picture 16-08). It was really surprising to learn that the Burj Lake is spread over an area admeasuring about 30 acres, in which the fountain jets were laid over perhaps 300 m length in such a pattern and power that thousands of liters of water could be thrown up to 140 m height to create a spellbinding display of water, music and light. Furthermore, we saw a long floating platform within 10 m of the fountain to walk along and enjoy the display. We also saw from a distance a boat taking visitors close to the fountain. After all, a display of this magnitude and aesthetics is rare to come by.

*Burj Khalifa Tower amidst a few other high-rise buildings (Picture 16-05)*

*Dubai city seen from the observation deck of Burj Khalifa Tower (Picture 16-06)*

*The setting of evening as seen from the Burj Khalifa Tower (Picture 16-07)*

*The Burj Khalifa Lake with illuminated fountain (Picture 16-08)*

Another feature of everlasting impression was our visit to Expo 2020, an international exhibition of 192 countries, which, due to the Covid pandemic, was opened to public after about a year on October 1, 2021 and remained open till March 31, 2022, making it possible for us to pay a visit there. The Exhibition ground was closer to the border between Dubai and Abu Dhabi. If you haven't been there, it would be difficult for you to appreciate its vastness and meticulous planning. It was a small township spread over 1000 acres of land. Wide paved roads, individual pavilions of the larger countries, combined pavilions of the smaller countries, well organized internal transportation systems, care centers for safety and emergency requirements of the visiting public, numerous hotels, restaurants, entertainment facilities made the exhibition an unforgettable one. The most interesting was the basic layout of the township. There was a Central Plaza named after Al Wasl, around which there were three thematic districts: Opportunity, Mobility and Sustainability. Depending on the selection of the theme, the pavilions of different countries were located. For the illustration purposes, the photographs of Al Wasl Plaza and a pavilion are presented below (Pictures 16-09 and 16-10). It is no wonder that Expo 2020 had 24 million visitors. Though the exhibition is over now, the built facilities are strong and durable with magnificent architecture, and will stay as a useful addition to Dubai's infrastructure.

*Expo 2020: a part of Al Wasl Plaza (Picture 16-09)*

*Visitors moving from pavilion to pavilion inside Expo 2020 (Picture 16-10)*

Let me take my readers from the exhibition to another unique landmark of Dubai – "Museum of the Future". Though the name itself is oxymoronic, the thematic thrust in the museum is intensely futuristic with multitudes of displays pertaining to Artificial Intelligence and Robotics. The architecture itself is distinctly different from the high-rise construction culture of the city. It is an oval tubular structure situated in the heart of the financial district of Dubai. Over the entire body of the huge structure, three Arabic poetic verses, composed by the Ruler of Dubai, are inscribed in the calligraphy of Mattar bin Lahej.

*A view of the Museum of the Future (Picture 16-11)*

The inscribed verses basically convey the following messages:

- We won't live for hundreds of years but we can create something that will last hundreds of years.
- The future will be for those who will be able to imagine, design and build it. The future does not wait; it can be designed and built today.
- Renewal of life, development of civilization and progress of humanity singularly mean innovation.

The façade with such inscription is made of over 1000 segments of stainless steel manufactured with the help of robotic technology to cover a surface area of 17,600 m$^2$. The entire museum structure is 97 m high and occupies an area of 30,548 $m^2$. The oval shaped building sits atop a green mound. It is said that the oval structure represents humanity, the green mound is the earth, and the void of the oval structure represents the unknown future. There is also an excellent landmark sculpture of a human palm with fingers on the road passing by the museum (see Picture 16-12).

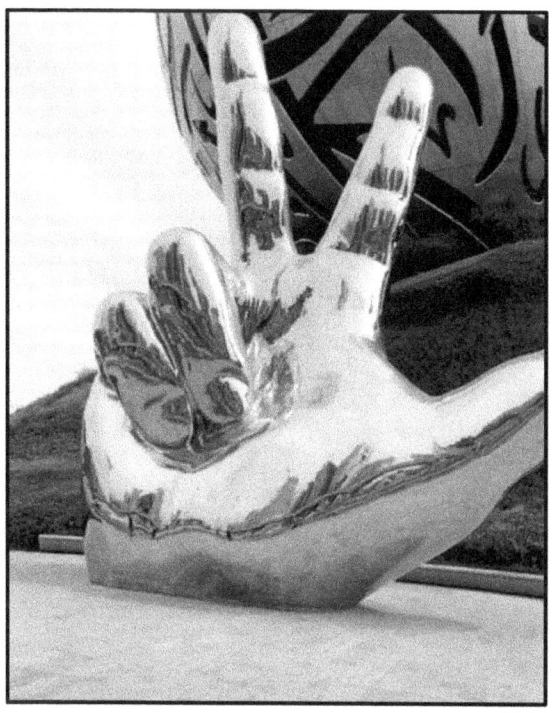

*Sculpture of a palm near the Museum of the Future (Picture 16-12)*

Now it is the turn to look at another innovative project in progress in Dubai – the creation of patterned man-made islands and archipelagoes. Creating new land masses in seas and oceans is certainly not an unknown phenomenon. Thanks to the efforts of several island nations and archipelagic states, there are many such instances in the world. However, the endeavor already initiated and being pursued intermittently in Dubai has the distinction of creating groups of land masses off the coast in innovatively conceived patterns in an organized manner.

There are four such interesting projects at various stages of execution: Three Palm Islands and a Multi-islet World. Each of the Palm Islands (Palm Jumeirah, Palm Jebel Ali, and Palm Deira) had the basic plan of building a flat configuration of a date palm tree consisting of a trunk, a crown with fronds or branching leaves, surrounded by a crescent island as a breakwater. There have been interruptions and changes in the Jebel Ali and Deira plans. The Palm Jumeirah, however, was finished in 2006, making use of billions of tons dredged sea sand vibro-compacted in place with the help of a huge labor force, maybe, 14000 strong over a five year period. The basic plan of the Palm island can be comprehended from Picture 16-13. It is quite interesting to see that the Palm Jumeirah is now packed with villas, hotels and many other attractions for tourists. Layout wise hotels are built in the trunk and homes in fronds.

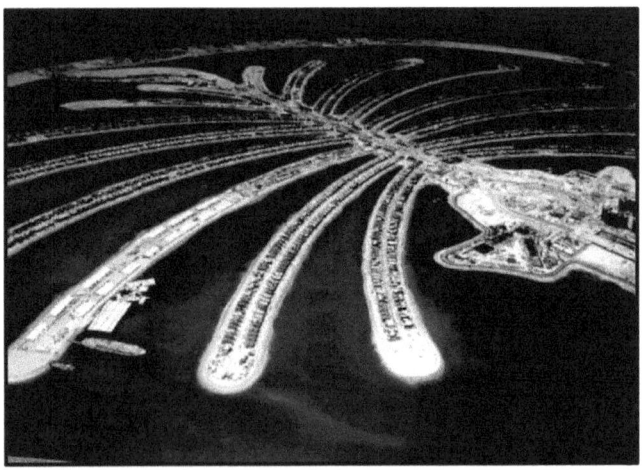

*A schematic layout of the Palm Jumeirah (Picture 16-13)*

The other project of World Islands was planned to create a replica of a world map as shown in Picture 16-14 and the construction work is in progress, though there are several barriers in execution including viability here and there. It was reported that the construction of 300 islands began in 2008. It appears that in the past few years the construction of the Lebanon Island has been completed and it is opened up for commercial exploitation. As we heard, the work on islands like Europe, Sweden and Germany has been taken on hand. In this context it is interesting to note that all the islets are called by the actual names of countries or regions that they represent. The construction engineering for this project remains more or less the same as in making the Palm Island. The project, no doubt, is an ambitious one and will take years to complete.

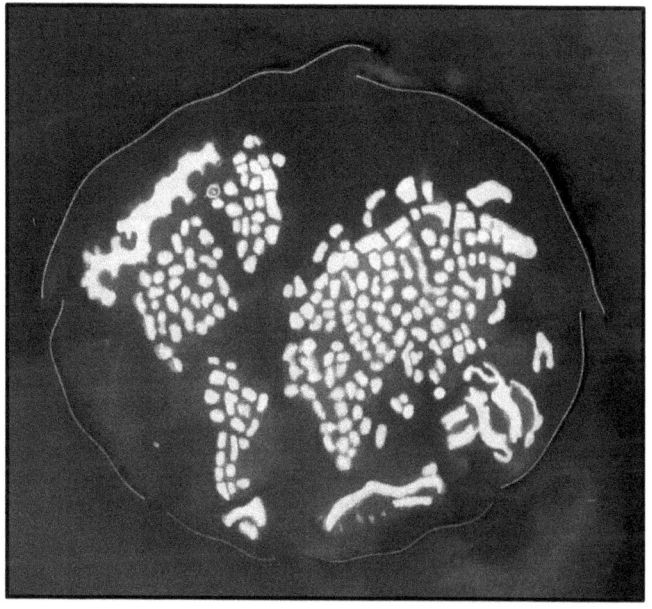

*Artificial archipelago planned to look like a world map (16-14)*

## Closing Remarks

As stated at the beginning, Dubai is a wonder city in many aspects. What struck me most that though the city and the state are administratively managed primarily by expatriates from multiple countries, for all intents and purposes, the law and order situations remains peaceful. It is also claimed that the crime rate in the state is zero and the HDI (Human Development Index) in 2021 was as high as 0,911. The country has already achieved the sixth highest GDP per capita on PPP basis in the world. The infrastructure of the country rivals the best of the most developed nations. It is not that the country has not been criticized for labor exploitation and even abuse of human rights but these barriers have been and are being overcome, keeping the country's future above all obstacles. The desert could not stop the prosperity of the country. The vision and the will of the leadership played the most significant role in transforming a fishing village of the past into a magnificent metropolis of the present.

# EPILOGUE

This is a humble attempt of a scribbler like the present author to build up stories of travels to some places that were personally more attractive to him than many other cities and global landmarks that are commonly visited by others. The stories have been built up from the author's desultory notes, fading memories, hearsays, and multitudes of unrestricted websites. However, the readers owe an explanation why most of the popular destinations for sightseeing have been left out by the author. It is for the simple reason that this book is not a guide for tourists. It is more an autobiographical story with a personal bias to share the pre-historical and historical stories of some places of interest, relevant archeological findings there if known in the public sphere, layman's geology and geography of those places, some pictorial snaps, unusual social and cultural traces encountered there, and other rarities.

The seed of this endeavor was unknowingly sown in the author's growing up as a young school boy and later as a college lad in an institution of great heritage, introducing in him an innate urge for *wanderlust*. Though the word *wanderlust* has a German root, its inbuilt appeal and spirit are universal. It is one of those words that is not buried in its own language and conveys to you something definitive and tangible. An equivalent of this word is seldom found in other languages, though the etymology of the word is simple; wander comes from the word *wandern* meaning "to hike or roam about" and *lust* meaning "pleasure or delight". Is the word in reality limited to its etymology? Perhaps, it is not. To me, it reflects more what Robert Louis Stevenson once wrote "For my part, I travel not to go anywhere, but to go. I travel for travel's sake. The great affair is to move." In the context of forwarding his book on "Travels with a Donkey in the Cevennes" to Sidney

Colvin, he further wrote "But we are all travelers in what John Bunyan calls the wilderness of this world – all, too, travelers with a donkey; and the best that we find in our travels is an honest friend. He is a fortunate voyager who finds many."

Talking about *wanderlust*, I must say that I enjoy looking at the frontispiece of the book by Stevenson again and again. It appeals to me as a symbol of *wanderlust*. Perhaps it expresses the deeper sense of the word more vividly than many definitions. For the appreciation of my readers, the impression of the frontispiece created by Walter Crane in 1907 (Chatto and Windus, London) is reproduced below. I wonder how the artist captured in this small space the diversity of the planet as conceived then. *Wanderlust* is certainly an endeavor to unravel the diversity then and is so even now.

*Frontispiece of the book by R L Stevenson*

To my mind, *wanderlust* does not end there. It creates invaluable intangible assets that we treasure as our memories. Surprisingly these memories last for decades. How these memories are encoded and stored safe in our body and mind for retrieval from time to time I do not know. I am not sure if the medical professionals in the field have succeeded in unraveling these mechanisms. Yet they happen. You look back deep into your past. You will find many events and incidents of your daily life have faded away but you will recall your travel memories as vividly as shots captured in a camera.

It is often said that painful memories hang on for longer periods of time. The specialists believe that it happens because of increased biological arousal during the negative experience in life. I am not sure if any similar mechanism works during our positive experience of travels and sojourns. The memories, however, remain indelible deep inside us and reappear with unknown triggers of recalling.

Over the decades, *wanderlust* has changed its color. It is no more an aimless exploration of the unknown world. It has become more purposeful. A social, economic and environmental approach has been added to the intrinsic lust for traveling. This has resulted in a more mindful and responsible outlook for travelling, be it local or global. Urge for respecting the local sensibilities of the places we visit and to lower the carbon footprints in our travel activities, a lot of technological advances are being taken recourse to. At the same time, bike rides and walking tours are receiving wide attention of "wanderers". In a nut shell, "conscious travelling" is the name of the game today. You cannot but think, while you travel, how your actions extend beyond yourself and into the future. This thought reminds me of two lines of a poem by Kevin Quero that I read in the website [PoemHunter.com]:

> "I would like to time travel to see the future me,
> Wouldn't that be great to see what I really be."

While such a self-exploration may be relevant at present times, the very thought of containing or curbing the delight or pleasure of wandering by the emerging social chains make me feel uneasy. Can you really overcome the thrill of travelling to a different country to experience the diversity of cultures, to experience the cuisines that you are not familiar with, to witness multitudes of social practices, and above all, to enjoy the Nature's varied gifts to different parts of the planet that is so dear to us? Given an opportunity, will you ever abandon the idea of cruising on the seas and oceans, or even experiencing the life in an igloo, or standing on the icy continents and looking at the white wilderness? My wish list is long. Perhaps it is too long for most of us to realize in a life span. So I thought that I must pacify my mind with the sense of a poem written by Rabindranath Tagore in "Gitanjali: Song Offerings":

"The time that my journey takes is long and the way of it long.

I came out on the chariot of the first gleam of light, and pursued my voyage through the wildernesses of worlds leaving my track on many a star and planet.

It is the most distant course that comes nearest to thyself, and that training is the most intricate which leads to the utter simplicity of a tune.

The traveller has to knock on every alien door to come to his own, and one has to wander through all the outer worlds to reach the innermost shrine at the end.

My eyes strayed far and wide before I shut them and said: "Here art Thou".

The question and cry "Oh, where?" melt into tears of a thousand streams and deluge the world with the flood of assurance "I am".

The above quote is the prose-poetry translation made by the poet of his own Bengali composition, which, to my sensibility, is more expressive and rhythmic. The first stanza of the original Bengali version is quoted below just to facilitate those who read Bengali to recall the poem:

> "অনেক কালের যাত্রা আমার
> অনেক দূরের পথে,
> প্রথম বাহির হ'য়েছিলেম
> প্রথম-আলোর রথে।
> গ্রহে তারায় বেঁকে বেঁকে
> পথের চিহ্ন এলেম এঁকে
> কত যে লোক-লোকান্তরের
> অরণ্যে পর্বতে"।

All will agree that the most difficult journey is to reach your inner self. In your journey of life, you discover yourself many times in many places in many reflections but still you keep your search on. Is *wanderlust* also a search for your own self?

# ABOUT THE AUTHOR

Anjan Kumar Chatterjee is a Materials Scientist and spent almost five decades in the corporate sector in various capacities including the position of directorship on the boards of different companies. He is an alumnus of the prestigious Presidency College (now University), Kolkata. He holds a doctorate degree from Moscow State  University, Russia. He carried out extensive research studies abroad in various countries in the technical fields of his interest. Professionally, Dr Chatterjee started his career as a faculty member of Indian Institute of Technology, Kharagpur, India and later moved to different organizations for industrial research and corporate management in New Delhi and Mumbai. He has been on various international assignments with UNIDO and other organizations He has been elected as a Fellow of the Indian National Academy of Engineering. He has been conferred lifetime achievement awards by several professional bodies. Amongst his numerous technical publications, there are books authored and edited by him and published by the international publishing houses.

One of the many diverse passions of Dr.Chatterjee is to indulge in literary activities in order to escape from the pulls and pressures of professional life and also to give vent to his own ways of looking at the surroundings and the world at large. There have been sporadic publications to this effect. He has been a regular contributor to a travel magazine. Recently, a collection of his poems, both in English and Bengali, entitled *Abasor Binodan* (The Leisure Fillers) has been published. A book on international travels is on the anvil.

www.ingramcontent.com/pod-product-compliance
Lightning Source LLC
LaVergne TN
LVHW061541070526
838199LV00077B/6863